"TURN TO THE SOUTH"
Essays on Southern Jewry

"TURN TO THE SOUTH"

Essays on

Southern Jewry

Edited by

Nathan M. Kaganoff

Melvin I. Urofsky

Published for the

American Jewish
Historical Society
Waltham, Massachusetts

by the

University Press
of Virginia
Charlottesville

THE UNIVERSITY PRESS OF VIRGINIA
Copyright © 1979 by the Rector and Visitors
of the University of Virginia

First published 1979

Library of Congress Cataloging in Publication Data

Main entry under title:

"Turn to the South."

Based on papers presented at a conference on southern
Jewish history, held in Richmond, Va., in Oct. 1976.
1. Jews in the Southern States—History—Addresses,
essays, lectures. 2. Rabbis—Southern States—
Addresses, essays, lectures. 3. Southern States—
History—Addresses, essays, lectures. I. Kaganoff,
Nathan M. II. Urofsky, Melvin I. III. American
Jewish Historical Society.
F220.J5T87   975'.004'924   78-9306
ISBN 0-8139-0742-X

Printed in the United States of America

He who desires to become wise
should turn to the south,
and he who desires to become rich
should turn to the north.

Talmud *Baba batra,* 25b

In Memory of

Bernard C. Ehrenreich

Contents

Foreword

Rabbi Isaac said: "He who desires to become wise should turn to the south [when praying], and he who desires to become rich should turn to the north." (Talmud *Baba batra,* 25b)

To be a Jew in the American South is to be affected by the culture of the South. Regional and national cultures shape the style and sometimes the substance of Jewish life, as every student of Jewish history knows. Southern distinctiveness has been a tantalizing concept by which to test generalizations about the American experience as a whole. Foreign observers invariably have noted about American life such factors as class fluidity, individualism, social informality, optimism, and energy. When Americans have written about the South, they usually called attention to the exceptions such as Southern aristocracy, the significance of community and extended kin, the dominance of color caste, the pervasiveness of evangelical Protestantism, the rules of Southern propriety and servility, and especially the strong sense of regional tragedy.

Since Southern distinctiveness illuminates the general condition by contrast, scholars have turned to the South for wisdom. Here, scholars turn to the Southern Jewish past in the same quest for understanding of more than the South itself. Throughout Proverbs, Jews are constantly instructed to seek wisdom, and we have taken the title of this volume from the Talmud, as noted above. Rabbi Isaac tells us to look to the South to achieve wisdom and to the North to obtain riches. We know that Southern Jews have not been particularly poor, at least not by the second or third generation, and they have not always been wise. But we turn to the South because their story tells us something special about ourselves as Americans and, for those of us who are Jewish, about that peculiar chemistry of acculturation which constitutes the American-Jewish experience.

The essays result from a conference on Southern-Jewish history held in Richmond in October 1976. A milestone in American-Jewish history, it resulted in the re-creation of the Southern Jewish Historical Society and a commitment to future research, publications, exhibits, and meetings.

The conferences included professional and lay participants dedicated to a better understanding of the Jewish experience in the South. Over 200 persons attended the various meetings and functions.

To Professor Melvin I. Urofsky, Chairman of the Conference, who arranged and planned the program, we acknowledge our gratitude for putting together a successful program and for making the initial selections for this book. Saul Viener, as Conference Co-Chairman, and the local arrangements committee deserve special thanks too.

Appreciation goes also to Dr. Nathan M. Kaganoff, Editor-Librarian of the American Jewish Historical Society, who edited for publication the papers presented.

Finally, we would like to thank Mr. and Mrs. Milton J. Krensky of Chicago, who are the sponsors of this publication. They have both our appreciation and our respect for supporting this endeavor.

Lawrence H. Fuchs
Meyer and Walter Jaffe Professor
of American Civilization and
Politics, Brandeis University

Chairman, Academic Council
American Jewish Historical Society

Preface
The Tip of the Iceberg

The South, in American literature and folklore, has long been the most exotic part of the United States, a fanciful mixture of fact and myth. Within the South there has existed for over two centuries a flourishing Jewish community that is, in its own way, just as exotic and unknown. When writers and analysts have talked about American Jewry, they have almost always meant the large urban communities of the North, especially New York. The experience of American Jews, immigrants and their children, in New York and other large Northern cities has dominated American-Jewish historiography and sociology; almost invariably, the protagonists of American-Jewish fiction are Northerners.

Within the past few years, however, there has been an increase in studies of Southern Jewry. Graduate students, seeking out areas unploughed by earlier dissertations, discovered virtually virgin territory below the Mason-Dixon line. More established scholars in a number of fields—as well as the popular media—have also begun to focus our attention on Southern-Jewish communities. Two national trends can account in large part for this sudden spurt of interest. One has been the rediscovery of ethnicity, with blacks, Irish, Italians, Chicanos, Poles, and, of course, Jews seeking to sketch out the details of their group's communal life in the United States. The other trend is the final emergence of the South as a major region and influence in contemporary America. Following Appomattox, the defeated Confederate states withdrew unto themselves and erected social and cultural barriers not only to keep Yankee influence out but to preserve as much of the old ways as possible. Not until after the Second World War did the South begin to move back into the mainstream of American life, a development that culminated in the election of a Georgian to the White House. And as the South grew and prospered, so did interest in it and in its particulars.

The interest in these particulars is phenomenal. In October 1976 a scholarly conference on Southern Jewry in Richmond, Virginia, drew a surprisingly large crowd, not only of academics but of interested lay people as well. Nor were these men and women only from the South; they came from as far away as Boston, Chicago, and Los Angeles. The essays in this volume represent the principal papers of that conference, sponsored by the American Jewish Historical Society, the Richmond Jewish Community Council, and the Department of History and the Judaic Culture Committee of Virginia Commonwealth University, and underwritten by a grant from the National Foundation for Jewish Culture.

A number of conclusions emerged from that gathering. First, despite extensive work done on Southern-Jewish history, very little is known about twentieth century issues, and we are only beginning to chip away at the iceberg of ignorance. Nearly every speaker prefaced his or her remarks with comments on the large amount of work that remains to be done and the vast areas of Southern-Jewish life about which we know virtually nothing.

Second, from what we do know, it appears that the Southern-Jewish experience differed both qualitatively and quantitatively from that of Northern Jewry. Far fewer Jews, both in absolute numbers and as a percentage of the total population, settled in the South, and this fact significantly affected their self-perceptions, as well as the way others saw them. In New York the large Jewish population had a major impact on the culture and lifestyle of that city; New York, after all, is the largest Jewish city in the world, and its greater metropolitan area contains as many Jews as the entire State of Israel. But the Jews in the South always remained a minority, at times an almost invisible minority. They did not affect the South so much as they imbibed its values and became part of it. Speaker after speaker commented on the "Southernness" of the Jews.

Despite their becoming the most assimilated part of American Jewry, however, despite their being so Southern, it can be seen that these communities and individuals retained a strong sense of Jewish identity. Ironically, much of this might be attributed to the demands for religious affiliation and practice imposed by their Southern Gentile peers.

A final conclusion that emerged from these essays is that old stereotypes often bore little relation to reality. The South has long enjoyed the dubious reputation of being the most prejudiced section of the country, with the dominant white, Anglo-Saxon, Protestant group discriminating against any and all outsiders—especially blacks, Catholics, and Jews. The South, after all, gave birth to the Ku Klux Klan and was the scene of the only lynching of a Jew in this nation's history. Yet here we must follow historian John Higham's warning to distinguish between the Jew as symbol and the Jew as a real, flesh-and-blood neighbor. The Southern white may have hated the alleged international Jewish banking conspiracy headed by the Rothschilds, but he rarely connected the sinister Rothschild with Sam Cohen who ran the dry-goods store down the street and was practically a "good ole boy."

Finally, we now realize that, just as the South is nowhere as monolithic in character as had been thought, so too there is great variety in Southern Jewry as well. Although the original conference originated with the American Jewish Historical Society, we sought to have representatives not only from history but from other fields as well, including political science, sociology, psychology, and literature. Their findings, we believe, reflect the great diversity of the Southern-Jewish experience. But it will take many more conferences and studies before we can limn the portrait of Southern Jewry that it so richly deserves.

Melvin I. Urofsky
Professor of History
Virginia Commonwealth
University

"TURN TO THE SOUTH"
Essays on Southern Jewry

Portrait of a Romantic Rebel Bernard C. Ehrenreich (1876–1955)

1.

Byron L. Sherwin

Bernard C. Ehrenreich was a man of his times, yet ahead of his times. Though deeply committed to assuaging the social ills and the religious perplexities of his time, Ehrenreich's gaze was persistently directed toward confronting the challenges of the future. Since the future is determined by what youth does with destiny, Ehrenreich invested much of his boundless energy in youth work. For Ehrenreich, only an inspired and informed Jewish youth could insure a vibrant and creative future for American Jewry.

Born in Hungary in 1876, Ehrenreich and his family immigrated to New York City in 1879. The child of immigrants, the young Ehrenreich perceived the attainment of symbiosis between Americanism and Judaism to be the primary desideratum. To immigrants who believed America to be a *trefa medinah,* an "impure land," hostile to Jewish existence, Ehrenreich continually stressed the unique hospitality toward Jewish life afforded by America and a toleration there of Jews and Judaism that was unknown in European lands. To children of immigrants who were convinced that Judaism was a European obsolescence to be discarded in America, Ehrenreich ·demonstrated both by his words and by his deeds that acculturation need not entail assimilation, that Jewish identity need not be mortgaged to achieve Americanization.

Ehrenreich's long and distinguished career was pervaded by an obsession with the need for the physical, spiritual, and intellectual development of youth. Long before the founding of Jewish youth movements, he strove to make spiritual inroads in the hearts and minds of Jewish youth. When

The author wishes to express deep gratitude to Professor Harold Wechsler of the University of Chicago for his research efforts and advice and to Terry Dick for her personal insights and technical assistance.

formal Jewish education in America was still in a chaotic, nascent stage and informal Jewish education was as yet an unconceived idea, Ehrenreich attempted to reach out to youth in every way, in both formal and informal settings. For Ehrenreich, as for the educational "progressives" of his day, education of youth was society's insurance policy for the future. Youth is the most precious natural resource, but requires the refining influence of education to insure the future amelioration of society's ills. In Ehrenreich's words, "We are told . . . that the nature of man is bad from his youth (Genesis 8:21), which means that unless the refining influence of education, culture and civilization are brought to bear on the child, one may expect the very conditions which now confront us."[1]

Ehrenreich's commitment to the spiritual, physical, and cultural development of youth was manifest early in his life. While an undergraduate at New York University, he helped establish the playground system of New York City. Though the playground system was still in an experimental stage, Ehrenreich's efforts demonstrated its viability as a means of helping to insure the physical stamina of urban youth and to build their self-reliance. Generations of New York youth of diverse ethnic backgrounds are indebted to his efforts to transform this experiment of the late nineteenth century into a reality taken for granted in the twentieth century.

Ehrenreich perceived the community playground not merely as a vehicle for recreation but as an opportunity for character education. He worked with newly arrived Jewish immigrant children and endeavored to convince them that dispensing with their Judaism was not the necessary corollary of their achieving Americanization.

While he was laboring in the teeming streets of the urban ghetto, a notion began to percolate in Ehrenreich's mind which took almost twenty years to become translated into actuality. To provide a proper atmosphere for the total development of youth, an urban setting was inadequate. Only in a natural environment could the physical and spiritual potentialities of youth be truly and totally nurtured. Thus, long before summer camps—much less Jewish summer camps—existed, Ehrenreich conceived of establishing a Jewish summer camp to serve as a vehicle for human development and character education. What was an adolescent's fantasy on the blistering streets of New York in 1898 was to become a reality in the northern woods of Wisconsin two decades later.

But ownership of a summer camp, implementation of a new idea, was out of the grasp of an impoverished undergraduate. Consequently, Ehrenreich continued to pursue his studies at New York University, from which he was graduated with a Bachelor of Philosophy degree in 1900. Seeking a career of service to the Jewish people, Ehrenreich pursued rabbinical studies at the fledgling Jewish Theological Seminary and was among the first rabbis to be ordained by that institution.

In the twilight years of the nineteenth century, Ehrenreich–like so many of his fellow students at the Jewish Theological Seminary–became intoxicated with the newly emerging Zionist cause. A lifelong Zionist, he was a founder of the Federation of American Zionists and of the first American Zionist youth organization.

In the wake of the Dreyfus trial (1894) and with the emergence of Theodor Herzl, the Central Bureau of the Federation of American Zionists was established.[2] On December 27, 1897, Ehrenreich was named recording secretary of this first American Zionist organization. In 1898 the Young American Zionists, the first intercollegiate Zionist society, reorganized itself into the first intercollegiate Zionist fraternity–Z.B.T. (i.e., *Zion B'mishpat Tipadeh*: "Zion will be redeemed through justice"–Isa. 1:27). Ehrenreich was one of its founding members as well.

For Ehrenreich, the establishment of Z.B.T. represented not only a vehicle for promoting Zionism but an opportunity for encouraging Jewish identity and for stimulating Jewish solidarity upon college campuses where secularism dominated and anti-Semitism persisted. He hoped that Z.B.T. would attract college men who would later become leaders of the American-Jewish community. The presence of a Jewish fraternity on college campuses, he anticipated, would help arouse feelings of Jewish identity amongst Jewish collegiates, which–he felt–"conditions and environments have almost deadened."

In 1898, the year in which Z.B.T. was founded, Ehrenreich delivered an address, apparently in New York, in which he set out to define American Zionism. In this statement, entitled "Israel's Hope is Palestine" and published in the *Jewish Gazette,* he characterizes Zionism more as a moral imperative than as a political program.

> Anti-Semitism, a German product, has planted its seed in Austria. It has extended to the remote districts of Rumania and even to the liberty loving people of France. The seed is carried by these human insects from land to land, their missionaries are everywhere. . . . Are we who in this land enjoy the rights of American citizens to look upon the sufferings of our brethren indifferently? Are we to keep our eyes shut to these miseries? . . . Your fellow Jew's interest

is your interest. His suffering should be your suffering. . . . From the chasid to the atheist, from the most fanatic to the most liberal thinker, men of our religion meet in brotherhood to assist in this noble undertaking. Their love for the suffering cannot be extinguished.[3]

For Ehrenreich, Zionism entailed, not the immigration of American Jews to Palestine, but the responsibility of American Jews for their European brethren—a moral necessity required to insure the physical safety of European Jewry. Persecution of Jews in eastern Europe was then rampant and was moving westward into Austria; anti-Semitism flared in France in the wake of the Dreyfus trial, even though by 1897 Dreyfus's innocence had been established. Ehrenreich, therefore, called upon Jews of all persuasions and beliefs to support the establishment of a Jewish homeland in Palestine as a place of refuge for oppressed and endangered European Jewry. Thus Zionism was not antithetical to Judaism, as American Reform Judaism then maintained; nor was it hostile to Americanism, as a number of prominent American Jewish leaders then claimed. For Ehrenreich, Zionism expressed the highest concerns of the American penchant for justice and of the Jewish passion for compassion. Like Solomon Schechter, Ehrenreich perceived Zionism as an ideology which could reawaken Jewish identity among disaffected American Jews. Zionism was not only a plea for European Jewry but a promising catalyst for re-Judaizing extremely assimilated American Jews. Ehrenreich's Zionism and his concern for Jewish youth—specifically for Jewish collegiates—therefore, were mutually inclusive. Through the Zionist ideology and by means of the Jewish Zionist fraternity, he hoped the "deadening" of Jewish concerns amongst Jewish youth would be halted and a renaissance of Jewish culture in America would be initiated. Education would be the key to precipitating this rebirth. Consequently, Ehrenreich played an active role in the then recently formed (1893) Jewish Chautauqua Society, which, like Z.B.T., was committed to disseminating knowledge of Judaism on the college campus. In a speech delivered to the Jewish Chautauqua Society in July 1900, he characterized the activities of that organization as "one of the noblest undertakings of the Jew in America: the propagation of learning, the spreading broadcast of knowledge of our beloved faith."[4] In the course of another sermon delivered to the Jewish Chautauqua in 1900, Ehrenreich's conviction regarding the essential role that education in general, and Jewish education in particular, must play in the development of human character was forcefully stated. His hope for a renaissance of Jewish life in America was unabashedly announced: "Edu-

cation is the axis around which the earth revolves. Jewish learning is necessary for an upright life . . . today we love the secular and hate the religious.
We need a reawakening. We need a reanimation. 'The Book of the Law
shall not depart out of thy mouth' (Joshua 1:8) must again be made a
motto."[5]

In 1900, after having completed his studies at New York University and
at the Jewish Theological Seminary, Ehrenreich began his long distinguished rabbinical career. Ehrenreich's first congregation (1900) was
Beth Israel in Atlantic City, New Jersey. A summer resort, Atlantic City
swarmed during the summer, but was virtually deserted the balance of the
year. Once fall came, Ehrenreich found his congregation numerically de-
pleted and himself despondent. Despite small synagogue attendance, he
diligently continued to prepare his sermons carefully. The young rabbi's
conscientiousness was soon rewarded.

Some influential members of Philadelphia's prestigious Congregation
Adas Jeshurun chanced to visit his synagogue and were so singularly impressed with the youthful preacher's pulpit presence that they invited him
to replace their retiring rabbi the following fall. On August 24, 1901,
Ehrenreich commenced five years of intensive activity in Philadelphia.
Both local newspaper reports and congregational records testify to the
extraordinary impact he made upon the Jewish community of Philadelphia
in general and upon his congregation in particular.

While in Philadelphia, Ehrenreich experienced little of the loneliness
or despondency he had felt in Atlantic City. His work was exhausting, but
gratifying. His brother, Herman, studying medicine at the University of
Pennsylvania, provided companionship. Nevertheless, Ehrenreich felt un-
fulfilled. He sought romance; he strove to advance his education. Dis-
satisfied with the scope of his knowledge, he began to pursue graduate
studies in literature and philosophy at the University of Pennsylvania.

The overworked rabbi never forgot his family obligations. He supported
Herman through medical school and aided in the support of his parents for
many years. The time had come, however, for him to establish a family of
his own. On December 17, 1902, Ehrenreich married Irma Bock of New
York, whom he had been courting for some three years. Bernard's enduring
infatuation with Irma began in 1899; it was love at first sight. The match-
maker was Irma's mother Rosa Waterman Bock; the catalyst was Stephen
S. Wise.

The Bocks were members of Wise's congregation in New York. An

established American-Jewish family, the Bocks traced their ancestry to
Germany. Irma Bock's maternal grandfather, Sigmund Waterman, had
arrived in America in 1840. An eminent physician, he also taught German
for a time at Yale University. Members of this family, scattered throughout
the United States, attained positions of prominence. In-laws of the family,
the Weils, established the Kahl-Montgomery congregation in Alabama.
Active in the Confederacy during the Civil War, members of the Weil family
were on close personal terms with Judah P. Benjamin. Another cousin,
Philip Stein, was the first Jew to be appointed to the judicial bench in
Chicago, serving first as judge of the Superior Court of Cook County and
later in the appellate court.[6] Branches of the Waterman-Bock family thus
set down roots in two cities in which Irma and Bernard Ehrenreich would
later make their home—Montgomery, Alabama, and Chicago, Illinois.

In 1899, the year she met Bernard, Irma was graduated from Normal
College of New York, presently Hunter College. A gregarious young
woman, she was president of her graduating class. Rather than seeking a
mate among her more established, wealthy, and assimilated German-
Jewish confreres, Irma sought to pledge her troth to the foreign-born
young rabbi. Romance triumphed over social expectation. The Ehren-
reich-Bock marriage articulated Solomon Schechter's hope for American
Jewry—that the method characterized by German Jewry and the madness
which epitomized East-European Jewry would coalesce into a creative
union, that there would be method to madness, that regularity and spon-
taneity would insure a vital future.

In 1906 Ehrenreich left Philadelphia to accept a call to the pulpit of
Congregation Beth Or in Montgomery, Alabama. The reasons for his
departure are unclear. Ehrenreich was popular in Philadelphia. His abilities
were widely recognized. His services were being continually courted by
other congregations. Why then did he choose to go to Alabama?

Irma Ehrenreich's cousin, David Davidson, had been the rabbi of Beth
Or. Davidson was the officiating rabbi at the Ehrenreichs' wedding. Davidson sealed the match between Bernard and Irma and apparently arranged
the courtship between Rabbi Ehrenreich and his new congregation. Further-
more, Irma's relatives, the Weils, were among the founders of the Montgomery congregation. The Ehrenreichs perceived the South as an area of
fertile promise. It was a romantic region, providing a young family with
challenges to overcome. While in Philadelphia, Ehrenreich's activities were
largely restricted to congregational matters. The less oppressive nature of his
Montgomery ministry and the encouragement of his congregants allowed

Ehrenreich's abilities to blossom. In Alabama he expanded the scope of his ministry to embrace communal affairs.

While Ehrenreich believed in the strict separation of church and state, he nevertheless maintained that it was the obligation of Jews—both as Americans and as Jews—to be involved in seeking to assuage the moral ills of society at home and abroad. For Ehrenreich, "Judaism is not alone a religion of creed; it is a religion of action. [To] labor for the welfare of the government in which he lives is an inseparable part of the religious duty of every Jew."[7]

The above statement, printed in the Montgomery press, was made by Ehrenreich in a sermon on the need for establishing juvenile courts, delivered shortly after he arrived in Alabama in 1906, and his remarks blended his concern for youth with his passion for social justice. Shocked by rising juvenile crime, the lack of special judicial review, and the penal treatment available for minors, Ehrenreich pleaded for special courts and rehabilitation for juvenile criminals. Deploring the brutal treatment then received by juvenile offenders, Ehrenreich declared:

> Instead of the whip and the lash, we find the persuasive method; in the place of force and threats we find moral stimulants. And if we have adopted these methods with the insane; if we have found that kind and humane treatment is conducive of better and higher results in the education of children—is it not surprising that we have not tried it with the young offender? . . . [Is it not] a moral imperative upon us to do what we can to rescue these unfortunates?[8]

Ehrenreich's social activism in Alabama's state capital not only stimulated a raising of moral consciousness and conscience but evoked legislative activity. Besides trying to influence local legislators to effect general social improvement, Ehrenreich also activated local concern regarding injustices to Jews at home and abroad. For example, when Russia ceased to grant visas to American Jews to visit Russia, Ehrenreich helped convince the Alabama state legislature to pass a resolution to be forwarded to the federal government, demanding that the United States abrogate its longstanding treaty with Russia until American citizens of the Jewish faith were no longer denied the rights accorded other Americans wishing to visit Russia. In a letter dated September 20, 1913, from Emmet O'Neal, the governor of Alabama, Ehrenreich was appointed an official delegate representing the people of Alabama to a conference in New York convened to protest the persecution of Jews in Rumania. The governor expressed his "full trust in your [Ehrenreich's] prudence, integrity and ability."[9]

Ehrenreich's wife Irma joined in and supported his social activism. Irma was a national leader in the struggle for woman suffrage. In a speech to Alabama suffragettes, she correctly predicted, "Suffrage is coming whether you want it or not."[10] Indeed, Bernard's interest in establishing juvenile courts in the South seems to have been awakened by his wife, who had worked in the juvenile courts of Philadelphia. The rabbi's manifold efforts to ameliorate social conditions in Alabama were clearly attested to in the Montgomery press and by the fact that he was chosen to serve as vice-president of the United Charities of Alabama.

No doubt Ehrenreich's social activism was controversial. However, two areas of his social concern were inevitably dangerous as well: his interest in higher education for blacks and his Zionist beliefs. As an eminent rabbi, the late Jacob Weinstein, pointed out in a eulogy for Ehrenreich, for a Jew to be pro-Zionist and pro-black in Alabama in the first quarter of the twentieth century was physically dangerous. The Ku Klux Klan was powerful; the social position of Jews was insecure; and Zionism was considered by Southern Jews and Gentiles as a "snare and a delusion fostered by Yankee Jews."[11] Nevertheless, Ehrenreich persisted.

In 1915 Seth Low, former president of New York's Columbia University, and Julius Rosenwald, a Chicago Jew who was President of Sears Roebuck, visited Montgomery. They had recently met in Montgomery to encourage the growth of Tuskegee Institute. At a dinner meeting of local civic leaders, Low and Ehrenreich spoke forcefully of the need to support higher education for Southern blacks. Subsequently, at a meeting of the Peanut Association attended by Ehrenreich in 1917 in Montgomery, George Washington Carver had to enter the hall via a freight elevator. This experience made a shocking impression upon Ehrenreich.

During his ministry in Montgomery, Ehrenreich endeavored to make new inroads for Zionism among the Reform Jewish anti-Zionist congregations of the South. He literally brought Zionism to many Southern communities. His persuasive, magnetizing speaking abilities "converted" many Southern Jews, from Arkansas to Louisiana.

Both Irma and Bernard Ehrenreich continually insisted that social action undertaken by Jews must be rooted in Jewish values. Bernard maintained that Jewish social activism which did not emanate from the Jewish soul and which did not enrich Jewish culture would be unkindly evaluated by posterity. "We will not be judged by the social activities in which we have been engaged . . . but from the culture of the Jewish soul shall we be judged."[12] Thus, social action was crucial for Bernard, but penultimate to Jewish identity and to Jewish cultural creativity. In a similar vein, Irma admonished her fellow members of the Council of Jewish Women to seek social justice without denying their Jewish identity. In one address, she asked: "Are we ashamed to own up to our religious affiliations? Are we ashamed of our Jewishness? Why do we try to curry the favor of others by stamping ourselves with false colors and sailing under a flag which is not ours?"[13]

Ehrenreich's concern for his fellow Jews was also evident in a proposal he made in 1908. Convinced that the huge waves of Jewish immigration to the United States could not be quickly and easily absorbed by the large industrial cities of the North, he proposed the founding of an organization which would encourage Jewish immigration to the South. Southern Jewry, he believed, would be enriched by absorbing immigrants who could not be integrated into the already teeming Jewish ghettos of New York. Though Ehrenreich's plan was never realized during his lifetime, demographic shifts in American Jewry during the 1960s and 1970s have fulfilled his expectations.

The latter part of Ehrenreich's service in Montgomery coincided with World War I. The needs of the hour evoked both Ehrenreich's patriotic sentiments and his concern for human needs. Throughout the war years, Ehrenreich worked unstintingly as a civilian chaplain under the auspices of the Jewish Welfare Board, and he was assigned to serve the needs of soldiers stationed at Camp Sheridan.

The Buckeye division, stationed at Camp Sheridan, had many young Jewish soldiers from Ohio, away from home for the first time. Consequently, Ehrenreich opened his home to them. Acknowledgment of his service was carried by Jewish newspapers in Toledo and Cincinnati. In 1917 a mother of one of these soldiers wrote to the *American Israelite:* "Without Bernard Ehrenreich who would know what would become of the Jewish soldiers. To him they look up as a father, to him they confide their troubles. When they cry, when they are homesick . . . to him they go for money and his hand is always in his pocket, never refusing one. He feeds twenty-five to forty twice a week out of his own pocket."[14] One of these Jewish soldiers, Michael Aaronsohn, who was later to become a rabbi, reports in his autobiography how, after attending a Hanukkah service and a large meal at Ehrenreich's house, "the real Jewish spirit was awakened within me."[15]

Besides opening his home to the soldiers, Ehrenreich also made regular visits to the army base. There he not only visited the sick but taught hundreds of illiterate soldiers how to read and write English. Gentiles as well as Jews sought Ehrenreich's counsel, which was always freely and enthusiastically given. According to one report of his chaplaincy, "They [i.e., the soldiers] storm his house and none is ever refused. Not only Jews, but Gentiles wait for him."[16] Reflecting upon his experiences as a civilian chaplain, Ehrenreich wrote: "Looking after the boys of the Buckeye division is a pleasure. I love them all and the response that I am receiving from them makes me feel that there is a vast field for work for some rabbis who are inclined to work among young men that we Jews have neglected."[17] True to his interest in Jewish youth, Ehrenreich found time—despite his burdensome wartime duties—to translate his early vision of a summer camp into a reality.

In 1915 he purchased the campsite of Camp Kawaga in Minoqua, Wisconsin. The camp opened in 1915 with twelve campers. There were no cabins—only tents—no running water, no electricity, and no phone, but there was enthusiasm and hope. By 1920 Camp Kawaga had grown sufficiently to warrant Ehrenreich's complete attention. He therefore resigned from Congregation Beth Or to become a pioneer in a new adventure—Jewish summer camping.

Ehrenreich's departure from Alabama evoked a deep sense of loss among members of his congregation and the community at large. On that occasion, Thomas Kilby, governor of Alabama, wrote of his work:

> Dr. B.C. Ehrenreich is leaving Montgomery to engage in religious and welfare work in another State. He takes with him the respect, esteem and all good wishes of the people of Montgomery and thousands of friends throughout Alabama.
>
> His leaving is a great loss to the city and State for during his stay here for fifteen or twenty years he has been a material factor in the religious, educational and social life of both the city and the State.
>
> To those among whom he is to cast his lot I commend him as a man of high character and deep devotion to truth, justice and duty.[18]

In accepting Ehrenreich's resignation, Isidor Weil, president of the congregation, remarked: "No man nor preacher in our community was more sought after and held in higher esteem than he, and that not only for his learning but for his work. . . . When Dr. Ehrenreich leaves us he leaves a host of friends and admirers—he leaves more—he leaves the stamina of his character; he leaves the echo of his teachings and preachings–religious zeal and example."[19]

Ehrenreich plunged into camping with all his energy. In synagogue work he had felt hampered by congregational pressures and politics. As a camp director he was free to pursue his lifelong goal of bringing Jewish youth to God, of building a new and vital generation of American Jewish youth. Ehrenreich chose to be an inspiration to boys who would one day become leaders of movements. As a resolution of Ehrenreich's congregation put it: "Dr. Ehrenreich decided, or rather decreed, that he would follow . . . his aim, wish and desire for the last twenty years . . . to train and teach young men so that when they return to their homes they would become leaders of Jewish thought and Judaism."[20]

Camp Kawaga was not simply an opportunity for recreation, it was also a laboratory for religious education. To his generations of campers, Ehrenreich was a spiritual guide. He taught them that nature was but a reflection of divine beauty. Surrounded by the magnificence of Wisconsin's northern woods, he led his charges to seek oneness with the cosmic throb.

Reflecting upon the need for the summer-camp experience in the development of youth, Ehrenreich wrote:

> Life in the open is necessary to make a youth sturdy, strong and self-reliant. The pampered city boy becomes a slave of luxury.
>
> Reared in homes of comfort, he too often is allowed to shirk all responsibility of work–servants are at his beck and call–his desire to be of use is atrophied. But out in the open in camp life–with other boys his energies are forced into play. Not only are his muscles strengthened by hiking, canoeing, boating, swimming, and all other athletic sports, but his will power is strengthened by his enforced initiative.
>
> During the period of a boy's free-time–the summer months–a boy should be associated with men who will direct his thoughts into proper channels. He should receive the training that will make it possible for him to meet the difficulties of life, accepting success with understanding and failure without loss of courage.[21]

In 1940 Ehrenreich retired as the director of Camp Kawaga. When World War II broke out, he felt obliged to serve. Unable to enlist in the active chaplaincy due to his advanced age, Ehrenreich volunteered for the civilian chaplaincy, replacing rabbis called to the military chaplaincy. Though this meant arduous travel and the difficulty of moving his belongings, Ehrenreich was not one to shirk what he considered his moral responsibilities. In 1942 he served the Congregation Tree of Life in Columbia, South Carolina, and in 1943 and 1944 he ministered to Temple Israel in Stockton, California. Even as late as 1946, at age seventy, Ehrenreich became the first rabbi of the Liberal Synagogue of Baton Rouge, Louisiania, a synagogue which had seceded from a larger Reform synagogue because of the anti-Zionism of its rabbi.

In the early 1950s the indomitable Rabbi Ehrenreich began to feel the passing of the years, and on March 10, 1955, the soul of Bernard Ehrenreich entered the realm of eternity.

As Ehrenreich perceived the presence of God in nature, so did he see a spark of divinity in each human soul. No person was too lowly for him to minister to. No personal problem was too trite to evoke his concern. Not only in his camping and congregational career but also in his chaplaincies during two world wars, Ehrenreich's profound kindliness and sincere humanness were manifest.

An engaging speaker and an inspiring preacher, Ehrenreich left his mark wherever he went. His initial impact upon the lives of hundreds of individuals was profound. His correspondence demonstrates that he maintained intense personal relationships with many individuals though geographically distant from them. Members of his Montgomery congregation, former campers at Kawaga, servicemen and congregants he ministered to during the world wars continually sought his advice and counsel, and he responded freely, generously, and enthusiastically.

Despite a life of perpetual motion, despite a career of service to others, Ehrenreich never neglected his family. He was a devoted husband and a doting father. His correspondence with his wife reveals their marriage of over half a century to have been a perpetual honeymoon. Despite many moves, professional travail, and financial difficulty, their courtship ended only with his death.

Bernard Ehrenreich was a spiritual pioneer. He forsook national prominence during his lifetime to help insure capable leaders for American Jewry after his death. He withdrew from building institutions in order to build individuals. After a career marked by remarkable diversity, Ehrenreich's legacy endures. The indelible impression he made upon the hearts and minds of the many hundreds, if not thousands, whom he encountered guarantees the permanence of his presence.

2.   Reflections on Southern-Jewish Historiography

Stanley F. Chyet

In 1791 a Jewish woman living in a Virginia town wrote to her parents in Germany that she saw no prospect of raising her children as Jews. "Here they cannot become anything else [but Gentiles]. Jewishness is pushed aside here. . . . My children cannot learn anything here, nothing Jewish, nothing of general culture."[1] The problem was certainly not confined to Virginia or to the South, but it would not overstate the case very much to say that the problem there was and would long remain particularly acute. More than a century later a Texas rabbi lamented that most Southern rabbis were "far removed from intellectual centers." "We pine for Jewish intellectual companionship," he declared.[2] To be sure, intellectual malnutrition had more than a strictly Jewish aspect: no one has summed up the problem more strikingly than the South Carolinian Wilbur J. Cash in his memorable book, *The Mind of the South*. "In general," Cash observed, "the intellectual and aesthetic culture of the Old South was a superficial and jejune thing, borrowed from without and worn as a political armor and a badge of rank; and hence"—and here Cash calls "the authority of old Matthew Arnold to bear [him] witness"—"not a true culture at all."[3] Again—and worse from a Jewish perspective, as the Virginia letter writer had already recognized in 1791—there was little enough in the South to nourish either a robust *yiddishkeit* or a searching inquiry into intellectual and aesthetic concerns, Jewish or general.

To be sure, there were intriguing fits and starts—Charleston's Reformed Society of Israelites in the 1820s, for instance, or the Southern Rabbinical Association of a later generation—and there is no gainsaying the existence of such Southern-born or Southern-raised notables of the last hundred years as Louis D. Brandeis, Bernard M. Baruch, Adolph S. Ochs, Lillian Hellman, Lewis L. Strauss, Ludwig Lewisohn, Karl Shapiro, and Robert Strauss; nor would one omit Robert Strauss's fellow Texan, Kinky Friedman of "Ride 'em Jewboy" musical fame. As Lewisohn felt it necessary to say some forty years ago, however, from the Nullification controversy to the end of Reconstruction—and perhaps Lewisohn was too restrictive in setting these termini—"the South was in its psychical character an armed camp in which any expression deviating from the strictest group conventions was held the last and foulest of disloyalties . . . [and] since it was held dishonorable and disloyal in any Southern gentleman to differentiate himself in any manner from the experience, opinion, emotion, of his dominant, aristocratic and yet subtly menaced group, it is clear that there was no place for art in this society."[4] What wonder, then, that the overriding tendency of Southern Jewry should have been to attenuate its Jewish sensibilities and to move inexorably in the direction of discomfort with Jewish self-assertiveness? The Jew who felt somewhat chagrined by his origins or who cultivated a certain indifference to the indicia of Jewish identity would seem to have suited rather well the elementally agrarian South, the South Willard Thorp has called "racial intolerance and Negro slums, eroded hillsides and silt-choked rivers, demagogues and the one-party system," the South in which (Cash reminds us) Jews "were usually thought of as aliens even when their fathers had fought in the Confederate armies" and in which they stood "in the eyes of the people as a sort of evil harbinger and incarnation of all the menaces they feared and hated—external and internal, real and imaginary."[5] Even a classical turn-of-the-century *y'feh nefesh* like Rabbi David Marx of Atlanta could not deny the existence in the South of "widespread and deep-seated prejudice against Jews as an entire people."[6] To the phenomenon represented in France by the Dreyfus affair and in Russia by the Beilis case, the American South contributed the agony of Leo Frank.

This condition would not remain unaltered, however. As Northern economic interests and Northern mores pressed southward, and especially as what might be called a technological infrastructure took shape in the region, a new South began emerging. Did a new Jew begin emerging as well? For most of the century following Appomattox, the South—burdened with a tributary "raw-material economy, [and] with the attendant penalties of low wages, lack of opportunity, and poverty"[7]—was not a region which could be hospitable to the growth of Jewish life, but the post–World War II decades have witnessed a rather dramatic volte-face. Regrettably, insufficient research has been undertaken for us to be in a position to say authoritatively to what degree and in what ways a new Jew has been emerging in the New South.

The bicentennial year 1976 was incontestably the Year of the South, but was it also the Year of Southern-Jewish Historiography? Jimmy Carter and Robert Strauss are proof of the changes recent decades have wrought in the old southern pattern that Cash described as "high romantic histrionics, violence, and mass coercion of the scapegoat and the heretic."[8] Can anything comparable be said of a historiography which is yet to give priority to the question of Jewish life within the context of the South during the second half of the twentieth century? There are indeed a number of quite respectable and, in some instances, even impressive works relating to and illuminating Jewish life and history in the South, but alas, they do not add up to a keen, mind-stirring Southern-Jewish historiography, for they do not, in general, address themselves to any far-reaching changes which might be detected in the patterns of Southern Jewish life.

Apart from earlier, and what it might be proper to call classical, chronicles of Jewish beginnings in South Carolina, Virginia, Maryland, Georgia, and Texas,[9] the contributions of modern writers have added substantially to our knowledge of the Jewish experience in the South, and to prove this point one need not undertake an inevitably tedious review of works by scholars as accomplished as Bertram W. Korn, Jacob R. Marcus, Leonard Dinnerstein, Leo Shpall, Malcolm H. Stern, Isaac Fein, Charles Reznikoff, Mark Elovitz, Fedora Frank, Arnold Shankman, Janice Rothschild, Stephen Hertzberg, Louis Ginsberg, Elaine Maas, Alfred Hero, Myron Berman, and others who have labored in this vineyard.[10] The problem is that, with some few exceptions, these studies have been episodic or they have focused on the Old South and have paid minimal attention to the New South–especially the South in the years since World War II. What has resulted is a certain provincialism in the presentation of Southern Jews and Southern-Jewish history.

Now provincialism in the establishing of historiographical foundations is not necessarily–and, in any case, not entirely–a stumbling block. Certainly there are worse defects. Without a measure of provincialism, without a concentration–even an insular one–on the immediate matter at hand, chronicling the events and personalities of a given community or locale might never begin. But ultimately provincialism is nothing less than asphyxiating, and it must be set aside–which American-Jewish historians in general–and within their number, of course, many of those who have devoted themselves to recapitulating the Southern-Jewish experience–have been loath to do. We have, on the whole, been unwilling to deprovincialize our work, or we have simply not comprehended the need for an ampler, more thoroughgoing construction of the data at our disposal— a construction which would allow us to judge what we take to be Jewish phenomena in connection with, or against the background of, both the development of Jewish tradition and the life of the surrounding non-Jewish society. How have the Jews of a particular place and time seen themselves related to, on the one hand, the ancestral norms secured from the Jewish past and, on the other hand, the usages of the non-Jews in whose midst they have lived and by whose values, more often than not, they have been governed in a variety of crucial ways quite apart from anything theological? It is at least as important to ask such questions and to seek answers for them as it is to gather data and to determine who came and when and from where or to establish when and by whom Jewish institutions were founded in a specific locality. Often enough, admittedly, the answers could be no more than partial or speculative, but that is what makes for a historiography worthy of the designation. After all, there is no good reason, no historiographical reason, to ignore or to dismiss the question of the role of Jews in general social and economic, as well as in cultural and religious, development; further, there is no justification for avoidance of probing— again, however tentatively—the meaning or meanings of Jewish identity within the framework of both Jewish communal experience and the larger non-Jewish world. Wilhelm von Humboldt, writing "On The Historian's Task" a century and a half ago, understood that nothing could be allowed to jeopardize "that more general concern with humanity which history requires even when it is dealing with an isolated phenomenon."[11]

Those who profess a desire to reconstruct the history of Jews in the South are surely no more derelict than their colleagues who want to reconstruct Jewish history elsewhere in North America—but in a way, the weakness of Southern-Jewish historiography *is* a greater pity. With all its complexities, Southern Jewry does constitute a smaller, somewhat more self-contained and more homogeneous group, the study of whose experience might very well shed light on certain otherwise ill-defined dynamics pertinent to North American Jewry as a whole—social history, the fabric of its religiocommunal life, the socioeconomic gradations within Jewish communities, the impact of Jews as Jews on the general society, and the impact of the general society on Jews, on their values and their lifestyles. How much, to supply a concrete instance, have Southern Jews, whether newcomers or members of older families, been influenced by the flamboyant evangelical religiosity for which the region is famous in American life and history? Is Jewish congregational life in the South distinctive in any way? Does it differ appreciably from Jewish congregational life elsewhere in North America? Have rabbis in the South achieved any greater authority than rabbis elsewhere?

C. Vann Woodward speaks of "theological orthodoxy" as "the essence of Southern religious solidarity" and assures us that in the years between the Civil War and World War I "modernism and liberalized theology were rejected, or ignored in favor of 'the old-time religion.' Unorthodox sects such as Unitarianism and Christian Science made [little] progress in the South," while "Evangelistic revivalism . . . continued to flourish" there. Cash, too, speaks of the "swing back to primitivism in religion . . . the sweep of the so-called Fundamentalism through the region, until even men of great dignity in the community could be brought to grovel and weep at the mourners' bench of Mr. [Billy] Sunday." And he tells us of the time— decades after Reconstruction—when "the ministers of the evangelical sects finally towered up to their greatest power, until almost literally nobody in the South dared criticize their pronouncements or oppose the political programs they laid out."[12]

But how is it that no comparable mood has been characteristic of Jewish religious life in the region? Reform Judaism, of the so-called classical, pointedly rationalistic nineteenth-century variety, would seem to have found itself nowhere more welcome than in the South, where to this day the high-minded and altogether chaste rhetoric of the *Union Prayer Book* is probably most appealing to the synagogue-affiliated and where, as one sociologist has written, "rejection of all but the most superficial of the rituals and ceremonies"[13] appears more often than not to be the Jewish norm. Nor was it at all a typically Southern idea that a Nashville rabbi voiced seventy years ago in contending that Jewish "children should be made acquainted with the ethical history of all religions" and that Judaism would "not suffer in comparison, even if it be shown to be but one agent in God's providence."[14] The ethical history of all religions is not what has interested most Southern churchmen.

Henry W. Grady tells a charming story about "an old preacher [an evangelical Protestant, of course] . . . who told some boys of the Bible lesson he was going to read in the morning. The boys, finding the place, glued together the connecting pages. The next morning he read on the bottom of one page, 'When Noah was one hundred and twenty years old

he took unto himself a wife, who was'—then turning the page—'140 cubits
wide, built of gopher wood—and covered with pitch inside and out.' He
was naturally puzzled at this. He read it again . . . and then said: 'My friends,
this is the first time I ever met this in the Bible, but I accept this as an evidence of the assertion that we are fearfully and wonderfully made.' "[15] The
story is wonderfully made and no doubt hilarious in the context of Southern Protestantism; it is virtually unimaginable in a Southern-Jewish context. Jewish religiosity in the South has apparently been a phenomenon
very much at variance with what writers like Woodward and Cash say of
the Protestant Christianity that is virtually supreme below the Mason-
Dixon line. To understand and account for this phenomenon is not an
undertaking for theologians alone; it is something a respectable historiography might be expected to illuminate. A probing of Jewish values and
Jewish life-styles is appropriate to any Jewish historical research worthy
of the name, but the overall patterns of Southern life might very well
make this research more manageable. The South has remained distinctive
longer than any other region. That distinctiveness may be fast waning
today; it may no longer be possible to say, as one Northern writer did in
the mid-1950s, that the South is "the most exotic . . . region in America,"[16]
or, as a Southern scholar put it a few years earlier, that the South is notable
for "the chains of habit and custom and the deep groove of agrarian tradition that confined thought in ancient patterns."[17] Still, some precipitate
must be expected to survive and to be recognizable. Humboldt put the
matter this way: "Nations and individuals . . . leave behind them forms of
spiritual individuality . . . which are more enduring and effective than deeds
or events."[18] Will the life of Southern Jews be quite mute on this score?

Another problem on which historiography ought to offer us some gui-
dance is the relationship between blacks and Jews in the contemporary
South. What is known of relations between blacks and Jews in the South
of Jimmy Carter and Robert Strauss? There is no clear, unblurred picture.
On the one hand, we have no reason to dismiss what a transplanted North-
erner, Mark Pinsky of Durham, means us to understand when he chides
fellow Durhamite Eli Evans, now resident in the North, for going "easy
on certain Jewish mayors of certain large Southern . . . cities who have
experienced great difficulty in dealing with black sanitation workers."[19]
We have no warrant for being shocked by Rabbi Elovitz's report that the
Birmingham Jewish establishment preferred to see black-white conflicts
as a "Christian" problem. The earlier research efforts of Allen Krause and

Leonard Dinnerstein have prepared us for such a report.[20] Nor are we likely to imagine that Harry Golden is only the humorist when he declares: "The studied attempt to avoid all debate, except on purely Jewish matters, has been in force so long that it would be hard to find six Jews below the Mason-Dixon Line who hold sufficiently strong convictions to be accused of anything."[21] On the other hand, we are told that a black, Memphis-born Chicago businessman apparently encounters no obstacle in buying a large house in a predominantly Jewish neighborhood in Memphis and moving there with his three children.[22] Is this datum without significance? Unfortunately, no serious work of historical and sociological research is available today to help us secure a sharper focus.

What do we know with any certainty of Southern-Jewish life today, and what would we be safe in predicting for tomorrow? Today we confront a rapidly industrializing South, a South of increasingly deregionalized lifestyle. Will this South spark some counter tendency of ethnic consciousness, of ethnic emphasis, among Southern Jews—so many of whom have for decades or longer seemed bent on stressing their Southernism and on diluting their Jewishness? What impact might such a countertendency have on Southern Jewry? If Theodore Lowi is to be believed, the seeds for such a consciousness are apparently not lacking. Lowi suggests that, for Jews who are not newcomers to the South, Jewishness has long been "an ethnic rather than a religious experience." Such Jews "display virtually every feature of ethnicity save its acceptance." Ironically, Lowi observes, the member of a typical well-established Southern-Jewish family "is a living refutation of his own argument that 'Judaism is a religion, not a nationality.' Religion is quite superficial to him, but Jewry is not."[23]

What impact will another related, and not at all putative, by-product of industrialization and deregionalization—the settlement in larger numbers of Northern Jews—have on Southern-Jewish life? According to *Time* magazine, Miami has long been a suburb of New York—but how far is Atlanta from that status? How far behind is Birmingham or Charlotte or Memphis or Houston? It may be that Miami has never been anything but a suburb of New York—how often has it been said in Florida, "the further south one goes, the more north one is"? But a hundred years ago—and, indeed, even more recently—Baltimore and Washington and Louisville were quite Southern, and now a nationwide periodical like *Time* excludes them from its map of the region.[24] (My Louisville-born mother-in-law, of blessed memory, would have been pained.) And how has all this affected, and how is it going to affect, the by-no-means-negligible Jewish communities of the meta-morphosed Southern metropolises? Much more is known of Jewish life in antebellum Charleston and Richmond and New Orleans than of the Jewish experience during the past three decades in those cities. We may know something of the experience of notables, but the patterns of life lived by the less distinguished or less articulate or less heralded Jews in the South have gone without much notice. Not that Jewish historiography in the North and in the West has so much to boast of, but it may be said without outrageous exaggeration that historiographically Southern Jewry—a group whose communal roots go back to at least the early 1700s—has had to endure something of a shadow existence since the Civil War. It is time for a true Southern-Jewish historiography to begin taking shape.

The Role of the Rabbi in the South

3.

Malcolm H. Stern

Although the organized American-Jewish community proudly traces
its origins to Nieuw Amsterdam in 1654, it was almost two hundred years
before an ordained rabbi made his home in North America. The reason for
this hiatus was the traditional role of the rabbi in the European-Jewish communities. There the rabbi was primarily a scholar, versed in the laws and lore
of Judaism. The more scholarly he was, the less he had to do with any aspect
of congregational life except answering the ritual questions of individuals.
He devoted his days and nights to study and to raising up disciples who
would become the next generation of rabbis. He rarely preached, was more
oracle than pastor, and if he had any contact with children, it was only to
supervise their Hebrew education. He was supported by the community
or by a wealthy patron—often a father-in-law whose prime choice of husband
for his daughter would be a rabbi. In the emancipated North American
scene, no Jewish community before 1840 was large enough to warrant, or
dedicated enough to want, a rabbi.[1]

The seventeenth- and eighteenth-century North American congregations—all but one of which followed the Sephardic ritual[2]—made the distinction between the *hacham,* or "scholarly rabbi," and the *hazzan,* or
"cantor" (Americanized to "reader" or "minister"). Among the founders
of Charleston's Congregation Beth Elohim in 1749-50 was one Moses
Cohen, who was accorded the title of *hacham*—although the title in all likelihood was honorific, there being no record of Cohen's rabbinic training
in the London community. He may have been knowledgeable in Hebrew
lore, but he earned his livelihood as a "shopkeeper."[3] Until 1840, no ordained rabbi settled in America, and it was long after the Civil War before
most of the Southern communities acquired a rabbi whose credentials could
be verified.

As each community established a congregation, it used laymen to con-

duct the worship; as communities and congregations grew, these functionaries became full-time professionals. Modeling themselves on the dominant
Protestant community, they became preachers and pastors, organized Hebrew schools, and eventually set up Sunday schools (or frequently Sabbath
schools, meeting on Saturday). By the time any sizable group of trained
rabbis arrived on these shores, the role had become totally "Protestantized,"
with some interesting variations practiced by individuals.

The pioneer rabbi was Abraham Rice, who arrived in New York from
his native Bavaria on July 25, 1840, as part of the tide of Bavarian Jews
which flowed across the Atlantic from 1836 on. After unsuccessfully trying
to revive the Newport, Rhode Island, congregation, Rice met a *landsman*
in New York who was then president of Baltimore Hebrew Congregation.
By Rosh Hashanah of 1840 Rice was ensconced in that pulpit, dutifully
attempting to preserve Orthodox Jewish practice among his assimilating
flock. He inveighed against those who opened their businesses on the Sabbath and who used Masonic rites at funeral services. Within the congregation, however, he met with stubborn opposition when he sought to shorten
the worship, especially on Yom Kippur, by dropping some of the less
intelligible mediaeval Hebrew poetry (*piyyutim*). Frustrated by his inability
either to preserve his Judaism in such an environment or to institute
moderate reforms, he resigned in 1849. Eking out a living as a shopkeeper,
he functioned without salary for a small clique which gathered for worship,
until in the last six months of his life he was called back to Baltimore
Hebrew Congregation.[4]

Prior to the outbreak of the Civil War, Baltimore was the only city below
the Mason-Dixon line that seems to have had a strong enough Jewish community to import trained rabbis from Europe. The rest of the communities
in the South settled for what Rabbi Marcus Jastrow, at a Baltimore meeting
as late as 1885, described as self-qualified, self-ordained, and self-taught
"rabbis."[5] This state of affairs made the Central Conference of American
Rabbis—organized by Isaac Mayer Wise and others in 1889—open membership not only to ordained rabbis but to "all autodidactic preachers and
teachers of religion who have been for at least three successive years dis-
charging those duties in any one congregation."[6] It is evident that the
Conference was trying to establish standards for congregational functionaries.

Many of these "readers" were given the honorific title of rabbi by their
congregants and by the Gentile community, and a number of the pioneering
ones served with real distinction. Most notable was Westphalian-born,

Richmond-trained Isaac Leeser (1806–68), whose ministry was spent totally in Philadelphia. Through his periodical *The Occident,* his translation of the Bible into English, and his other writings, Leeser was certainly the most influential Jewish clergyman of his era. His younger contemporary, Isaac Mayer Wise, himself probably never ordained, was the prime mover for the creation of a seminary to train American rabbis.[7]

But America was on the road to producing its first rabbi. This was Hungarian-born Simon Tuska, the son of the reader of Congregation B'rith Kodesh, of Rochester, New York. Acquiring in 1851 the first scholarship to that town's university, young Tuska was prevailed upon–partly because of his own dreams, and with much encouragement from Isaac M. Wise–to enroll in Germany's well-established Jewish Theological Seminary at Breslau in 1858. Two years later Tuska returned to America without having completed the course, attracted by an opening at New York's Temple Emanu-El, but his thin voice and small stature eliminated him from consideration there. He accepted an invitation to Memphis, where he ministered for eleven years before dying of a heart attack at age thirty-six. His career set the standard for the training of American rabbis–a university degree plus seminary rabbinic education, preaching and teaching in English, and American training. Among his papers was a proposal for an American seminary.[8]

In 1867 the Philadelphia rabbinate, led by Leeser, opened Maimonides College, which aimed at combining university and Hebrew education. This attempt to train American rabbis lasted a bit more than five years, dying for lack of interested and eligible students. Only three men completed a portion of its academic program, although no formal graduation or ordination was ever held. Two of them came south. David Levy served Beth Elohim of Charleston from 1875 to 1893. In 1879 he published his own prayer book, *The Service of the Sanctuary,* totally Reform in its approach. A painter and poet, Levy's verses became a fixture in three editions of Reform Judaism's *Union Hymnal.* Samuel Mendelsohn, the other alumnus of Maimonides to settle in the South, served the traditional congregation, Beth El, in Norfolk, Virginia, from 1873 to 1876 and spent the remainder of his career, until his death in 1922, in Wilmington, North Carolina. The Russian-born Mendelsohn had an excellent Hebrew background and devoted his energies to Jewish scholarship, translating the Book of Haggai for the Jewish Publication Society's *The Holy Scriptures* and contributing to the Talmudic dictionary of his father-in-law and teacher, Rabbi Marcus Jastrow.[9]

A word should be said about the nature of the Southern congregations served by these men and their contemporaries. Most students of American Jewish history are unaware of the three eighteenth-century congregations: Mickve Israel of Savannah (founded in 1733, but with gaps in its subsequent history); Beth Elohim of Charleston (1749); and Beth Shalome of Richmond (1789). The founders of the Savannah and Charleston congregations were predominantly Sephardic Jews, and although both congregations—like their Northern counterparts in New York, Newport, and Philadelphia—quickly acquired a majority of Ashkenazic (German-Polish) Jews, they retained the Sephardic rite, primarily for two reasons: In building their synagogues, they relied for financial help on the wealthy and established Sephardic communities in London and the Caribbean, and the dignity of the Sephardic service (compared with the lack of decorum in the Ashkenazic) made it more acceptable in the eyes of non-Jews. *Mah yomru hagoyim?* ("What will the Gentiles say?") was to influence American Judaism—especially in the South—until after the establishment of the State of Israel. Of the twenty-eight founders of Richmond's Sephardic-rite Congregation Beth Shalome, only one, Aaron Nunes Cardoza, could claim to be of Sephardic origin.[10] With the exception of Baltimore (which cannot strictly be considered a Southern city), the South was slow in establishing congregations. At the outbreak of the Civil War there were only twenty-one congregations in the entire Confederacy or bordering it.

By 1860 the leaders of most of these congregations were English-speaking, some of them second- and third-generation Americans. They were beginning to be swamped by the growing population of German immigrants which would overrun the South in the Reconstruction period. Many of these German Jews started out as peddlers, found a suitable sales territory, and settled down as shopkeepers and merchants. City directories show the majority to have been operating clothing or dry-goods emporia, with a smattering of small-time manufacturing. A native son might infrequently achieve professional status as attorney or physician. The German-speaking element originated from two sources. The earlier migration, beginning about 1836, came from the Rhineland, Bavaria, Baden, and Württemberg. These areas had been somewhat emancipated under Napoleon, and despite the post-Napoleonic restrictions and the anti-Semitic activity to which they were increasingly subjected, they had tasted some of the fruits of Western culture and had adjusted to Christian mores. The failure of the revolution of 1848 produced the far larger wave of Prussian Jews, whose traditions were far more ghettoized. They followed the Polish rite, since their parents and grandparents were predominantly from Posen, a province annexed from Poland by Prussia in the 1790s. Because of the divergent culture of these two groups (the Rhinelanders called the Prussian immigrants "Polanders"), the growing number of German congregations split into groups which either evolved as Reform, led predominantly by the Jews from southern Germany, or Orthodox, led by those of Prussian-Posen origin.[11]

The decade of the Civil War saw Rabbi Isaac Mayer Wise of Cincinnati emerging as the most important single Jewish influence on Southern congregational life. Wise's two newspapers – the English-language *Israelite* and the German *Die Deborah* – appealed to a growing audience. Although he identified himself with a Talmudic-based Judaism, Wise editorialized strongly for an Americanized practice, a view that struck a responsive chord in the hearts of Jews scattered through the South and elsewhere. Recognizing that observing kosher dietary laws was almost a physical impossibility for Jews in isolated communities, Wise borrowed a concept from the New Testament, stressing that what came out of one's mouth was more important than what entered it. Thus, when Wise issued in 1873 his call for the creation of what became the Union of American Hebrew Congregations, almost half of the delegates who came to the first meeting were from the South. It was this gathering which agreed to help create the Hebrew Union College, born two years later and now the oldest surviving Jewish seminary in the world. There were four members of the first graduating class in 1883, of whom one, Henry Berkowitz, went south to Mobile, Alabama. By the time of Wise's death in 1900, one-fourth of the sixty-three men he had ordained were serving in southern pulpits. At long last, the South had acquired trained rabbis.[12]

What was the role of the rabbi in the South? As in the case of Abraham Rice, America's first ordained rabbi, the impact of America weakened Orthodox Jewish practice, even though the congregations organized in the South between 1850 and 1880 were founded by men who sought to preserve Orthodox Judaism. The immigrant German Jews sought to transplant to America what they had known in Europe, and the Norfolk story is perhaps typical.

In 1844 Jacob Umstadter, an Orthodox Jew from Hanover, arrived in Norfolk. Trained as a cantor and kosher butcher, he complained that the local Jews were eating non-kosher meat, and set about establishing what became four years later *Chevra B'nai Jaacov* (literally, "Association of the Sons of Jacob," but Americanized to "House of Jacob"). By 1853, the

Norfolk Jews were incorporating their institution with an Americanized name, the Norfolk Hebrew and English Literary Institute, to indicate its function as a parochial school for children. Umstadter and a variety of other laymen conducted the worship and performed the marriages; presumably they performed the other traditional rituals as well. Following the Civil War, the Norfolk community reorganized and became Congregation Ohef Sholom (being Germans, they pronounced the Hebrew word *Ohev* as "Ohef"—and Ohef Sholom it has remained). By 1869, however, assimilationist members, mostly of South German origin, were demanding reform of the ritual. The engagement of Rev. B. L. Fould as reader and preacher became a step in the direction of Reform, causing the traditionalists, including Umstadter, to drop out of the congregation and create, a year later, Congregation Beth El—consisting predominantly of Prussian-Posen Jews. Reform came gradually to Ohef Sholom: the prayers were shortened (the minute book actually lists the deletions); an organ was installed; and a Christian organist was engaged. By 1871 the bylaws had been amended to allow election of a president and vice-president who did not close their businesses on the Sabbath. Rabbi Fould tried to introduce the radical Reform prayer book created by Rabbi David Einhorn, but that was moving too fast. An attempt to alternate this book with the more traditional one of Rabbis Szold and Jastrow also failed. A committee was set up to compile a ritual composed of readings from both of these and from Isaac M. Wise's, but the outcome is not recorded. A vote taken in 1876 to remove head-covering found only two supporters; there is no record of when this step was ultimately taken. (Probably the influx of east-European immigrants in the following decades encouraged a more rapid assimilation in the effort to distinguish the second- and third-generation German-American from his too-often-caricatured "Russian" counterpart.) Fould was succeeded by English-born Rev. Bernard Eberson, who functioned—with the affection and admiration of the majority of his congregants—until 1899, when the congregation acquired its first Hebrew Union College graduate, Simon R. Cohen. Like a number of the Reform rabbis of his day, Cohen wore the collar and garb of an Episcopal minister and became a symbol of the strong assimilative trend that was to pervade Reform Judaism until 1948 and the birth of Israel. The typical Southern Reform rabbi was in the vanguard of assimilation.[13]

The major impetus toward assimilation was the growth of public anti-Semitism. In 1877 the prominent Joseph Seligman family of New York, friends of President Grant, were denied admission to the fashionable Grand Union Hotel in Saratoga Springs, New York. The resultant battle in the press, and a growing feeling of "America for the Americans" resulted in a social anti-Semitism, which, until World War II, kept Jews out of clubs and resorts, set up quota systems in colleges and professions, and otherwise discriminated against the Jews. A prime function of the Southern rabbi became interpreting the Jew to the non-Jewish community. It was no accident that the Jewish Chautauqua Society, founded by Rabbi Henry Berkowitz in 1893 with a view to training Jews in Judaism, changed its function. In 1910 the Society received a request from the president of the University of Tennessee, at Knoxville, for a speaker on the Bible. Berkowitz sent Julian Morgenstern, then a young professor and later president of the Hebrew Union College. Fundamentalist preachers in Tennessee raised a storm against having a Jew indoctrinate their young people, but so successful were Morgenstern's three lectures that the Chautauqua Society changed its entire program from instructing Jews to instructing Christians about Judaism. My longtime predecessor on the Norfolk pulpit, Dr. Louis D. Mendoza, was well appreciated by his congregants for his oratory but was even more heralded for the fact that he was welcome on every Christian pulpit in the area. This was an attitude which my generation of Reform rabbis in the South inherited, and our attempts to reverse the assimilative trends and to build Judaism within the congregation moved slowly.

From 1880 onward, the growth of east-European immigration into Southern Jewish communities had its own effect. Former Orthodox congregations, like Beth El of Norfolk or its Richmond namesake, found themselves more Americanized than the immigrants and moved toward what became Conservative Judaism—where some of the more assimilative among the immigrants joined them, while other immigrants attempted to transplant shtetl Judaism to the American South. Such was the case with Rabbi Tobias Geffen, who served Atlanta's Orthodox Congregation Shearith Israel from 1910 until his death in 1970. The epitome of the European-style rabbi, he wrote scholarly books, gave responsa to ritual questions, and organized a yeshiva which prepared a remarkable number of young men to enter rabbinical seminary. In the aftermath of World War I and the later Holocaust, his home became the Atlanta refuge and resettlement center for many a Jew. On a sea of assimilationism, he managed to keep the bark of Orthodox Judaism afloat.[14] Few of his Southern Orthodox colleagues were so successful, although they envisaged their role as that of preservers of Talmudic Judaism. The assimilative power of American life has influenced many Orthodox congregants to abandon strict Sabbath observance, dietary laws outside the home, and even membership in an Orthodox synagogue. The traditional rabbi, whether Conservative or Orthodox, has often become his congregation's unimitated model of Jewish observance.

The emergence of political Zionism at the turn of this century was to play a major role in separating the immigrants from those Jews who were already established in America and their descendants. The Southern Jew, predominantly American-born by the beginning of this century, accepted with fervor the pronouncements contained in the Pittsburgh Platform created by fifteen Reform rabbis in 1885, especially the statement: "We consider ourselves no longer a nation, but a religious community, and therefore expect neither a return to Palestine, nor a sacrificial worship under the sons of Aaron, nor the restoration of any of the laws concerning the Jewish state."[15] For the majority of Southern Jews and their rabbis, America was their Zion, and they wanted no other. For them, solution to any problems lay in overcoming anti-Semitism and in achieving America's fullest potential for "life, liberty, and the pursuit of happiness." To be outspokenly Zionist before World War II in a Southern Reform congregation took courage on the part of a rabbi. At least two men of record had that courage. One was Maximilian Heller, a graduate of the second class of Hebrew Union College, who became rabbi of Temple Sinai of New Orleans in 1886 and served there with distinction until his retirement in 1927. An outspoken Zionist, he nevertheless maintained a career of stature within the New Orleans community, where his philosophy was anything but popular.[16] Similarly, Bernard C. Ehrenreich, a strong Zionist, served the Montgomery, Alabama, congregation for a number of years before, during, and after World War I. He subsequently left the pulpit rabbinate for other Jewish activities, including the operation of a Wisconsin camp for Jewish boys.[17]

The Central Conference of American Rabbis, meeting in Columbus, Ohio, in 1937, included in its "Guiding Principles of Reform Judaism" a statement to the effect that Zionism and Reform Judaism were not necessarily incompatible, but so divided was the Reform rabbinate on the issue that a truce was declared on debating that subject or issues pertaining to it. It was a presumed violation of that truce at the 1942 conference—when a vote was taken on a resolution supporting the idea of a Jewish Army to fight with the British in Palestine—that provoked a group of anti-Zionist rabbis, led by Louis Wolsey and William Fineshriber of Philadelphia, to summon a meeting of like-minded rabbis and to create the American Council for Judaism. Of the ninety-three rabbis who signed Wolsey's original manifesto, a large majority were serving in Southern pulpits. In the aftermath of the birth of Israel, most of these rabbis recognized that history had passed them by and resigned from the American Council, leaving it to some ardent laymen to keep the organization alive. The 1967 war gave the Council its coup de grace. As late as 1947, however, my own election to the pulpit of Ohef Sholom of Norfolk had been predicated on my being an anti-Zionist, and the major opponents to my election were congregants who opposed that viewpoint.

The one issue that has affected every aspect of Southern life since the birth of the United States has been race, the issue that eventually split the nation in one of the bloodiest wars in all human history. The Northern rabbinate remained divided on the issue. Isaac Leeser–living in Philadelphia but with strong ties to Richmond–tried hard to remain aloof and neutral and was condemned by both sides. In Baltimore, a city of divided sympathies, Rabbi David Einhorn had been writing and preaching against slavery since 1856. In April of 1861 rioting broke out in the city, with Confederate sympathizers molesting anyone suspected of abolitionist views. Young men from Einhorn's Har Sinai Congregation sought to protect him and his family, but after four days of riots he was prevailed upon to flee north. That was as close as any rabbi in the geographical south came to expressing Northern views. So far as we can tell, every one of the functionaries in the Southern congregation–like the overwhelming majority of their congregants–actively supported the Confederacy. In the 1863 Yankee occupation of New Orleans, Rev. James Gutheim chose to move his family to the home of his in-laws in Mobile rather than take an oath of allegiance to the United States. Similarly, Rev. Henry S. Jacobs, who had served Beth Shalome of Richmond for three years (1854-57) before moving on to Charleston, fled the bombing of Charleston and joined a number of his congregants in Columbia, South Carolina. There he functioned for Congregation Tree of Life, until Sherman's army set fire to that city. He denounced Rev. Samuel Isaacs of New York for writing an appeal for loyalty to the Union. When General Grant's infamous Order no. 11 was issued–prohibiting Jews, as a group, from trading with his Union Army in Tennessee–Rabbis Tuska and Peres of Memphis denounced Northern merchants who were crossing the line to deal in contraband, but they made no recorded complaint against the anti-Semitism implicit in the order itself.[18]

In the decades between the Civil War and World War II, no Southern rabbi seems to have made any attempt to deal with the race question. The fear of anti-Semitism, which reached its peak with the trial of Leo Frank in Atlanta in 1913, remained so pervasive throughout the South, that few (if any) Jewish laymen or rabbis would have had the courage to speak out on so unpopular an issue as the rights of blacks.

In the era of good feeling that followed World War II, small interracial projects and gatherings were originated. My own experience in Norfolk can perhaps convey the nuances of the Southern rabbi's role in the civil-rights struggle of the 1950s. I had come to Norfolk in 1947 from an assistantship in my native Philadelphia, where I had taken an active part in Fellowship House, a community center which generated numerous activities aimed at bringing whites and blacks together in harmony and under-standing. I was delighted to discover in Norfolk an Interracial Ministers' Fellowship, as well as an active Women's Council for Interracial Coopera-tion. On Washington's Birthday in 1951, we held, under the auspices of these two groups, an interracial service in Ohef Sholom Temple, possibly the first such service in the history of Norfolk. With the help of the Methodist Minister of Music from the church across the street, I organized an interracial choir which sang for the occasion. When the announcement of the service appeared in print, members of the temple board panicked. Only the presence at the service of the Rev. Beverley Tucker White of the socially elegant St. Andrew's Episcopal Church rescued me from more than a repri-mand from the angry temple board. By the 1954 Supreme Court decision, we could point to fifteen interracial projects in Norfolk. But from then on race relations deteriorated. In June of 1958, seventeen black children were ordered to be integrated among the 10,000 students of the white junior and senior high schools of Norfolk, despite a state law threatening to close any integrated school. To me and to many others, it was then unthinkable that public schools could be closed. I preached to a Methodist congregation, "If we don't rise above our partisan feelings of segregation versus integra-tion, we'll have disintegration in our public schools." Those comments, enunciating what so many were feeling at that time, evoked favorable com-ment, and I wrote to the mayor and the city council, with copies to many communal leaders, suggesting a public meeting to inform the citizenry of where they stood in view of federal and state law. As I was about to leave for a month's vacation, the mayor called to report that his hands were tied by state law, though he expressed appreciation for the suggestion. September came, and the schools failed to open. Frantic parents organized with the teachers a series of tutoring groups and prevailed on the churches and synagogues to open their classrooms, despite my own qualms and those of some of my leadership about encouraging closed schools. When convinced that nothing would get the schools open, we agreed that the lesser evil was to get the children into classrooms. So successful were the tutoring groups that, when a second semester was approaching, some wanted to renew the program, despite public statements by me and by other rabbinic colleagues—who had finally become involved—that these groups were unaccredited and would preclude college entrance.

Attempts by the Jewish Community Council to silence rabbinic voices speaking out on the issues, led to a sermon in which I told the congregants that, although I had no intention of making any public statement at that moment, I would not be muzzled should a further situation arise. This led to a petition from five board members to have a special congregational meeting to censor me. The president, who sympathized with what I was trying to do, took me to lunch, and on the assurance that I would clear any public statement with two of the more liberal board members before issuing it, prevailed on the petitioners to withdraw their demand.

By January 28, 1959, massive resistance was legally dead, and Norfolk's schools were scheduled to reopen on an integrated basis. Even earlier, I had recognized that die-hard segregationists might create violence and had proposed to the governor and several legislators that, for the good of all, those who so wished should be allowed to remain in the segregationist private schools—which had been set up alongside the tutoring groups. Evidently the legislature agreed with this view, because this course was followed.

My story is only one of many that could be reported from rabbinical colleagues during this period. Probably the bravest of all was Rabbi Charles Mantinband, a quiet self-effacing individual whose fervent belief in the equality of mankind led him, as the rabbi of Hattiesburg, Mississippi, to take the presidency of that state's Council on Human Relations and a leadership role in the Southern Regional Council and to otherwise publicly proclaim his creed. Despite the understandable qualms of his congregation, the very threats on his life led them to rally to his support even though most did not agree with his views. Other colleagues like Jacob Rothschild in Atlanta, Perry Nussbaum in Jackson, Mississippi, and Milton Schlager in Meridian, Mississippi, had to contend with the bombing of their synagogues by bigots. In the calm which inevitably followed the eras of violence, all of us were proclaimed heroes of a sort. When I left Norfolk in 1964, newspaper editorials spoke of my having been in the forefront of the battle for integration; and members of the congregation, many of whom had fought my efforts, were equally effusive.

It has become evident that the South is not the same today as it was during my years in Norfolk. In the first place, many Northerners have moved south and have assumed some places of leadership in the congregations. No longer do the older Reform congregations limit the presidency to children and grandchildren of old-guard families. The emphasis is far less on pleasing the non-Jews than on attracting the congregant to his Judaism. And the demands for more intensive, more authentic Judaism from the rabbi—despite the protests of the more classic members of the congregation—make him much more concerned with program. The birth of Israel and the influence its culture is having on every Jew who visits our historic homeland, and especially on our youth, is creating a laity who have been educated not only in universities but in Jewish lore. They are demanding more adult education, more participation in worship. The major problem confronting today's rabbis in these communities is that so much of the good leadership has been absorbed by federations, and the major share of Jewish communal funds go to Israel. Consequently, the synagogue and American Jewish culture often suffer for lack of strong leaders and adequate funding.

In sum, the rabbi in the South was slow to emerge as an influential force in the Jewish community. In the early years, he was, for the most part, a follower. In the era of interfaith activity, he became a leader. In the civil-rights era, a prophet. Today he has become a facilitator, channeling the interests and talents of his membership in creative Jewish directions. While the Messianic Age remains as elusive as ever, Judaism, thanks to the rabbis, is alive and well and flourishing in the South.

4.   The Rabbi in Miami—
A Case History

Gladys Rosen

It is an old and often repeated truism that in traveling south along the east coast, the farther south one goes, the more Northern it becomes. Thus Miami has the peculiar distinction of being typically Northern in many ways while lying farther south than the Deep South. Greater Miami—which includes Miami, Miami Beach, twenty-four incorporated municipalities, and unincorporated territory—is located at the southern tip of Florida in Dade County. It is the easternmost part of what Kirkpatrick Sale calls the Southern Rim,[1] the section of this country which underwent the most massive population explosion in history between 1945 and 1975. Florida's population grew by 400 percent, and Greater Miami became the newest of the very large Jewish communities. Its current estimated population of 200,000 places it fifth or sixth among American Jewish communities, and Daniel Elazar predicts that this new community will probably emerge as a major regional center during the coming generation.[2]

Like the rise to prominence on the American scene of the Southern Rim, the Jewish community of Miami is a twentieth-century phenomenon. Initial efforts to develop the Miami area and to take advantage of its natural resources and climate made little progress until the extension of the Florida East Coast Railroad in April 1869. Within three months of that date, the city of Miami was incorporated, and among the 500 residents there were 25 Jews. Those pioneers came largely from other nearby southern cities in search of business opportunities in the newly opened region. Most drifted off, but one Isidor Cohen remained to play a major role in the early growth of Miami and its Jewish community. Miami's Jewry did not develop through the orderly succession of the German wave of immigration from western Europe followed then by a major influx from eastern Europe, a pattern which characterizes most of American Jewish communal history. Rather, it grew very slowly at first, augmented periodically by the arrival of merchants and peddlers, professionals and small businessmen, willing to brave the rough pioneering conditions. By 1912 there were seventy-five Jewish settlers, and the first synagogue was founded. But it was not until the Florida land boom of the twenties that there was any sizable influx of Jewish settlers. Among them were the lawyers and builders who were to become the true founders of the Miami Jewish community. In addition, there was a growing number of winter visitors from the northeast and the Chicago area who encouraged the establishment of local branches of national organizations. Some of those visitors ultimately invested in Miami and settled there. Some vacationers who had made fortunes elsewhere helped to shore up the sagging economy of the area in the wake of the 1926 collapse of the land boom of the 1920's by buying real estate and unfinished buildings begun during that boom.

The community, however, remained small and was characterized by the communal patterns of a small town. New social and communal organizations constantly appeared, only to disappear again in most instances. The pioneer synagogue, Beth David, Conservative in concept, originally encompassed all groups, but soon witnessed the birth of a Reform Temple and two Orthodox synagogues. There was considerable give-and-take between groups and a frequent change of professional leadership, but these four institutions served the needs of Miami's Jewry until the 1940s. Indeed it was World War II and the postwar immigration which increased Miami's Jewish population from 7500 in 1940 to 40,000 in 1949 and 69,000 in 1960. The rapid rate of growth, the incapacity of existing agencies to cope with such numbers, and the communal inexperience of the newcomers, many of them soldiers who had been stationed in the area during World War II, left a leadership vacuum which was filled by the rabbis, particularly those of the war-born congregations. Some indication of the ever-new suburbanlike status of the Miami Jewish community is reflected in the statistics of the National Jewish Population Study done by the Council of Jewish Federations and Welfare Funds in 1972, which reported that only 2.8 percent of Miami Jewish household heads have always lived in that community.[3] The national figure is ten times that size.

Little wonder that here, as in most new Jewish communities, the locus of organized Jewish life is the congregation. Most such congregations represent first-settlement efforts, with all that this implies—particularly reliance on a publicly attractive rabbi to whom congregants are loyal and upon whom they depend for their sense of belonging. Although communitywide institutions began in Miami as early as 1920, when a Jewish Family Service was established, they have only begun to develop as serious community forces in the last ten years. It has been the synagogue and its rabbi that have served as stabilizing and leadership forces and have given to each new wave of immigrants some sense of cohesion and communal identity. Unlike the rabbi in the midwestern community studied by Kenneth Roseman—who found that the laity is firmly entrenched and that "the rabbis are consulted not to make policy but only out of deference to their position and stature in the community"[4]—the rabbis of the major congregations in Miami have assumed strong leadership roles in the community.

In Miami, the rabbi epitomizes Salo Baron's description of him as "the Jack of all trades in an age of specialization."[5] He is called upon to serve as cultural, spiritual, and communal leader and as representative to the general community. The rabbi must be preacher, pastor, and chief executive officer of the congregation. His fund-raising responsibilities extend beyond his own congregation and involve him in the United Jewish Appeal (UJA), the Greater Miami Jewish Federation, and all other major causes affecting Jews. Unlike the rabbinic images produced by east-European tradition—that of the profoundly learned master of the Lithuanian school or of the Hasidic rebbe whose strength lay in true holiness—the American rabbi is, in Arthur Hertzberg's words, "a cross between a pastor or a parish priest and the leader of an ethnic group."[6] In Miami he is also the liaison between his local congregation and community—both Jewish and general—and the larger American-Jewish community for whom Miami serves as a winter retreat or a part-time residence. The growing Miami community offered a unique outlet for the creative abilities and communal energies of rabbis willing to take on the challenge of a rapidly changing inchoate community.

One such case was that of a small Orthodox congregation, the Miami Beach Jewish Center and Congregation Jacob Joseph, founded in 1940 and soon transformed by the swollen wartime population and the arrival of Rabbi Irving Lehrman—young, gifted, and perfectly attuned to the nature and needs of the Jews of Miami Beach.

Prior to Lehrman's arrival, the Miami Beach Jewish Center boasted 200 members (including the part-time ten-dollar-a-week tourists), and its major activities revolved around the many Jewish soldiers stationed in Miami. The center served as a meeting place, offered food and entertainment, and provided housing where necessary. A director of education and clubs was appointed, and the foundations of a rich activity program were laid. But it was Irving Lehrman who gave direction to the center and established it as the largest and most important Conservative synagogue in the South. Lehrman was young, and his previous experience had been limited to that of a part-time rabbi of a congregation in Montclair, New Jersey. He heard about the position from his brother-in-law and decided to try out for the job. After the position was offered, he was advised by friends against accepting it, and he himself confessed to being put off by the heat and the potential physical discomforts of the area. But he seemed to know instinctually that he should take the gamble. He agreed to stay for a year, and that year extended to the present.

When Lehrman arrived, he faced the disorganization that followed in the wake of internal dissension among the leading laity in regard to his predecessor. From his kitchen office he proceeded to tighten and give direction to the loosely organized, soldier-oriented congregation. He introduced the Conservative prayer book and the late-Friday-night services that were to become a hallmark of the renamed Temple Emanu-El and a weekly community event. He went on to modernize the center's school, which had resembled an old-fashioned heder, and at the first Yom Kippur services which he conducted, Lehrman announced that at least two years of schooling would be required before a boy could become Bar Mitzvah at the Miami Beach Jewish Center. Subsequently the idea was picked up by the nascent Board of Jewish Education, which made it a community regulation.

Because of the large number of transient or part-time residents, continuity and adherence to regulations were difficult to achieve in Miami congregations. Indeed, Beach synagogues, in order to attract membership, quoted special winter membership rates for temporary residents, and many who came down for the season took advantage of the offer. In such an atmosphere, great effort and ingenuity were required of the more permanent religious leaders in order to lend stability and content to their congregation programs. These efforts were especially difficult during wartime because of Miami's enormous and constantly changing soldier population.

Rabbi Lehrman's approach to the problem emphasized education. His initial attempt to enforce the Jewish education of members' children was followed by the introduction of a special Sunday-morning breakfast service for teenagers, and in 1944 he hired a director of educaton. By the end of that year, the education-conscious congregation turned its attention to building plans. Public announcement of the plans to erect a half-million-dollar center were made in October 1945 and elicited a variety of responses. From New

York, the *Yiddish Morning Journal* criticized the young Miami rabbi for pre-suming to collect funds for an elaborate building while Jews were suffering; locally, *The Jewish Floridian* decried the effect of the drive on the eve of the often-postponed United Jewish Building Fund campaign on behalf of the Miami and Beach YMHA's, the Bureau of Jewish Education, and the University of Miami Hillel Foundation. Rabbi Stephen S. Wise, on the other hand, hailed the center's new building program and congratulated Rabbi Lehrman (his former student) and those who would bring "the program projected to triumphant conclusion."[7]

The first fund-rasing dinner yielded $180,000 in initial pledges to the expanded center. The theme of the campaign, "Build yourself a new Center for your Jewish life," was soon echoed in the plans of the other local syna-gogues which wanted to build new facilities for their growing memberships. (In November 1946 Beth David launched a building-fund campaign under the chairmanship of Harry Markowitz. The goal of $100,000 was to be raised by private solicitation; just one year later, however, the goal announced at a special-gifts dinner had risen to $525,000. Meanwhile, Temple Israel's mortgage-burning dinner did not preclude plans to raise $50,000 for additional improvements.) Irving Lehrman had initiated a trend and had launched an institution. Ground was broken for the new structure on December 22, 1946, and actual construction began in 1947.

The growing importance of the rabbi in a community like Miami was enhanced from within by the resurgence of the synagogue in the 1950's and by the tendency of such institutions to embrace a variety of functions. Much in the manner of the suburban synagogue, the Miami Beach Jewish Com-munity Center and similar Miami Jewish religious institutions began to undertake recreational and social-service functions in addition to providing Jewish schooling. To accommodate this expanded role, the synagogue had to develop into a large institution, capable of supporting its new functions in a viable manner. In most suburban areas throughout the country, this brought the synagogal leadership into conflict with the leaders of community federations whose concepts of their tasks and the role of the community as a whole were expanding. In Miami, however, with its many part-time and transient residents, communitywide institutions were late in developing and depended for their success upon the involvement and leadership of the charismatic and publicly attractive rabbis. Thus, a rabbi like Irving Lehrman was a key person in the Zionist Organization of America as well as in the National Conference of Christians and Jews. His assistance and cooperation were invaluable in fund-raising efforts within the Jewish community, and he twice served as chairman of the Combined Jewish Appeal of the Greater Miami Jewish Federation.

Despite the centrality of his role within his congregation, Lehrman did not hesitate to participate in other areas of communal activity. In fact, the roster of his active involvements over the years covers the entire spectrum of Jewish and general community interests. He was an organizer of the south-east region of the Rabbinical Assembly of America and honorary president of that group; he served as chairman of the Rabbinic Advisory Committee of the national UJA and continues his activities in many capacities in behalf of the Jewish Theological Seminary of America. As chairman of the Jewish National Fund, he led a delegation to Israel and participated in the ground-breaking ceremonies for Miami's sister city in the Galilee, MeAmi, and he became that city's first honorary citizen.

It is in the area of Jewish representation to the Gentiles, however, that Lehrman has been most influential. He has served as trustee and board member of every local agency from the Red Cross and the United Fund to the Travelers' Aid Society, of which he is a past president. Rabbi Lehrman, like many of his colleagues in Miami, represents the new type of American rabbi in the extent of his interaction with Christian colleagues and his involvement in social issues. For such leaders, Judaism cannot be confined to the synagogue alone; it must make its mark on public issues, political parties, and the struggle for social justice. Public expression requires courage and a sense of power on the part of the rabbi, particularly in such areas as civil rights and politics. In an interview, Nathan Perlmutter, who served as executive director of the Florida region of ADL during the fifties, noted Lehrman's pivotal position in the struggle to implement the Supreme Court's 1954 ruling. He stood to the fore in the struggle for civil rights and did not hesitate to use his influence through private conversations with local Jewish and non-Jewish leadership as well as through public statements. Perlmutter characterized him as "in the forefront of civil rights efforts and a strong proponent of what was constitutional and decent."[8]

In conversation, Lehrman recollected with pride the fact that his strong stand had prompted some of the members of his congregation to write letters suggesting that he "attend to his own business" and that others had even resigned. The author of a recent history of Miami Beach, however, has referred to Lehrman as "Miami's favorite rabbi" and described him as "a one man ecumenical movement for all South Florida and most of the southeastern states."[9] Lehrman is determined to stress a positive image of Miami

Beach as a place that "stands for churches, synagogues and good homes, not just the Club Gigi and the Fountainebleau." In fact, in the original design for Temple Emanu-El, he "especially wanted that big dome on our synagogue . . . so people could see that this is what Miami Beach stands for."

The difficulties encountered in efforts to create communitywide Jewish cultural institutions in Miami left the local rabbis responsible for developing appropriate synagogal programs to promote an understanding of the Jewish heritage in a nontraditional, rootless Jewish community. As early as 1950 Lehrman made arrangements to establish a permanent branch of the Jewish Museum of the Jewish Theological Seminary at Temple Emanu-El—as the Miami Beach Jewish Center came to be known after 1954. At that time, he stated: "The value of such a project is immeasurable. It will not only bring prestige to, and raise the cultural level of the community, but will afford an opportunity to the thousands of residents, as well as visitors, to see the vast storehouse of Jewish artifacts and learn more about our cultural heritage." It was in this spirit too that distinguished speakers and scholars in the field of Judaic studies were brought to Temple Emanu-El as part of the educational program. This approach, adopted by other Miami synagogues, gave the rabbis an important role in determining the cultural climate of an area not primarily oriented in that direction.

Miami's role as the winter headquarters for American Jews seeking to escape the rigors of cold weather has made it, in a sense, the campaign capital for fund-raising efforts of most national agencies and institutions. Although this may have had a retarding effect on the development of the local community, Lehrman has stated that this infusion stimulated local fund raising by creating a climate of giving. This giving was, until less than a decade ago, largely directed to the synagogues, rather than to the Federation's Combined Jewish Appeal, a good reason, no doubt, for the Federation's having twice co-opted Lehrman to its chairmanship. But times have changed, and while the rabbis of Miami continue as major communal influences by virtue of their long tenure, their charisma, and the loyalty of their congregations, the Greater Miami Jewish Federation is at last beginning to assume a major role in community planning and leadership. Lehrman feels that the community has grown not only in size but in depth and that Miami is approaching the "onset of maturity."[10] A clear sign of this development is that leadership has been taken over by young and enthusiastic Miamians, who in the words of one of their number, Hap Levy, regard Miami as "a sleeping giant" capable of unlimited growth.[11]

The centrality of the rabbi and the synagogue to Jewish communal

development in Greater Miami was due in large part to the unique internal
structure and dynamics of the community and of the area as a whole. However, despite its atypical and often Northern stance, Miami, particularly in
its early period, retained enough that was "Southern" to reinforce the predominantly Protestant congregational pattern in its local religious structure.
The local emphasis on independent congregational autonomy and on the
social desirability of membership in a religious institution paved the way for
the Miami version of Jewish community life. Without a centralized control
over standards of religious observance and behavior, the individual rabbi
became the authoritative figure for those who chose to affiliate, as well as
the spokesman for the Jewish community. Each rabbi of a major congregation was able, and was indeed encouraged, to maintain his special fiefdom
with only limited reliance on existing communal agencies. It may well be
that the Miami rabbi is more suburban than Southern. In the large spectrum
of American rabbis, however, men like Irving Lehrman and his colleagues,
who thrived in the special conditions of Miami, belong to those congregational decision makers characterized by Daniel Elazar as "the more talented,
important, well known, or cosmopolitan who build upon their rabbinical
roles to become influences in the larger areas of Jewish communal life."[12]

5.

Rabbi in the South
A Personal View

Jack D. Spiro

As Wilbur J. Cash wrote in his great classic, the South is a "part of America and yet set apart most definitely from America, a nation within a nation." Sundry reasons are given by historians for this sense of separateness, this feeling of being different from the rest of the nation. But I think the most significant reason and cause for distinguishing traits of the Southern minds is what Cash calls "conflict with the Yankees."[1]

After all, what caused the governor of Alabama to remove the United States flag from his state capitol and to reluctantly replace it several years later, and months after the celebration of the nation's bicentennial had begun—and even then to receive negative reactions from many of his fellow Alabamians for so doing? Why do we refer so frequently to the Confederacy as though it were still alive in some respects? It goes back to the Southern conflict with the Yankees. And what is the basis of this conflict? Let me put it this way.

Some years ago I was in a very small Louisiana town called Natchitoches. In the town square there is (or was) a statue of a benign, humble looking, rather elderly black man with a bald head and thick lips grinning from ear to ear. He is slightly stooped over—and even though on a pedestal, it appears as though he's looking up to everyone who passes by. There is a caption underneath the statue which reads: "We love our darkies."

I think we can see three levels in the Southern mind, all of which play an extremely important role in understanding the Southerner, the Southern Jew, and the rabbis' positon in the South. One level is the mentality symbolized by that Natchitoches statue. The white Southerner loved his darkies—so long as they continued to have broad, rather stupid grins and to bend over in Uncle Tom submission. But then, when the darkie became the Negro—that is, a little more than slave but a little less than human, he was not to be tolerated, he was not permitted to vote or to share Caucasian bus seats and, heaven forfend, toilet seats. The Negro was then on the march for total freedom and humanization and, in only a few years, he was transformed from the acquiescent Negro to the militant black. So while the white Southerner loved his darkie and hated the Negro, he now harbors a deep fear of the black—of the black's newfound assertiveness and his aggressive fight for full equality.

This false love, this widespread hatred, and this deeply lodged fear throughout the decades have produced a kind of schizoid reaction. The South turned within itself and developed a sense of unreality about what was actually happening. It regressed into a state of romanticism and tried to avoid the relentless forces of history. It was like the fabled bird which flies backward because it's more interested in knowing where it's been than in where it's going. Along with this unrealistic outlook, there developed an intolerance for diversification and dialectic, for variety and freedom of thought, for intellectual give-and-take. Provincialism became typical, with exceptions. It's all changing now before our very eyes, but we are still living with it. How does the rabbi fit in?

With the exception of very few of us (and I'm one of the exceptions), most rabbis are not Southerners; they have not been born and bred in the Southland as I was. In addition to having a different outlook, they are, of course, labeled "Yankees." They are also dreamers, perhaps as unrealistic and romantic in their own right as is the South itself. They want to change things; they perceive themselves in Protestant robes and prophetic roles. They want to shout: "Are you not as the Ethiopians to me, saith the Lord?"[2] They want to say that the black man must come out of the dungeons of oppression and not have his houses joined one to the other. They want freedom and justice for all. They want an ephah to be an ephah for all human beings regardless of race or station. Like Amos, they come to preach God's demand for equality. But unlike Amos, they do not return to Tekoah and sheepherding. They stick around from year to year in the same place, and naturally they bear the brunt of the consequences—like a bruised reed—of preaching the prophetic message. You see, at least Amos was a Southerner. But these damn rabbinic Yankees come to disturb the waters of unreality. They come to rudely transform the status quo—which is not really a status quo anyway, as the South is always changing. But who likes to be reminded of it constantly, especially by an unrealistic dreamer, the self-appointed, or HUC-appointed, prophet? And especially if he has come from the North, where they think that they know everything and how to solve every problem and they can impose their standards on us in Dixie.

After I was here a few months, one person said to another: "The trouble with Rabbi Spiro is that he's a Yankee." The other person said: "How can you say that? He was born and raised in New Orleans." The first one said: "I don't care, he *acts* like a Yankee!"

And that's because I was being somewhat unrealistic in my desire to make everything right as I saw the right. After fifteen years in the rabbinate, the old spirit of Amos and Isaiah was still burning inside me—and I scorched a few others with that spirit. And yet, isn't it curious that the spirit of prophecy is expressed on every page of the *Union Prayer Book*, which has been used by generations of Southerners as well as Yankees? Why is it that conflict is generated when the rabbi utters these same prayer-book ideals in relation to black-white equality, educational reform, equal housing, and so on? The beauty of the prayer book is its prophetic generalizations. But it doesn't ever hit home. It doesn't summon us to specific practice. The most specific thing it says is: "How much we owe to the labors of our brothers! Day by day they dig far away from the sun that we may be warm. . . . "[3] The rabbi, on the other hand, tries to apply these vague generalizations to local specificities.

There was a visiting preacher at a Baptist church in Mississippi who preached on the commandment "Thou shalt not steal." The response was so wonderful that the next week he decided to expound on the theme by preaching, "Thou shalt not steal chickens." That was the last sermon he ever preached there.

Leo Baeck said the detail is also divine. But the prophetic detail, the great ideals of our heritage put into the detail of personal application and local implementation, can be a threatening experience.

That is, in part, what the rabbi—usually a Yankee—lives with in assuming a Southern position. The most important thing that I can suggest for the transplanted rabbi occupying a Southern pulpit is a deep and broad understanding of these forces and a multitude of others at work in Southern history, which affect the Southern Jew and non-Jew alike.

The rabbi must try to penetrate the mind of the South—which, of course, is undergoing radical transformation now. But there is still a distinctive mind below the Mason-Dixon line. And the rabbi must not be all Amos or all Isaiah. A little bit of prophetic exuberance is expected of him; that's the name of the game. But it is terribly important for him to see himself as a real blend of Amos and Aaron and to place his greatest emphasis on being a calm, persuasive, patient, rational, composed teacher of his heritage. Isn't this blend, after all, his most genuine role historically? Prophetic zeal need not be subdued, but it will be expressed most constructively if it is subsumed under *talmud torah keneged kulam*. The study of, and therefore the teaching of, Torah is equal to everything else—north, south, east, and west.

6.   Judah P. Benjamin

Richard S. Tedlow

The most important American-Jewish diplomat before Henry Kissinger, the most eminent lawyer before Brandeis, the leading figure in martial affairs before Hyman Rickover, the greatest American-Jewish orator, and the most influential Jew ever to take a seat in the United States Senate were all one and the same man—Judah Philip Benjamin of Louisiana. Nevertheless, Benjamin is largely a forgotten figure today among the general public, if not among historians. Symbolic of this national amnesia is the current literature on Kissinger, whom one finds compared to Disraeli, Metternich, and Dr. Strangelove but never to the Confederacy's Jewish secretary of state.[1] After outlining Benjamin's career, this paper will provide some historiographical observations and will then suggest a direction for a revived discussion of him.

Benjamin was born on St. Croix in the West Indies on August 6, 1811. His father, an English Jew, was a drifter who has been described as "that *rara avis*, an unsuccessful Jew."[2] His mother was of Portuguese-Jewish descent and in contrast to her husband was industrious and strong-willed. The family moved to Charleston, South Carolina in 1822, and soon thereafter Judah's precocity attracted the attention of a wealthy Jewish patron who sent him first to private school and then to Yale—where his social climb was mysteriously interrupted. He claimed that he had left without taking a degree because of his financial straits, but there is considerable evidence that he was dismissed for disciplinary reasons. It is an indication of his desire for respectability that this man, who in the course of his career was to bear endless slanders with a seemingly inexhaustible equanimity, never ceased to be infuriated by allegations of his wrongdoing as a college youth. In the midst of the formation of the Confederacy, he actually took the trouble to ask two Northern friends to institute legal action against newspapers which were accusing him of having been a thief in New Haven.[3]

He departed Charleston—where more than one influential citizen had graduated from Yale—for New Orleans, where he arrived in 1828 with five dollars to his name. It was in this latter city, a cosmopolitan commercial hub "alive with music and sin,"[4] that Benjamin's ascent to prominence began in earnest, although not without one further painful setback. In 1833 he married Natalie St. Martin, a belle of Creole society whom he "endowed . . . with all the depths of companionship his nature required."[5] However, she soon found life with him at his new mansion *triste*.[6] She moved to Paris, where Benjamin saw her only on his annual trips to Europe. He managed to spirit her to his side of the Atlantic only once, for a few days in 1859. After one encounter with the *grandes dames* of Washington, D.C., however, she fled back across the ocean, and gossip about her continued unabated. Although he "idolised her and gave her everything she wanted, she left the impression that she resented being married to a Jew."[7] To the end of his career, his enemies thought of him as "the Jew whose wife lives in Paris."[8]

Professionally, though, his progress was untrammeled. In the mid-1830s he was practicing law before the state supreme court, and by the early 1840s he was an established leader of the bar. In 1842 he was elected to the state legislature as a Whig and in the following decade played a key role in writing two state constitutions. He was elected to the federal senate in 1852 and at some point in the winter of 1852-53 was offered a seat on the United States Supreme Court, the first Jew to be so honored. He preferred to remain in the Senate, however, where he neglected no opportunity to defend the institution of slavery. He himself was a large slaveholder.

In the Senate, even critics granted that his was a masterful intellect, and his oratorical skill was often admired. His valedictory in February of the winter of Secession prompted a British visitor to concede that his performance was "better than our Benjamin himself could have done."[9]

Jefferson Davis chose Benjamin to be attorney general, but in nine months transferred him from this least important of the Confederacy's cabinet positions to the most important, secretary of war. It soon became common knowledge that, next to Davis, Benjamin was the most influential man in the government. His mastery resulted from his ability and his imperturbability, but the root of his power derived from his relationship to Davis.

Some of Benjamin's early encounters with Davis had been anything but auspicious. In mid-1858 the two men had a disagreement in the Senate which almost resulted in a duel.[10] But this animus gradually abated. What impressed Davis the most during the early months of the war was Benjamin's spirit of self-sacrifice.

This spirit is illustrated by Benjamin's handling of the Roanoke Island incident early in 1862. Southern defenders had pleaded with Richmond for reinforcements prior to an expected Federal attack. Help was not forthcoming, and a Southern disaster resulted. This seemingly unnecessary outcome raised a storm, and the war secretary speedily became "the most unpopular and the most hated man in the Confederacy." Benjamin accepted this criticism without effective retort and in March was forced from office.

Not until a quarter of a century later did the true story of Roanoke Island become known. Benjamin did not send help because there had been none to send. He did not give this reason because he did not want the enemy to learn of Southern "poverty and . . . utter inability to supply the requisitions." After consulting with Davis, Benjamin decided it "best for the public interest that I should submit to censure."[11] In the midst of venality, ambition, and incompetence, Benjamin's gesture deeply impressed the harried Davis, who stood by his friend. He had to remove him from the War Office, but he kept him in the government, moving him to the State Department where he stayed until the war's end.

Space does not permit a discussion of Benjamin's efforts to secure the foreign recognition upon which the survival of the Confederacy depended. It suffices to say that he probably did as well in this impossible task as any man could. After the government was forced to abandon Richmond, he remained with Davis until May 3, 1865, when he determined that further resistance was pointless.

He then decided to flee to England, and his odyssey included near-capture by Northern soldiers and a long journey by open boat to the Bahamas. He was fifty-five years old when he reached his destination, but he immediately set out to build a new career. He was called to the bar in 1866, published a much-admired treatise two years later, and built a lucrative practice, which he finally relinquished when his health gave way early in 1883. He spent his final year in Paris with his wife, with whom he had not lived for four decades, and died on May 6, 1884.

Up to the turn of the century, Benjamin's detractors far outnumbered his partisans. For James G. Blaine, he was "a foe in whom malignity was unrelieved by a single trace of magnanimity." Not only had he favored secession but after the defeat he "did not share the disasters and sacrifices with the sincere and earnest men whom he had done so much to mislead . . . " Rather, he "took refuge under a flag to whose allegiance he was born." Goldwin Smith took this line of criticism one step further, arguing in an 1891 article that the Jew "adopts . . . the language of the country in which he lives, reserving that of Judea for the interior of the synagogue. But he changes his country more easily than others. When the Southern Confederacy fell, its leaders generally stood by the wreck and did their best for those whom they had led, but Judah Benjamin went off to pastures new."[12] This portrayal of Jews as a people who could not give heartfelt allegiance to their country of residence raised a torrid controversy in the pages of the *North American Review* and resulted in meticulous, if flawed, investigations of the role of Jews in the Civil War.[13]

From the South, too, there was criticism aplenty. Throughout his political career, Benjamin had been subjected to attacks on himself as a Jew by Southerners. Names on this dishonor roll included Henry S. Foote, General Thomas R. R. Cobb, Andrew Johnson, and sundry plain folk who asserted that Confederate prayers would have more effect if "Judas Iscariot Benjamin" were dismissed. "All the distresses of the people," wrote one, "were owing to a Nero-like despotism originating in the brain of Benjamin, the Jew." Soon after the war, Southern memoirs complained of Benjamin's alleged incompetence. For at least one of the authors, Foote, anti-Semitism was an important factor in shaping his indictment.[14]

Thus Northerners held Benjamin in low esteem because he had been a leader of the rebellion and a slaveholder, while Southerners did so because they thought him incompetent. And in both sections his Jewish background intensified the criticism.

American ethnic groups have often sought eminent men and women that they could exhibit as proof of their contribution to the nation, just as they have insisted that malefactors within their group are exceptional and that each man should be judged as an individual. The first important effort to use Benjamin as a positive stereotype for Jews came from the pen of Jewish attorney Max J. Kohler in 1905. Kohler viewed Benajmin as an admirable statesman of great oratorical skill, legal proficiency, and acuteness of intellect. He forgave Benjamin's support of slavery because "himself a slaveowner, [Benajmin] accordingly became familiar with the institution under its most favorable conditions, and knew how false were the pictures of it, claimed to be typical, which the fevered brain of some of the abolitionist agitators created." He concluded that "instead of being ashamed to be identified with Benjamin, American Jewry can today point with pride to the remarkable career of the greatest statesman, orator, and lawyer it has yet produced, notwithstanding his identification with the 'Lost Cause.'"[15]

Kohler's call for a biography worthy of its subject was answered with the publication of a lengthy study by Pierce Butler of Tulane in 1907. Like

Kohler, Butler was impressed with Benjamin's legal talent, and their views on his support of slavery were so alike that Butler closely paraphrased (without attribution) Kohler's above-quoted remark about abolitionists. Butler saw Benjamin as constant in his devotion to his family and "steadfast in adherence to political principles and ideals." He was not however, a "patriot of the highest type" like Davis and Lee, because he left the Confederacy after its defeat. "The perfect patriot is so much of the soil that he cannot survive transplantation. . . . But of that lofty, Puritanic type of patriotism Mr. Benjamin could not boast. Thus remains a flaw in his character which I would not seek to conceal. . . . " Unlike Goldwin Smith, Butler explained Benjamin's departure by reference to his profession rather than to his religion. "He was a born lawyer," wrote Butler, and having, as it were, "taken a brief for the South, he earnestly and zealously fought for his client as long as his abilities could avail. When the cause was lost . . . , he accepted the decision as absolving him from further useless effort." [16]

Other Southern historians have also sought explanations for Benjamin's departure, but none has turned to his religion again, although his exposure to non-Western cultural traits has been thought influential. Rembert W. Patrick, for example, wrote that Benjamin's "philosophy of life was to live in and for the present, and it had a quality of Oriental fatalism. . . . When the cause of the Confederacy was lost, he forgot it, turned his back upon the scene of his labors, and took up life anew in another country" [17]

On the whole, however, Southern writers and celebrants of the Lost Cause came to accept Benjamin as an honorable member of their pantheon. The charge of incompetence which so exercised his contemporaries disappeared, as did aspersions on his religion. In the view of his foremost biographer, the Virginian Robert D. Meade, he attained the rank of statesman despite his sometime absorption "with crasser forms of money getting" and his occasional willingness to follow rather than to lead public opinion. In the opinion of another Southern biographer, Martin Rywell, he was more than a statesman. He was the "unsung rebel prince." [18]

Also indicative of the increasing acceptance of Benjamin has been his recognition by Southern fraternal associations. A small pin in the Benjamin Papers at the American Jewish Historical Society attests to a commemoration of the centennial of his birth. In 1925 the Judah P. Benjamin chapter of the Daughters of the Confederacy donated a mansion where Benjamin hid during his escape to the state of Florida, and the legislature appropriated $10,000 for its restoration. In so doing, the legislature singled Benjamin out for his "conspicuous and invaluable services" to the South and remarked that he "only fled after the government had collapsed." Five years later, the Stonewall Jackson Camp of the Sons of Confederate Veterans was authorized by the City of Richmond to erect a monument to Benjamin.[19] This gesture is noteworthy, because Benjamin and Jackson had clashed sharply when the former was at the War Department.

The ease with which Benjamin has been accepted by historians and memorialists of the South has not been paralleled among his coreligionists, but not for lack of effort. Kohler's attempt to use him as a model has already been mentioned. In 1948 the Jewish Publication Society of America published a brief novel, *Mr. Benjamin's Sword*, designed to portray the man as worthy of emulation by Jewish youth.[20] This novel and the Rywell book prompted a neat bit of detective work by Rabbi Bertram W. Korn. Korn showed that various tales linking Benjamin with Jewish worship or conspicuous ethnic loyalty were untrue. It is difficult to disagree with Korn's conclusion that "Benjamin had no positive or active interest in Jews or Judaism."[21]

As the true enormity of the slave regime became generally understood, his identification not only with the South but specifically with slavery has become a greater stumbling block for Jews who wish to use Benjamin as a model. In 1961 Korn pointed out the irony that Benjamin's honors were "in some measure dependent upon the sufferings of the very Negro slaves he [and others] bought and sold with such equanimity," and Rabbi Abraham J. Karp defended Jewish attitudes on slavery by noting that the institution's major Jewish apologists, Benjamin and Senator Yulee, "were totally estranged from Jewish life and Jewish affiliation." The suggestion of these recent authors is that the best way to treat Benjamin from the standpoint of the reputation of American Jewry is to read him out of it as far as possible rather than to use him as an exemplar of its traditions. A recent article professes to find "mysteries, " deep-seated contradictions, in Benjamin's "true feelings" about slavery. His stand on this issue is indeed what must be gotten around if there should be a second rehabilitation of his reputation, but this is an unpromising tack to take. Few politicians are as consistent in anything as Benjamin was in support of the "peculiar institution." Indeed, there was truth in Ben Wade's clever slur that he was an "Israelite with Egyptian principles."[22]

Korn believes that Benjamin's importance to historians of American Jewry lies in a role he couldn't help playing: that of a lightning rod for the anti-

Semitism of his age. As such, he provides support for Korn's thesis that the Civil War, rather than the great immigration at the turn of the century, marks the beginning of modern anti-Jewish feeling in America.[23] Clearly Benjamin's Judaism not only heightened dislike of him but brought into sharper focus an animus against Jews in general on both sides of the Mason-Dixon line. And unlike John Kennedy's Catholicism, which may have been as much of a help as a hindrance politically, Benjamin's faith failed to stimulate any significant support.

On the other hand, what seems most impressive about his career is, not how much, but how little his religion mattered. Here was a man born to poverty under a foreign flag–a Jew who, if he never flaunted his background, never disguised it either, living in an overwhelmingly Protestant and largely evangelical nation and achieving prominence in a section where, even as late as 1969, 80 percent of the dominant religious sect, the Baptists, believed that "the Jews can never be forgiven for what they did to Jesus until they accept Him as the True Savior."[24] Yet there was not one office short of the presidency which he could not have held had the Union remained whole. And when his region made its bid for independence, he was its second most powerful civilian. To judge from his career, Southern anti-Semitism appears to have been less important than logic would lead one to expect.

This is not to deny that it did exist or to minimize the suffering it caused. But the practical effect of anti-Semitism in Benjamin's case was minimal. The abuse he suffered was verbal, never physical, and no different in kind from that meted out to foreigners and Catholics, not to mention blacks and Indians. Perhaps the key is that neither Southern nor Northern anti-Semitism at that time had extensive institutional props; neither was organized. There was no anti-Jewish political machine with power similar to that of the Anti-Masons or the Know-Nothings. Without such organization, the attacks of bigots have been random. Without a widely accepted philosophical underpinning, the ulterior motives of these attacks have often blunted their force.

In the South, according to Leonard Dinnerstein, "it is rare for a Jew to support publicly controversial issues" for fear of exciting latent bigotry.[25] As Benjamin's career shows, this fear is not unwarranted. On the other hand, twentieth-century Southern Jews may have reaped some benefit from his exertions in behalf of the Confederacy. As we have seen, once they had accepted his departure from the South, Southern commentators began writing praiseworthy books about him and building monuments to him. The gift to Florida by the Benjamin chapter of the Daughters of the Confederacy, it should be noted, took place at the pinnacle of the power of the second Klan, and when the mansion was finally dedicated in 1942, a rabbi was among the speakers. One wonders how many might have taken this as a symbol that the Jews belonged in and to the South.

Benjamin had no love for biographers. "I have read so many American biographies which reflected only the passions and prejudices of their writers," he once said, "that I do not want to leave behind me letters and documents to be used in such a work about myself." He was as efficient in destroying his papers as he was in his other endeavors, and when he died, "he did not leave behind him half a dozen pieces of paper." Robert D. Meade, the most meticulous of his five biographers, complained that he was "one of the most secretive men who ever lived," and spent twelve years scouring archives and private collections for surviving material. Meade used this material in conjunction with published sources to construct what will be the standard work on Benjamin for the foreseeable future.[26] And even Meade's work, for all its careful scholarship, is similar in many important respects to Butler's. To be sure, heretofore unknown letters may occasionally surface, but unless wholly unexpected material casting light on such important issues as Benjamin's attitude toward slavery or Judaism is unearthed, Meade's book will stand. In the future, Benjamin will probably be more interesting as a historiographic, rather than a monographic, topic. As we have just suggested, he can, for example, be used to reflect changing Jewish views on slavery (from Kohler to Korn and Karp) and to illustrate changing Southern views on Jews (from Foote to the Benjamin chapter of the Daughters of the Confederacy).

Another promising direction for future Benjamin scholarship is comparison. The figure that immediately comes to mind in this context is Benjamin Disraeli.[27] Both men have appeared in Jewish lore as defenders of the faith and the race. The anecdote is told of both—and only of these two— that their Judaism having been referred to in a derogatory fashion, they responded, "It is true that I am a Jew, and when my ancestors were receiving their Ten Commandments from the immediate hand of Diety, amidst the thunderings and lightenings of Mt. Sinai, the ancestors of my opponent were herding swine in the forests of Great Britain."[28] To the best of my knowledge, neither man ever made such a statement. Disraeli might have, but for Benjamin it would have been quite out of character. And therein lies the difference between the two men's attitudes toward the faith of their fathers.

Although it doubtless influenced his outlook as a private person, Judaism simply did not matter for Benjamin the public man. He seems never to have paid it heed after his youth, nor did he seize opportunities to speak up for the rights of his adherents. It was a personal matter for him, like his relations with his wife, and in this realm he was intensely secretive, as symbolized by his destruction of his papers. As Mrs. Jefferson Davis rightly said, "No more reticent man ever lived where it was possible to be silent."[29]

Although buried in consecrated ground at the insistence of his devoutly Catholic wife, Benjamin lived his life a Jew. Disraeli, on the other hand, joined the Church of England at the age of twelve and a half, but despite that—or perhaps because of it—he developed an elaborate theory of the nobility of the Jewish race, which he consistently defended against civil disabilities and bigoted slurs. Disraeli's theological ideas were, as his shrewd biographer Robert Blake has pointed out, "in reality, the rationalization of his own psychological dilemma." He sought to blur the difference between Christianity and Judaism, almost seeming to regard Christ's Jewishness as more important than his divinity. He saw Jews as proto-Christians, Christians as completed Jews, and himself as the intersection of the two. Or as he put it, "I am the leaf between the Old and the New Testaments." "How else," remarks Blake, "could a person intensely proud of his Jewish ancestry which his less worthy enemies flung in his face, yet at the same time a convert to the very faith of those who sneered at him, justify both that pride and that conversion?"[30]

Charges of crypto-Judaism notwithstanding, there can be no question of Disraeli's "punctuality in performing his formal religious duties as a Christian. . . ." "He knew about Christianity in fact, in his shallow way, a very great deal," writes Professor Cecil Roth, "about Judaism he knew next to nothing."[31] Nevertheless, he flamboyantly identified himself with Jewish aspirations both in his statecraft and in his novels, and he praised the power of Jewish magnates and financiers across Europe.

More than one commentator has remarked on the oddity that "an insolent, mysterious, half-foreign adventurer with a libertine past and a load of debt, who had married a rich widow for money," "an alien, exotic figure of Jewish extraction," should have risen to the leadership of the most parochial branch of the mid-Victorian English aristocracy in an era when religious questions were constantly in the forefront of politics.[32] To reconcile himself to this anomalous position, Disraeli combined his peculiar conception of Judaism as a natural aristocracy surpassing that of the proudest

English lines with his (quite incorrect) belief that he was himself descended from a particularly noble branch of this group.

Moreover, Judaism was for him primarily a race, and his emphasis upon this characteristic unwittingly foreshadowed the emphasis of German anti-Semitism in the twentieth century. This belief is reflected most clearly in his novels. "All is race," avers Sidonia, the Rothschild-like banker in *Coningsby*, "there is no other truth." And from *Endymion*: "[Race] is the key to history. . . . Language and religion do not make a race . . . There is only one thing that makes a race, and that is blood."[33]

The contrast with Benjamin could hardly be more stark in this regard. For him the Caucasian race was the only one worth considering. It was for the cause of white ownership of property in black men that he gambled his career. Thus the remark attributed to both men about receiving the Ten Commandments and herding swine sounds more like Disraeli than Benjamin. Here also we may see a reason for Disraeli's flaunting of what he imagined to be his Oriental traits, while Benjamin acted the conservative in manner and mien as well as in politics. Disraeli took pride in his alien image, while for Benjamin such an image would have been an irrelevant hindrance.

Had Disraeli remained a Jew, he never would have reached the top of the greasy pole. Until 1858 the parliamentary oath had to be taken "on the true faith of a Christian," which would have excluded him from that body until his mid-fifties. This oath did not, of course, hinder Jews as a race.[34] And the importance of a politician's being a member of the established church should not be minimized. Benjamin, on the other hand, first held office in 1842 without the necessity of conversion, and through the next twenty-three years no position was denied him due to religion. Even had Benjamin converted, however, it is hard to believe that he would have been able to become head of government either in the Union, had the Civil War not intervened, or in the Confederacy, had it survived (supposing, that is, that he had not been disqualified from such office in the first place by virtue of his foreign birth). European nations have sometimes turned to members of alien minority groups to lead them in times of crisis. Thus Napoleon was from Corsica, Lloyd George from Wales, Stalin from Georgia, and Hitler from Austria. But this has not been the American way. The United States chose as its leader through depression and war in this century a man with the closest resemblance to aristocratic lineage it has ever elected. Only in 1960 would a Catholic attain the presidency, and in 1964 the nation took note of Goldwater's Jewish heritage, although it was certainly not that which cost him the election. Even as late as 1976 a major party's nomination of a Deep South politician raised eyebrows.

Benjamin, or any other Jew, would have had to win a national canvass to become head of government. Disraeli had only to win election from a single small constituency and then to wangle his way to the top among men who, though certainly not without their prejudices, might be more directly impressed with superior ability than the public at large.

Both Benjamin and Disraeli constantly encountered anti-Semitism. Benjamin met such attacks in silence, while Disraeli retaliated through his novels. Indeed, one of his victims was the same Goldwin Smith who was referring to Benjamin when he wrote in 1891 that Jews could not feel true loyalty to their country of residence.[35] Such anti-Semitism might have been sufficient to cripple the careers of lesser men. But both Benjamin and Disraeli were so able, and the feelings against men of their background in Britain and America so disorganized, that their ambitions were eventually rewarded.

It is to this kind of comparison that we believe thinking about Benjamin could now be profitably directed. And in addition to Disraeli, a comparison with Kissinger—another foreign-born and poverty-stricken Jew who, in a conservative cause, would push radical policies—might be highly suggestive.[36]

7.

Charles Jacobson of Arkansas
A Jewish Politician in the Land
of the Razorbacks, 1891-1915

Raymond Arsenault

The quarter century between the Populist revolt and the beginning of the First World War has generally been viewed as an era of decline for Southern Jews—a time when rising anti-Semitism drove many Jews from the mainstream of Southern life. As Leonard Dinnerstein and others have pointed out, it was an era which began ominously with an outburst of night-riding forays against Jewish merchants in Louisiana, Georgia, and Mississippi (called "the first serious anti-Semitic demonstrations in American history" by John Higham) and ended tragically with the horror of the Leo Frank case.[1] According to the prevailing view, this was the period when a large portion of the white South, goaded by economic colonialism and cultural insecurity, began its Gothic descent towards the KuKluxism and "cottonpatch fascism" of the 1920s and the 1930s.[2] As the Bourbons gave way to the rednecks, Southern Jews—many of whom were foreign-born merchants and all of whom were religious "dissenters"—were allegedly caught in a riptide of nativism, rural chauvinism, class hatred, militant fundamentalism, and political demagoguery.

In its essentials, the above indictment of the late-nineteenth and early-twentieth-century South is probably justified. Though additional research on the subject is needed, the corroborative findings of John Higham and Leonard Dinnerstein (the only two scholars who have studied the subject intensively) demonstrate that anti-Semitic behavior was on the increase in many areas of the South during the period. Nonetheless, as Higham himself has observed, it is crucially important to keep this trend in proper perspective.[3] While there is some evidence of a regional tendency towards increased

The author would like to thank Alvin Jacobson and Rabbi Ira Sanders, both of Little Rock, for their help in the preparation of this article.

anti-Semitism, there is no evidence that this trend was so pronounced that it fundamentally altered the lives and careers of most Southern Jews. In short, unlike that of the black man, the overall position of the Jew in Southern society remained fundamentally secure throughout the Populist-Progressive period. Whitecappers and demagogues notwithstanding, there was no mass exodus and no retreat behind closed doors, either literally or figuratively. In fact, the Southern Jewish community as a whole became, if anything, more active and more visible than ever before.

This pattern of continued security was present in all areas of Southern-Jewish life, but nowhere was it more evident than in the realm of politics.[4] Unlike his black counterpart, the Southern-Jewish politician did not disappear with the rise of the "Solid South." On the contrary, the number of Southern Jews elected to public office during the period 1890-1915 was probably (exact figures are unavailable) greater than during any other period in the region's history prior to the Second World War.[5] The list of those elected includes one congressman (Adolph Meyer of New Orleans, 1891-1908), numerous judges, more than a dozen state legislators, and literally scores of municipal officials—including the mayors of Montgomery and Mobile, Alabama; Pensacola, Florida; Shreveport, Louisiana; Pine Bluff, Arkansas; Brownsville, Texas; and Georgetown, South Carolina.[6] Admittedly, these men represented only a small part of the Southern political establishment; in a region where Jews made up less than 1 percent of the total population, it could hardly have been otherwise.[7] Nonetheless, the careers carved out by Southern-Jewish politicians stand as important testaments to the fact that many turn-of-the-century Southerners remained relatively tolerant in their attitudes towards Jews. To ignore the Jewish component of Southern political life is, at the very least, to write history with the rough edges removed. The story of men like Charles Jacobson, to whom the following pages are devoted, is a tale worth telling, not only for what it says about early-twentieth-century Southern society and politics, but also for what it says about Southern Jews.

Despite his relative obscurity, Charles Jacobson's career is particularly intriguing—primarily because of his long and close association with Jeff Davis, one of the early-twentieth-century South's most celebrated "demagogues." As Davis's trusted lieutenant, Jacobson did more than survive the "revolt of the rednecks"—he took part in it. Although he ultimately struck out on his own—serving two terms in the Arkansas state senate—for more than a decade Jacobson played a leading role in a political protest movement which was strikingly similar to the one led by Tom Watson, the Georgia rabble-rouser who helped to incite the lynching of Leo Frank.[8] Manned by angry rustics and laced with xenophobia, it was the kind of political movement which is often associated with virulent anti-Semitism—the kind of movement that Victor Ferkiss and other social scientists in the 1950s liked to characterize as "protofascist."[9] As we shall see in the following pages, such a characterization would be a mistake in the case of the Davis movement.

One of the post-Reconstruction South's most colorful politicians, Jeff Davis was an extraordinarily successful mass leader who earned such sobriquets as "the Karl Marx of the Hill Billies," "the tribune of haybinders," and "the wild ass of the Ozarks."[10] Elected Arkansas attorney general in 1898, he went on to serve three stormy terms as governor before moving up to the United States Senate in 1907. He died shortly after his re-election to the Senate in 1912.

Vilified as a demagogue by many of his contemporaries, Davis was famous for his picturesque crusades against Yankee trusts, city dudes, and "high-collared aristocrats." Although he occasionally resorted to racial demagoguery, he was essentially a neo-Populist. A sincere if ineffectual reformer (his administrations produced more politics than legislation), he consistently championed the interest of downtrodden white farmers—or as he called them, "the horny-handed sons of toil." As one scornful Arkansas editor described him, he was nothing more than "a carrot-headed, red-faced, loud-mouthed, strong-limbed, ox-driving mountaineer lawyer . . . a friend to the fellow who brews 40-rod bug juice back in the mountains."[11] Davis himself gloried in such descriptions and played the role of hillbilly folk hero to the hilt. A master of the common touch, he often ended his stump speeches with an open invitation to the governor's mansion: "If you red necks and hill billies ever come to Little Rock be sure and come to see me. . . . Don't go to the hotels or wagon yards, but come to my house. If I'm not at home tell my wife who you are, tell her you are my friend and you belong to the sun-burned sons of toil. Tell her to give you some hog jowl and turnip greens. . . . She may be busy making soap but that will be all right."[12]

Though he was primarily a class spokesman, Davis was also something of a political evangelist. The son of an ordained Baptist minister, he often spiced his stump speeches with religious allusions and professions of Christian piety.[13] As he told a crowd at Center Point in 1900, "I am a sort of hard-shelled Baptist in my faith. I believe in foot-washing. I believe in baptism by immersion, and I believe in using the straight edge." [14] For a brief period during his first administration, he even served as first vice-president of the Arkansas State Baptist Association. [15] "I love the Baptist cause and the Baptist church," he once declared, "better than anything except my mother and father, wife and children. . . . " [16]

Clearly, Jeff Davis was not the kind of politician that one normally associates with ethnic or religious tolerance. How did Charles Jacobson, a devout Jew, become involved with such a character? What forces drew the son of a Baptist minister and the son of an immigrant Jewish merchant together? How did Jacobson survive, and even flourish, in a political and social environment which was as intensely ethnocentric as any in American history? Hopefully, the answers to these puzzling questions will shed light not only on Jacobson's career but also on the general conditions which allowed other turn-of-the century Arkansas Jews to become political leaders. Considering the fact that there were less than 700 Jewish families in the entire state at the time, the list of Arkansas Jews who were either elected to public office or appointed to a position of public authority during the late-nineteenth and early-twentieth centuries is surprisingly long. [17] In addition to Jacobson, it includes Aaron Meyers, mayor of Helena from 1878 to 1880; Joseph Wolf, a Little Rock alderman from 1889 to 1893; Jacob Erb, county judge of Pulaski County from 1890 to 1894; Jacob Trieber, a United States District Judge from 1900 to 1927 and president of the Arkansas Bar Association in 1915; Joe Loeb, Little Rock city attorney from 1904 to 1906; Rabbi Louis Wolsey, president of the Little Rock Board of Education in 1906; Jacob Fink, mayor of Helena from 1908 to 1910; Joseph Gates, mayor of Roanoke from 1909 to 1911; Samuel Frauenthal, an Associate Justice of the state supreme court from 1909 to 1923; Rabbi Abraham Rhine (Hot Springs), president of the Arkansas Association of School Boards in 1910; Louis Joseph (Texarkana), a member of the state legislature from 1913 to 1917; and finally, Simon Bloom, mayor of Pine Bluff from 1913 to 1919. [18]

Born in Farmington, Missouri, on July 27, 1874, Charles Jacobson was the only son of Jacob and Josephine (Benda) Jacobson. Both parents were European-born Jews who had emigrated to the United States during the 1850s—Jacob from Prussia, Josephine from Bohemia. A storekeeper by trade, Jacob Jacobson was one of a handful of Jewish merchants who lived and prospered in southeastern Missouri's fertile Saint Francois Valley. [19] Although Farmington, with a population of nearly a thousand, was a relatively large town for its day, the nearest Jewish community of any size was located in Saint Louis, sixty miles to the north. Thus, like most small-town Jews of the Middle Border region, the Jacobsons practiced their religion in relative isolation.

In 1879, shortly after Charles's fifth birthday, the Jacobsons pulled up stakes and set out for the wild but promising land of Arkansas. Journeying more than 200 miles to the south, across the Ozark plateau and into the Arkansas River Valley, they resettled in the booming railroad town of Morrilton, in Conway County. Except for a brief interlude in nearby Perry County in the late eighties, the family would remain in Morrilton for the next twenty years.[20] It was here, on the western fringe of the Southern cotton belt, that Charles Jacobson grew to manhood and learned his politics.

Like most areas of Arkansas, the Conway County of Jacobson's youth was both overwhelmingly rural and unmistakably Southern. Nonetheless, in terms of its cultural makeup it was a rather unusual county. Stretching north-ward from the Arkansas River so that it straddled the southern edge of the Ozarks, the county was a physiographic anomaly which included both upland and lowland cultures. While the northern half of the county was a land of dogtrot cabins and mountain yeomen, the southern half (where the Jacobsons lived) was strictly Black Belt plantation country. Although the county as a whole was nearly 40 percent black in 1890, most of the upland townships were populated almost exclusively by whites.[21] At the same time, Conway County was also characterized by a surprising degree of ethnic and religious diversity. In 1890, 9.1 percent of the county's white males of voting age were foreign-born, compared to only 4.3 percent in the state at large. German Catholics constituted the county's largest single ethnic minority, accounting for more than half of the total foreign-born population, but there were also small communities of Swiss, Austrians, and French.[22] Although the local Catholic minority was not nearly as large as it would become in the early twentieth century (by 1906 white Catholics outnumbered white Baptists in Conway County), as early as 1890 Conway County boasted the sixth-largest Catholic population in the state.[23] Thus, far more than in most areas of the rural South, cultural heterogeneity here was an accepted fact of life.

Interestingly enough, however, Conway County's experience with cultural diversity did not extend to Jews—at least not until the Jacobsons arrived. At the time of their arrival, and for many years thereafter, the Jacobsons were the only Jewish family in the county.[24] Fortunately, this fact did not prevent them from prospering as never before. During his years in Conway County,

Jacob Jacobson became a highly successful cotton factor and supply merchant.[25] Consequently, his son Charles enjoyed a relatively privileged adolescence. Unlike most boys growing up in Arkansas during the 1880s, he was far better acquainted with the inside of a classroom than the backside of a mule. A serious student, he was sent to Little Rock in the late eighties to attend Peabody High School, considered to be one of the best secondary schools in the state.[26]

After graduating from Peabody in the summer of 1891, Jacobson returned to Morrilton to begin a legal apprenticeship in the law office of William Moose and Charles Reid. At the time, Moose, who later served as state attorney general, and Reid, who was later a five-term congressman, were both young but up-and-coming politicians. Only a year earlier, in 1890, Reid had lost a close race for the Democratic nomination for district prosecuting attorney to a young Pope County politico by the name of Jeff Davis.[27]

Despite his tender age, Jacobson soon followed his mentors' lead and became immersed in local politics. Relatively well-educated and savvy beyond his years, he quickly became something of a political prodigy. In September 1892, less than two months after his eighteenth birthday and nearly three years before he could legally cast a ballot, Jacobson served as the official clerk of the general election for Conway County.[28] Perhaps even more remarkable, a year later, at the age of nineteen, he was appointed Deputy Prosecuting Attorney for Conway County by District Attorney Jeff Davis (who was then beginning his final year in office).[29]

Jacobson's political precocity was a function not only of his own intelligence and enthusiasm but also of the competitive political climate which prevailed throughout the early years of the Populist revolt. In Conway County, as in the state at large, the Democrats were locked in a desperate struggle with the Union-Labor party, a biracial coalition of Republicans, Wheelers, Alliancemen, and Greenbackers. In 1888 and again in 1890, the upstart Union-Laborites came within a whisker of capturing the governorship. In fact, only through wholesale fraud and intimidation did the Democratic party manage to stay in power.[30] In short, the party had neither the luxury nor the inclination to quibble about the age (or, for that matter, the religion) of its supporters. As Jacobson himself explained, "Votes were needed. That was the reason why I had a poll tax before becoming 21 years of age."[31] In the unreconstructed Arkansas of Jacobson's youth, if you were a white man and a Democrat it was just that simple.

In 1895, after a year as deputy prosecuting attorney, Jacobson wisely decided to interrupt his budding career to attend college. With Charles Reid's help, he enrolled at the prestigious Vanderbilt University Law School (the alma mater of Reid, Moose, and Davis). He remained there for two years.[32]

Graduating from Vanderbilt in the spring of 1897, Jacobson—still only twenty-two years old—returned to Conway County to pick up where he had left off. By this time, his former employer Jeff Davis had gone on to bigger things. Rebounding from an unsuccessful bid for Congress in 1896, Davis was in the midst of planning a campaign for the state attorney generalship. Almost unknown outside of the Fifth Judicial District, he was then given little chance to defeat the acknowledged front-runner, Judge Frank Goar, a former dean of the University of Arkansas Law School.[33] Even in his home district, Davis faced an uphill struggle. During his years as prosecuting attorney he had made a great many enemies—particularly in Conway County where his relentless prosecution of "blind tigers" and other liquor-law violators had alienated the county-courthouse ring, which was more or less controlled by the liquor interests (at the time, Conway County was the "wettest" county in the district).[34]

It was in this context that Davis offered Jacobson the unenviable task of managing his Conway County campaign. "I am not even going in that county to speak," he promised his young friend, "but if you can carry it for me I will appoint you as my assistant [attorney general]." Despite the long odds, Jacobson accepted the challenge and set about to convince the locals that Jeff Davis was their man. To nearly everyone's surprise, his efforts were successful. Arguing that, despite Davis's past record, it would be highly beneficial for Conway County to have a man from an adjoining county in the attorney general's office (he also pointed out the obvious advantages of having a Conway County man as assistant attorney general), Jacobson persuaded the local Democratic machine to bury the hatchet.[35] As a result, Davis carried Conway County in the Democratic primary by more than a thousand votes.[36] No one was more surprised by this victory than Davis himself, who proceeded to name Jacobson as his statewide campaign manager. Even more important, as the eventual winner of the attorney general's race (Judge Goar dropped dead midway through the campaign), Davis was also able to make good on his original promise to Jacobson. Thus, on January 18, 1899, less than two years after he had received his law degree, twenty-four year old Charles Jacobson was sworn in as assistant attorney general of Arkansas.[37]

To be appointed assistant attorney general was a great honor for a fledgling lawyer, but, as Jacobson soon found out, it was an honor which also entailed an enormous amount of hard work, not to mention a measure of exploitation. Since Davis spent most of his attorney generalship running for governor, Jacobson became the workhorse of the attorney general's office. While Davis was out beating the bushes for votes, Jacobson was usually back at the court-house preparing or arguing cases. In fact, of the 150 cases handled by the attorney general's office during Davis's tenure, more than 100 were briefed and argued by the assistant attorney general.[38] Even on those rare occasions when Davis did appear in court, Jacobson apparently did most of the legal ground-work. In his biography of Davis, Jacobson describes how he orchestrated one of his superior's most celebrated appearances before the state supreme court:

I had a large array of books brought down, none of which had ever been examined by Senator Davis. When we got up to argue the case, I would simply hand him the book open at the case and he would read the syllabi—for the first time and then pro-ceed to argue the same. Very few would or could realize that he had not given the matter deep attention.[39]

Despite such a casual attitude towards his official duties, Davis's attorney generalship proved to be the most memorable in the state's history. By render-ing a radical and highly controversial interpretation of an antitrust law passed by the 1899 legislature, he triggered a bitter political struggle which threw the attorney general's office into the spotlight and the state into an uproar. As Davis interpreted the new law, it prohibited *any* trust from doing business in Arkansas—regardless of where the trust had been organized. To make his point, he filed suit against every fire insurance company then doing business in the state, demanding that they withdraw from industrywide pricing agree-ments. When the fire insurance companies responded by threatening to cancel policies by the hundreds, the donnybrook was on. Outraged business-men held mass protest meetings across the state, but Davis, supported by the legislature, refused to back down. In the end, Davis's interpretation of the antitrust law was overruled by the state supreme court; legally this ended the controversy, but politically it simply added fuel to the fire.[40]

Styling himself a martyr, Davis vowed that he would take his case to the people. Leaving Jacobson behind to take care of things in Little Rock, he announced for the governorship and embarked upon a year-long campaign, haranguing the court and shadowboxing with the trusts at every stop. He had tried to throw the rascals out, he told the voters, but he had been betrayed by the "five jackasses" of the supreme court and the "high-collared crowd" in Little Rock.[41] "The war is on," he declared, "knife to knife, hilt to hilt, foot to foot, knee to knee, between the corporations of Arkansas and the people. . . . If I win this race I have got to win it from 525 insurance agents scattered all over the state. I have to win it from every railroad, every bank and two-thirds of the lawyers and most of the big politicians. But if I can get the plain people of the country to help me, God bless you, we will clean the thing out." In the Arkansas backcountry–where antitrust sentiment was an article of faith–the response to Davis's populistic rhetoric proved to be over-whelming. Carrying seventy-four of seventy-five counties in the Democratic primary, he won the most resounding political victory in the state's history.[42] Arkansas politics would never be quite the same again.

Of course no one was more affected by all this than Charles Jacobson. No longer just an obscure bureaucrat, he now became the chief lieutenant of the most powerful politician in the state. For the next six years of his life, as private secretary to the governor, he would be part of a mass-political-protest movement and an important cog in a powerful political machine.

Despite a relatively unimpressive-sounding title, the private secretary to the governor was an important public official in Arkansas. An official member of the state government, he received an annual salary of $1500 (the governor received $3000) and was required to serve as adjutant general of the Arkansas state militia (a position which traditionally took up only a small part of his time). In effect, he performed many of the functions performed by lieutenant governors in other states. (Although Arkansas had a lieutenant governorship of sorts, it was largely a ceremonial position. Elected by his colleagues at the end of each legislative session, the lieutenant governor was a member of the state senate and served in the executive office only when the governor was out of the state.)[43] While the position of private secretary clearly lacked the prestige of a lieutenant governorship, it did offer its holder numerous opportunities to exercise a measure of power and influence.

Under any Arkansas governor the position of private secretary would have been an important one, but under Jeff Davis, who spent well over half of his six years in office out on the campaign trail, it was particularly so. Although Jacobson sometimes accompanied Davis on the stump, he usually remained in Little Rock attending to the various administrative duties of the executive office; answering the governor's correspondence, drafting legislative proposals, arranging future campaign speeches, dealing with legislators and various state boards, handling pardon requests, and most importantly, keeping the patronage mill running. In other words, in a limited way Jacobson acted as a surrogate governor for several months out of each year. Although he rarely if ever made important decisions entirely on his own, on occasion he did exercise real power. In several areas, most notably in screening pardon requests and in determining who received low-level appointments, Davis seems to have given Jacobson a wide range of discretion.[44] To some degree, such delegation of authority was inevitable, since consultation between the two men was often impossible. Some decisions had to be made unexpectedly and immediately, and when Davis was away on one of his many extended hunting trips or was out in the backcountry chasing the farm vote, he was often beyond the reach of telephone or telegraph.

Of course, even when Davis was in town, Jacobson still shouldered most of the administrative burden. According to Jacobson, campaign or no campaign, "it was hard to confine Jeff to an office. He wanted to be out in the open, talking, hunting, training dogs. . . . The Governor was not an office man and he was as quiet, restful and peaceful in his office as a lion in a cage during a circus parade."[45]

Jacobson's importance to the Davis administration becomes even clearer when we realize that Governor Davis's entire staff consisted of only three people: Jacobson; Davis's eldest daughter Bessie, who served as a stenographer; and a janitor.[46] In short, the governor and his private secretary were pretty much the whole show. Admittedly, Davis was also aided by a small coterie of unofficial political advisers—a protective ring of a half dozen or so close personal friends whom he knew he could trust. At various times—usually in times of political crisis—these advisers played important roles within the Davis organization. However, none of these men regularly took part in the day-to-day affairs of either the governor's office or the Davis machine. Unlike Jacobson, they all had competing demands on their time: Jeptha Evans, J. G. Wallace, Jesse Hart, and J. V. Bourland were judges; Webb Covington and Hal Norwood were state senators; and John Page was secretary of the State Board of Charities. Thus, aside from Davis himself, Jacobson was the only man who was almost always at the center of things, who knew the entire Davis organization inside and out, and who kept his fingers on the pulse of the Davis movement day after day and week after week.[47]

By almost any standard, Jacobson was the number-two man in the Davis administration. Although his authority tended to be more de facto than de jure, there was never any doubt that he, and he alone, was the boss's right-hand man. While it is true that most of his power was exercised behind the scenes, he was not just an anonymous back-room politico. His name often appeared in the press, and on a few occasions he was even in the spotlight. For example, at the close of the 1902 legislative session he created a sensation when, at Davis's request, he unloaded a wheelbarrow filled with more than a hundred vetoed bills onto the floor of the secretary of state's office.[48] On another occasion he engaged in a much-publicized fistfight on a Little Rock street corner with one of the city's more belligerent anti-Davisites. Though he apparently got the worst of the fight, his willingness to stand up for Jeff made him something of a hero in the backcountry.[49]

A key element of Jacobson's importance within the administration was his close personal relationship with Davis. Despite the measure of exploitation in their relationship, the two men were close friends. Jacobson was a frequent guest in the Davis home and often socialized with Davis after hours. They attended baseball games together, went drinking together, and sometimes even vacationed together.[50]

Interestingly enough, they did all this despite striking differences in their respective temperaments and attitudes towards politics and government. In point of fact, to a great degree it was their differences which held them together. Personally as well as professionally, each had what the other lacked. Davis, the flamboyant and unpredictable rabble-rouser, was a master politician who had little interest in, or aptitude for, administration. Jacobson, the calm and efficient bureaucrat, was an administrative wizard who had neither the background nor the skills to become a powerful politician on his own. Complementing each other almost perfectly, they formed an unbeatable combination—one which totally dominated Arkansas politics for more than six years. As it turned out, the only thing that could break their hold over the state was their own success. With Davis's triumphal elevation to the United States Senate in 1907, the Davis machine—bereft of its patronage base—quickly lost most of its power.[51]

After Davis's election to the Senate in 1906, Jacobson agreed to stay on indefinitely as an administrative assistant. Correspondingly, when Davis relinquished the governorship in January 1907, Jacobson became the senator-elect's legislative aide. As it happened, he also became his law partner. Faced with an interim year between the end of his governorship and the beginning of his senate term, Davis—whose finances had been sapped by years of almost continuous campaigning—decided to spend his time recouping his personal fortune. Accordingly, he and Jacobson opened a law office in Little Rock.[52]

The legal partnership between Davis and Jacobson proved to be a striking financial success for both men. Unfortunately, however, it also had the unintended effect of poisoning the relationship between two men who were not accustomed to working together as equals. After enjoying a measure of equality as Davis's law partner, Jacobson was unwilling to go back to the status of an unquestioning subordinate. For the first time in his political career, he began to demand a degree of personal and political independence. When Davis refused to adjust, the two men came to a parting of the ways.

According to Jacobson, the break was triggered by a disagreement over what his new duties as a legislative assistant should be. Davis, who hoped to spend most of his senate term in Arkansas tending to his political machine and his hunting dogs, wanted Jacobson to run his Washington office. In short, he wanted to continue the pattern of the previous decade: he wanted his assistant to do most of the work. Jacobson, on the other hand, insisted on staying in Little Rock. As he later explained, with a wife and two small children to support, he simply could not afford to live in Washington year-round.[53]

The disagreement over Jacobson's new duties would never be resolved—primarily because the two men soon had a political falling-out which rendered the original problem academic. During his years as Davis's private secretary, Jacobson had become a close personal friend of Secretary of State O. C. Ludwig. Thus, when Ludwig announced that he would run for a third term in the 1908 primary, Jacobson immediately offered him his whole-hearted support. At the time, it was assumed that Davis, who had supported Ludwig in the past, would do likewise. To nearly everyone's surprise, however, the governor threw his support to Ludwig's opponent, Julius Clary. Everyone in the Davis organization was ordered to follow suit, but many Davisites, including Jacobson, stubbornly refused. Later, when Ludwig won the primary by a narrow margin, the relationship between the senator and his assistant became, in Jacobson's words, "exceedingly strained."[54] Before long the break was complete, so much so that when Davis ran for re-election to the senate in 1912, Jacobson actually worked as a campaign aide for his opponent, Congressman Stephen S. Brundidge. At the time of Davis's death in January 1913, the two men were not even on speaking terms.[55]

The break with Davis provided Jacobson with the opportunity to stake out his own political career. However, he did not do so right away. From 1908 to 1911, he ran the Little Rock office of Arkansas's senior senator, James

P. Clarke. Elected with Davis's help in 1902, Clarke was a maverick progressive whom Jacobson deeply admired.[56] Fortunately, working for Clarke proved to be far less demanding than working for Davis, and Jacobson was able to spend most of his time developing his private law practice. A close student of the law and a clever speaker, he quickly gained a wide reputation as a "lawyer's lawyer," particularly after he compiled and published an authoritative digest of Arkansas's criminal statutes. By the end of the decade he was one of the most sought-after attorneys in Little Rock.[57]

Buoyed by his booming legal career, Jacobson—with Clarke's encouragement— decided to run for the state senate in 1910. The district in which he ran, the tenth, consisted of rural Perry County, where his family had lived briefly during the late 1880s, and Pulaski County, which included the cities of Little Rock and Argenta (later known as North Little Rock). Incredibly, though he had been actively involved in politics for nearly twenty years, this was his first race for elected office. Even so, he proved to be a vigorous and effective campaigner. Brandishing a progressive platform which called for a sizable expansion of governmental services, he finished a strong second in a primary race in which three candidates vied for two seats (see table).[58] In the general election that followed, he won easily over his Republican opponent.

Once in office, Jacobson proved to be an unusually conscientious and energetic state senator. During the 1911 legislative session he introduced more than thirty-five public bills, far more than any other senator. Deeply committed to governmental reform and expansion, he quickly established himself as one of the legislature's most forceful advocates of business progressivism. Appointed chairman of the Committee on Cities and Towns, he worked particularly hard to modernize municipal governments and services.[59] Though hardly a radical, his proposals touched upon a wide variety of progressive reforms: the substitution of electrocution for hanging as the only legal method of execution; a commission form of government in large cities (i.e., over 45,000 population); the inspection of plumbing and drainage facilities in urban areas; regulation of building and loan associations; stricter incorporation laws for insurance companies; juvenile delinquency laws; and stricter licensing requirements for everyone from peddlers to plumbers. Although most of these measures were defeated, Jacobson received a great deal of attention for his efforts. In 1912 he was easily re-elected to a second term.[60]

The highlight of Jacobson's career in the state senate was his coauthorship of the Turner-Jacobson bill, a controversial tax-reform measure designed to remedy a severe financial crisis which struck the Arkansas state government

TABLE 1

1910 Democratic Primary Vote for State Senator, Pulaski County, Arkansas[a]

Precincts	% for Jacobson	Jacobson	Vote for Pittard	Miles	Total Vote
Urban Precincts[b]	31.3	1741	1847	1972	5560
Little Rock City	30.9	1436	1545	1662	4643
Argenta City	33.3	305	302	310	917
Rural Precincts	34.2	487	414	525	1426
Ashley	27.6	8	10	11	29
Badgett	50.0	10	0	10	20
Bayou Meto	35.1	53	39	59	151
Big Rock	29.5	92	108	112	312
Brodie	30.0	15	21	14	50
Campbell	31.8	7	7	8	22
Eagle	38.8	40	6	57	103
Eastman	44.0	48	38	23	109
Ellis	34.8	16	16	14	46
Fourche	30.6	22	18	32	72
Gray	35.3	53	37	60	150
Mineral	38.0	30	24	25	79
Owen	42.5	51	32	37	120
Roland	30.8	8	12	6	26
Union	20.8	10	17	21	48
Worthen	22.7	17	28	30	75
Young	50.0	7	1	6	14
TOTAL	31.9	2228	2261	2497	6989

Source: Little Rock *Arkansas Gazette*, April 1, 1910.

[a]The tenth senatorial district consisted of Pulaski and Perry Counties, but primary returns for Perry County are unavailable.

[b]Virtually all of Pulaski County's Jewish population lived in Little Rock or Argenta. The Jewish population of Little Rock was approximately 1500, or about 3% of the total population. (*AJYB, 1918–1919*, vol. 20 [Philadelphia, 1918], p. 51.)

during the spring of 1911. Introduced during an emergency legislative session, the bill attempted to restore the state to solvency by simultaneously instituting 100 percent evaluation and lowering the tax rate. After much debate, the bill managed to pass both the house and the senate and was submitted to the electorate for approval in a September 1912 referendum. Unfortunately for Jacobson and his business-progressive allies, the bill was overwhelmingly rejected by the electorate–57,176 to 79,899–in part because the Democratic candidate for governor, Joseph T. Robinson, vehemently opposed it.[61]

Despite this setback, Jacobson's reputation as a talented and diligent legislator continued to grow. By the end of the 1913 legislative session, he had emerged as one of the acknowledged leaders of the senate. Still only thirty-eight years old, he seemed headed for a long and distinguished career as an elected public official.[62]

However, this was not to be the case. Despite his growing reputation, he did not seek re-election to the senate in 1914. In fact, though he would live into the 1950s, he never ran for public office again. In 1915 he was appointed to a United States commissionership by Federal Judge John E. Martineau, a position which he held until 1927. Thereafter, until his death in 1957, he devoted all of his professional energies to his private law practice.[63]

Why such a sudden departure from the political arena? Unfortunately, the answer to this question is unclear. Since neither Jacobson nor any of his contemporaries ever offered any explanation for his seemingly premature retirement, we can only speculate about his motivation. Such speculation produces at least two plausible lines of argument.

On the one hand, his retirement may have been wholly voluntary. Perhaps he was simply tired of politics; after more than a decade with Davis and after more than three years of wrangling with reactionary legislators, such an attitude would not have been all that surprising. Even more likely, he may have quit for financial reasons. A state senatorship was hardly a lucrative position, and he may have preferred a job such as the United States commissionership, which gave him more time to engage in private law practice.

A second and very different line of argument would suggest that Jacobson's retirement was involuntary–that he was driven from the political arena by a wave of anti-Semitism. Although there is no conclusive evidence that this was the case, the circumstantial evidence is highly suggestive. Clearly, it may have been no accident that Jacobson's retirement coincided with the Leo Frank controversy–that it occurred at a time when Southern anti-Semitism was approaching flood tide. If Jacobson had decided to run for a third term, his reelection campaign would have taken place in the spring of

1914, a period when Tom Watson's anti-Semitic diatribes against Frank and other "moneyed Jews" were sending shock waves across the South.[64] In Arkansas, as elsewhere in the region, the Frank case caused a sensation and led to a noticeable increase in anti-Jewish sentiment. Though most of the state's major newspapers, such as those in Little Rock and Fort Smith, reported the case in a relatively responsible and dispassionate manner (in the spring of 1914, for example, the Little Rock *Arkansas Gazette* joined several of the South's leading dailies in demanding a new trial for Frank), some small-town papers used the case as a pretext for indulging in anti-Jewish harangues.[65] As a result, tensions between Jews and Gentiles reached unprecedented levels in many areas of the state.

Without corroborating evidence, it would be risky to assume that Jacobson's retirement from politics was related to the Frank case. One thing is clear, however: if his retirement was prompted by the anti-Semitic fallout from the Frank case, he was not alone. In the aftermath of the Georgia tragedy, there was a sharp drop-off throughout the South in the number of Jews elected to public office. In fact, in many Southern states—including Arkansas—the Jewish politician (excluding judges) had all but disappeared by 1916.[66] Although Louis Joseph of Texarkana was elected to a second term in the state house of representatives in September 1914 and Simon Bloom was re-elected mayor of Pine Bluff in September 1917, both men were gone from the public scene by the end of the decade. With the exception of Eli Newman, who served as a Helena city councilman from 1922 to 1924, there was not another Arkansas Jew elected to public office until 1933, when Samuel M. Levine was sent to the state senate from Pine Bluff.[67]

Of course, speculation about the causes of Jacobson's retirement is somewhat extraneous to the purposes of this essay. Regardless of how it ended, Jacobson's political career was impressive while it lasted. The possibility that his retirement was part of the anti-Semitic purge which swept the South after 1914 should not obscure the fact that he enjoyed considerable political success throughout the Populist-Progressive era. For more than a decade—as assistant attorney general, as the chief lieutenant of the most powerful governor in the state's history, and finally as a state senator—Jacobson was a full-fledged member of the Arkansas political establishment. Though he was a Jewish politician in an overwhelmingly Gentile society, he was a man of influence who wielded more than his share of political power. Perhaps, most significantly, he did so without provoking an anti-Semitic backlash. Remarkably, a close examination of the public record—as reported

in the newspapers of the period—fails to reveal even a single instance in
which Jacobson was attacked because of his religion.[68] While this finding
does not preclude the possibility that he suffered from more subtle forms
of anti-Semitism—such as whispering campaigns and social discrimination—
it does indicate that anti-Semitic campaign tactics were frowned upon. In
other words, regardless of what happened behind the scenes, the fact that anti-
Semitic harassment (if such harassment did exist) was kept outside the
bounds of public debate is in itself striking.

Although it is impossible to be absolutely sure about such things, prior
to 1914—and perhaps afterwards as well—Charles Jacobson's religion seems
to have had relatively little impact on his political career. How did this
happen? How did a Jewish politician have such an easy time of it in a political
culture that was saturated with ethnocentrism and Anglo-Saxon zealotry?
Although there is no simple answer to this question, one thing is clear:
Jacobson did not succeed by repudiating or camouflaging his Judaism.
Admittedly, as a youngster in Conway County (where there was not a synagogue within forty miles), Jacobson often attended Protestant church
services (usually Methodist or Presbyterian) with his friends—a gesture which
may have facilitated his initial entry into the political arena. Nonetheless,
there is no evidence that he ever considered himself to be anything other
than a committed Jew. In the late-nineteenth-century South, it was apparently relatively common for devout but isolated Jewish families to worship
with their Christian neighbors on Sunday morning—the intent usually being
an act of courtesy rather than an act of conversion, either real or pretended.[69]

In any event, as an adult, Jacobson's identification with the Jewish faith
and the Jewish community could not have been stronger. Devoutly religious,
he joined the Reform congregation of Temple B'nai Israel immediately after
his arrival in Little Rock in 1899 and for the next two decades was probably
the most active lay leader in the entire congregation. A close friend and
frequent companion of Rabbi Louis Wolsey, Jacobson taught the temple's
confirmation classes throughout his career in state politics.[70] As the *Arkansas
Gazette* put it in January 1901, he had a distinct "liking for the ministry."
Whenever Rabbi Wolsey was absent from the city on the Sabbath, it was
invariably Jacobson who stepped in and conducted B'nai Israel's services.
In addition, he also served several terms as secretary of the Concordia Club,
Little Rock's largest and most active Jewish social organization.[71] Finally,
even his marriage marked him as a leader of the local Jewish community. His

wife, Dillie Navra Jacobson (whom he married in 1904), was the niece of Ida Navra, a longtime president of the local Ladies Temple Aid Society, and the granddaughter of Morris Navra, the founder of the B'nai Israel congregation.[72] Considering all this, it is little wonder that Jacobson ultimately became both a member of B'nai Israel's Board of Trustees and the president of District 7 of B'nai B'rith.[73]

Clearly Jacobson's religion was no secret. The fact that he was a leader of the Little Rock Jewish community was almost certainly common knowledge among Arkansas politicians and, to a somewhat lesser extent, among Arkansas voters as well. This was true, in part, because Davis himself made no attempt to hide the fact that his assistant was a Jew. Not only did he sometimes refer publicly to his "Jew clerk," (a phrase which admittedly may have had some implicitly negative connotations) but in April 1904, along with Rabbi Wolsey, he officiated at Jacobson's wedding, which was held at the home of Charles Abeles, one of Little Rock's leading Jewish merchants.[74] Apparently Davis did not consider it to be a serious political liability to be publicly associated with the local Jewish community.

This is not to suggest that Davis acted under the assumption that his constituents were free of anti-Semitic prejudice. Rather, it is to suggest that he recognized the fact that many of his constituents believed that there were two distinct kinds of Jews. On the one hand, there was the stereotypic alien Jew, or in John Higham's words, "the shadowy, imaginary Jew who lived far away in the big cities."[75] Feared and mistrusted, the alien Jew sometimes served as a convenient symbol for a variety of threatening forces, such as immigration, urbanization, and big business. As such, he usually was perceived as having only a tenuous connection with a second kind of Jew: the homegrown Southern Jew. In most cases more distinctively Southern than distinctively Jewish, the Southern Jew tended to have more in common with his Christian neighbors than with his Jewish cousins in Boston or New York. In other words, despite their religious distinctiveness, most Southern Jews were part of the regional mainstream.[76]

The prevalence of this dichotomous conception of the Jewish world explains why Davis, without any sense of inconsistency and without any fear of reprisal, could attack "the usurers, the Rothschilds" (he used this kind of rhetoric very sparingly) one minute and socialize with his Jewish assistant the next.[77] While it almost certainly would have been political suicide for any Arkansas politician to publicly associate with a New York Jew, a similar relationship with a native-born Southern Jew did nothing more than raise a few eyebrows.

This double standard was an instrumental factor in Jacobson's success. Certainly there was never any doubt as to which variety of Jew Charles Jacobson was. Despite his open and fervent commitment to Judaism, there was little, if any, of the outsider about him. In his white supremacist racial views, in his romantic patronage of the Lost Cause, in his ambivalence toward. Northern business intersts, in his sense of place, in his style of speech and dress—indeed, in every respect but his religion—he was a classic New-South gentleman.[78] Moreover, throughout his political career, Jacobson's image as an insider was strongly reinforced by his participation in numerous voluntary associations. In addition to being active in the Arkansas Bar Association, he belonged to no less than five fraternal orders: the Woodmen of the World, which he joined at eighteen; the Knights of Pythias, which he joined at twenty-one; and three Masonic lodges—the Royal Arch Masons, the Ancient Free and Accepted Masons, and the Arkansas Consistory.[79]

Perhaps even more significant as far as his public image was concerned, Jacobson was also a leading figure in the sports life of the city. A passionate baseball fan, he was a frequent visitor to the clubhouse of the Little Rock Travellers, the local entry in what was then the Southern League. The manager of the Travellers, Bob Allen, was a close friend, and for many years Jacobson served as the team's attorney. A perennial powerhouse, the Travellers were the pride of the city, and anyone who was closely associated with them was bound to be something of a local sports celebrity. At the same time, Jacobson was equally well-known in local football circles; for more than a decade he served as a field judge in high school football games throughout the Little Rock area.[80]

Clearly Jacobson's Judaism did not prevent him from sharing the values of the dominant culture. In every way but one, he identified with and participated in the mainstream of Southern life. For six days out of every seven, he was every bit as Southern as Jeff Davis himself. Considering the intensity of sectionalist feelings in Arkansas throughout the Populist-Progressive period, one cannot help but conclude that this unmistakable Southernness was a key element in his ability to survive politically.

An additional factor which undoubtedly contributed to Jacobson's success was his exceptional intelligence, or more specifically, his uncommon aptitude for both law and politics. Throughout his political career, but particularly during his years with Davis, Jacobson's rather extraordinary abilities effectively overshadowed his ethnic and religious distinctiveness. Although we have no way of knowing for sure, it is at least arguable that he would have been excluded from the Arkansas political elite if he had not been a supremely talented and industrious individual. All other things being equal, Jeff Davis almost certainly would not have chosen a Jew to be his chief assistant, just as he would not have chosen a Catholic or a Mormon. In a state such as Arkansas, where the White Anglo-Saxon Protestant majority was so overwhelming, to become associated with a member of an ethnoreligious minority was to take an obvious risk (though, as noted above, the risk was apparently much smaller than one might think). Without being overly cynical, it seems safe to conclude that a shrewd politician like Davis would not have taken such a risk if there had not been compensating advantages involved. In Jacobson's case, the compensating advantages could not have been more obvious. Davis was well aware that Jacobson was one of the keys to his success—that, in large part, it was Jacobson's labors which gave him the freedom to remain out on the stump week after week and month after month, grinding his opponents into the dust and communing with the voters as no Arkansas politician had ever done before. As Jacobson's employer, Davis was able to exploit an unusually skilled legal and political operative who was unceasingly loyal and who was willing to work long hours for low pay. Jew or Gentile, such men were difficult to find.

However, we should be wary of taking this "exceptionalist" argument too far. Jacobson's indispensability to the Davis movement cannot explain the most crucial element of his political success: the refusal of the anti-Davis forces to exploit anti-Semitic prejudice. As a general rule, the factional warfare between Davisites and anti-Davisites was a no-holds-barred affair, with both sides using every means available—no matter how slanderous or how farfetched—to discredit the opposition. Although the anti-Davisites rarely got the upper hand in this mudslinging exchange, it was not for want of trying. At one time or another, they called Davis everything from a "whoremonger" and an "anarchist" to a "blasphemer and a liar."[81] They did all this, yet for some reason they never resorted to anti-Semitism. Why? Why didn't they attempt to exploit the fact that Davis's chief assistant was a Jew?

Perhaps the most obvious reason for this restraint was the considerable economic power (and to some extent the political power) wielded by Arkansas's Jewish business community. Despite the scarcity of Jews in the state as a whole, Jewish businessmen dominated the commercial life of Arkansas's two largest cities, Little Rock and Fort Smith.[82] Significantly, like their Gentile counterparts, the vast majority of Jewish businessmen were solidly ensconced in the anti-Davis coalition. Boosters of the new urban South, they were an important part of the economic and social core of the anti-Davis movement (which suggests that Davis was not the only one open to anti-Semitic attack).[83] As such, they were not to be trifled with. To alienate the Jewish business community was to risk the unraveling of the anti-Davis coalition and to endanger the state's chances for future economic growth.

Of course, if virulent anti-Semitism had been as rampant in the early-twentieth-century South as some historians have suggested, the anti-Davis leaders might have been willing to take such a risk. The fact that they did not do so reflects their judgment that anti-Semitic politics (unlike white-supremacist politics) would have drawn relatively little response from the electorate. In the final analysis, Charles Jacobson's political survival depended on an atmosphere of relative tolerance.

8.

Jews and Other Southerners
Counterpoint and Paradox

Stephen J. Whitfield

In his most recent collection of essays, *American Counterpoint* (1971), C. Vann Woodward did for Southern whites what W. E. B. Du Bois had done at the turn of the century for American blacks, underscoring their ambivalence toward the rest of the nation. Both minorities have been burdened with a double consciousness, have been Americans with a difference, have adhered to the national consensus even as estrangement has complicated their loyalties. Professor Woodward's book, however, is not unusual among major studies in Southern history in its neglect of Jews, whose cultural characteristics and social situation in the region can nevertheless be approached contrapuntally. Consider the possibilities.

Compared to the rest of America, the region has been characteristically agrarian; and the financier, the banker, the lien merchant have been special targets of rural hatred and resentment. Jews by contrast were rarely granted the right to own land in Europe and have traditionally earned their living in commerce, sometimes not by choice. Even in the South they have preferred to meet a payroll rather than to walk behind a plow, and when we focus on their economic activity we really mean business. They have rarely been confined to the rank of unskilled workers, which even in Russia's Pale of Settlement was termed "black labor." And even the most publicized of Jewish "farmers," Bernard Baruch of Hobcaw, South Carolina, was, of course, a cosmopolitan financier, which did not prevent him from eloquently praising the agrarian life that he so frequently escaped.

The romantic attachment of Southerners to the land must bewilder the rest of the United States—which is the most mobile, the most restless, the most active of nations. Southerners have often been suspicious of Yankee

The author is much indebted to the incisive and learned criticism that Professor Richard H. King offered of an earlier version of this chapter.

meddlers (and of Jewish peddlers) and have made "carpetbagger" and "outside agitator" terms of opprobrium. Mississippi's Willie Morris has claimed
that "Southerners of both races share a rootedness that even in moments of
anger and pain we have been unable to repudiate or ignore." Another Mis-
sissippian, Eudora Welty, clings to her roots as the very incentive of her fiction: "The place where I am and the place I know, and other places that
familiarity with and love for my own make strange and lovely and enlighten-
ing to look into, are what set me to writing my stories."[1] American-Jewish
fiction, by contrast, tends to be introspective or allegorical; when it is
attentive to environment, those surroundings are urban, depicted without
the warmth of nostalgia or the impulse to sentimentalize poverty and ugli-
ness. Eastern European Jewry was so cut off from its environment that its
Yiddish vocabulary contained no names for wild birds and only two names
for flowers (rose, violet). Yet try to imagine the Southern environment and
sensibility without the magnolia blossoms and azaleas and honeysuckle and
summers of wisteria and Robert Penn Warren's bearded oaks, without
"nature writing"!

The sense of place, which in Southern writers is as keen as an animal's, is
organically entwined with filiopietism. Apart from race, the distinguishing
mark of the Southern mind is embodied in the slogan of the French right-
wing propagandist Maurice Barrès: *la terre et les morts*. An echolalic passage
in Faulkner's "The Bear" is streaked with such romanticism, in which Ike
McCaslin honors "men who could believe that all necessary to conduct a
successful war was not acumen nor shrewdness nor politics nor diplomacy
nor money nor even integrity and simple arithmetic but just love of land and
courage"–to which McCaslin Edmonds adds "And an unblemished and
gallant ancestry and the ability to ride a horse. . . . Don't leave that out."[2]
After the inexorable defeat, nearly all the leaders of the rebel government
remained in their beloved South–except one. Belle Chasse plantation and
Louisiana meant so little to Judah P. Benjamin that after Appomattox he
escaped to Great Britain (where he rose to eminence again at the bar, becoming Queen's Counsellor, though not–like Disraeli–her counsellor). He died
and was buried in France. That Benjamin was also in flight from his Jewish
origin and identity does not revoke his membership among the people
that Joseph Stalin, in an ominous euphemism, once called "rootless
cosmopolitans."

Compared to the rest of America, the South is especially violent, with the
highest homicide rates in the nation. With 52 percent of all white Southern

families owning guns compared to 27 percent of non-Southerners, with rifle racks boldly displayed on pickup trucks, with manhood defined and achieved not only in the bedroom but in the wilderness, Southerners have created a syndrome of violence that Jews have generally found repugnant. The region has sent disproportionate numbers of its sons to serve and to die in the American armed forces, and military academies dotted its landscape even before the Civil War. It was almost as socially necessary for the academically inclined antebellum Southerner to take his guns with him to college as it was for his cousins to carry theirs while tracking runaways on slave patrols. An important theme of southwestern humor is the exaggerated violence and cruelty of fistfights, gouging, and wrestling with men and beasts.

Yet the narrator of Isaac Babel's "After the Battle" (1920) is not concerned about how to face death honorably as he rides with the Galician cavalry; instead he is "imploring fate to grant me the simplest of proficiencies—the ability to kill my fellow men." Militarism has played a paltry role in Judaic tradition, which has fashioned *shalom* not only into a greeting and a farewell but into the core of its aspirations. Jewish humor gets its effects not by exaggerating strength but by underscoring weakness and vulnerability, as in Woody Allen's admission that he was once even beaten up by Quakers. It is true that Baruch took pride in the game that could be shot at Hobcaw; but the Jewish immunity to the charm of killing animals for sport has been more typical because, as Heine once explained, in the Middle Ages, *we* were the hunted. It is true that some outstanding American gangsters have been Jews, such as Meyer Lansky (who, as a senior citizen residing in Miami Beach, might be listed as a Southern Jew as well); but even Lansky's contribution to the Syndicate reportedly consisted more of the application of business methods than of raw violence. Jewish values, by virtually any test that could be devised, are either indifferent or derogatory toward what is fashionably called machismo and are pacific and even antiheroic. The matriculation of Isidor Straus at Georgia Military Academy during the Civil War lasted less than a day, his brother Oscar recalled, because the other cadets subjected him to hazing: "He had not heard of hazing before, and the incident disgusted him so that he never returned to the academy. He embarked upon his career as a merchant the very next morning."[3]

Compared to the rest of the country, the South has had the lowest rates of literacy and probably the most deeply embedded tradition of anti-intellectualism. Lenny Bruce once said that he could not imagine a nuclear physicist with a Southern accent, a remark delivered prior to the candidacy of Jimmy Carter. Perhaps, as W. J. Cash has argued, the Southerner could not help associating the modern mind with the Yankee mind. The fundamentalism, the absolutism, the irrationality and lack of realism, and the discomfort with ambiguity that have been the stigmata of Southern culture might be contrasted with the daily greeting that one future physicist, Isidore Isaac Rabi, got from his mother: "Did you ask any good questions in school today?"[4] Within the religious culture of the shtetl, the capacity to ask good questions of the sacred texts was proof of a student's ability—not, as in much of the rural South, a disqualification to teach biology. It is unnecessary to elaborate upon the differences between Southern Protestantism—direct, immediate, profoundly emotional—and historical Judaism—with its ratiocination, its codification, its interpretive arabesques, its proclamation that "an ignorant man cannot be pious."

Perhaps the most striking instance of the Jewish distaste for the primitive and the irrational occurred after one phase of the trial of the Scottsboro "boys," when their attorney, Samuel Leibowitz, returned to New York from Alabama in 1933 to describe the jurors as "those creatures, those bigots whose mouths are slits in their faces, whose eyes pop out like a frog's, whose chins drop tobacco juice, bewhiskered and filthy." Travelogues like that have undoubtedly helped to keep the Jewish population of the South at 1 percent. What Leibowitz was promoting in the interview that he granted to a New York newspaper was a stereotype—which is usually not a falsehood but a refraction of reality, a distortion that is tinctured with truth. Even when such testimony is reasonably uncompromised by prior rumors and fears about the region, the Jew tends to see Southerners as though they were part of the supporting cast of *Deliverance*. From the nineteenth century, for example, here is Ludwig Lewisohn's memory of his family's arrival in Queenshaven, South Carolina, when he was eight years old: "I recall vividly the long, shabby, crowded car and its peculiar reek of peanuts, stale whiskey, and chewing-tobacco. Half of the passengers were burly Negroes who gabbled and laughed weirdly. The white men wore broad—rimmed wool hats, whittled and spat and talked in drawling tones. I very distinctly shared my parents' sense of the wildness, savagery and roughness of the scene, their horrified perception of its contrast to anything they had ever known or seen." And even in the eighteenth century, in a letter Joseph Salvador wrote from South Carolina in 1785, the symbolic overtones of the encounter between Jew and Southerner were already articulated: "I am now in a wild country. . . .

The inhabitants are descendants of the wild Irish and their ignorance [is] amazing. . . . They are as poor as rats, proud as dons. . . . They are naked and famished and immensely lazy. They have no religion or morals. . . . Their minds are wholly bent on their horses whom they prize more than their wives and families. They hate society and pass their days in the woods or, loitering about, they drink hard. Rum is their deity; they . . . [are] always happy when they can do any ill-natured thing and molest their neighbors."[5]

The contrast that Salvador, Lewisohn, and Leibowitz evoke is virtually that between civilization and savagery. The coarsened sensibility of the lower-class whites does more than shock these Jews. It seems to excite in them the fear of descent into the primitive, the horror that in the South membranes of restraint that bind a social order may be broken. The Jew who enters the region may thus be faced more starkly, than elsewhere in America, with the possibility of id overwhelming superego, of the return of the repressed.

The contrapuntal tension is thus between two character ideals. The ghetto and the shtetl that encased diaspora life for almost two millennia required calculation, patience, prudence, cleverness, and, above all, temperance as the conditions of survival, which is why so many Jews prospered when trans-posed to a country ostensibly grounded in the Protestant ethic. Their equiv-alent of "bull in a china shop" was "cossack in a sukkah"; and those rambunctious Southerners, those wool hat boys with their incessant drinking and talk of horses, must have seemed like the American equivalent of cossacks (and therefore to be avoided when aroused). The currently popular stereo-type of the white Protestant of British ancestry—some overrefined, aloof, inhibited, lifeless quasi-aristocrat contemplating the bust of William McKinley—should be treated with some skepticism, for it has very limited applicability to a region so steamy that it has produced Earl Long, Kissin' Jim Folsom, Pappy O'Daniel, Cyclone Davis, Lester Maddox, Elvis Presley, Janis Joplin, Zelda Sayre Fitzgerald, Tallulah Bankhead, Burt Reynolds, Jerry Lee Lewis, Martha Mitchell, and Elizabeth Ray, among other demotic types. The normative male character-ideal for the Jew has been first the scholar, and later the business and professional man, in contrast to the prestige at-tached to the role described in The Mind of the South: "To stand on his head in a bar, to toss down a pint of raw whiskey at a gulp, to fiddle and dance all night, to bite off the nose or gouge out the eye of a favorite enemy, to fight harder and love harder than the next man, to be known eventually far and wide as a hell of a fellow—such would be . . . [the Southerner's] focus. To lie on his back for days and weeks, storing power as the air he breathed

stored power under the sun of August, and then to explode, as that air ex-
plodes in a thunderstorm, in a violent outburst of emotion—in such fashion
would he make life not only tolerable but infinitely sweet."[6] Even the more
casual descendant of this hell of a fellow—the good old boy—is far removed
in his romantic exuberance and instinctual ease from the character ideal of the
Jew outside the South. Indeed, the stereotypical Southerner has been sufficiently distant from the image of the WASP that the dangers of exaggeration have set in. It has become a little too easy, indeed treacherous, to accept
Cash's "man at the center" (the average ex-hillbilly on the make) as exclusively a man in extremis. As Flannery O'Connor once remarked about
regional writing, "Anything that comes out of the South is going to be
called grotesque by the Northern reader, unless it is grotesque, in which case
it is going to be called realistic."[7]

Nevertheless, for all these differences of value and perception, the Jews
who came to live and die in Dixie generally did not witness the realization of
further nightmares. Though the region was less sinister than might have
been expected, its response to Jews in its midst was so distinctive that
further analysis is warranted.

In the June 13, 1945, entry in his diary, the British politician and belle-
trist Harold Nicolson distinguished between mass pathology that had
resulted in genocide and a personal attitude that governed social relations.
He wrote: "Although I loathe anti-Semitism, I do dislike Jews."[8] Nicholson's feelings might be contrasted with those expressed four years earlier
in William Alexander Percy's elegiac *Lanterns on the Levee*. Its author was a
patrician, or at least what passed for one in a nation that had done so much to
corrode claims of status based on blood and birth. Like Nicholson, he was
committed to paternalism rather than to egalitarianism, and to individuality
more than to individualism; he also cherished a personal code of honor. Yet
his memoir of the Mississippi Delta virtually reversed Nicholson's distinction, for Percy marveled at individual Jews like the small store-owner in
Mississippi who asked him, "Do you know Pushkin? Ah, beautiful, better
than Shelley or Byron!" Percy's schoolteacher Caroline Stern, the daughter
of another village merchant and a later convert to Episcopalianism, ranked
as Percy's "favorite friend," from whom he "learned more . . . of what the
good life is and of how it may be lived than almost anyone else." But though
this Catholic planter's war record included the fight against the Ku Klux
Klan in the 1920s, the Jewish people itself was another matter. Caroline
Stern was special, for Jews in general exhibited qualities "which have re-

currently irritated or enraged other people since the Babylonian captivity. Touch a hair of a Jewish head and I am ready to fight, but I have experienced moments of exasperation when I could willingly have led a pogrom."[9] In a book published the year that the German government's Final Solution was secretly and systematically organized, Percy expressed neither a loathing of anti-Semitism nor the slightest dislike of individual Jews.

It is this paradox that best illumines the life of Jews within the history of the South, that most intelligibly locates the peculiarity of their situation. In *The Sound and the Fury*, Jason Compson, after attacking "a bunch of damn eastern jews," comes as close as he can to making a civil-rights speech: "I give every man his due regardless of religion or anything else. I have nothing against jews as individuals. . . . It's just the race." The paradox was recognized by perhaps the most influential of Southern rabbis at the turn of the century, David Marx, who told his Atlanta congregation in 1900: "In isolated instances there is no prejudice entertained for the individual Jew, but there exists widespread and deep-seated prejudice against Jews as an entire people."[10] Marx himself was probably unaware of the most striking illustration of his generalization. During the Civil War, a grand jury in Talbotton, Georgia, issued a presentment critical of "the evil and unpatriotic conduct of the representatives of Jewish houses" of finance. There was only one Jewish-owned store in all of Talbot County and only one Jewish family in town; and its patriarch, Lazarus Straus, took the grand jury's presentment as a personal insult and decided to move. His son Isidor should be allowed to complete the story: "Father's action caused such a sensation in the whole county that he was waited upon by every member of the grand jury, also by all the ministers of the different denominations, who assured him that nothing was further from the minds of those who drew the presentment than to reflect on father, and that had anyone had the least suspicion that their action could be [so] construed . . . it never would have been permitted to be so worded."[11] As the Straus family left Georgia to activate Macy's, one can almost hear the citizens of Talbotton uttering the envoi so familiar to all Southerners: "Y'all come back."

Leonard Dinnerstein's "Note on Southern Attitudes Toward Jews" (1970) has emphasized the precariousness some Jews have felt in a region so scarred by bigotry and so hostile to outsiders. If anti-Semitism is defined as the unjustified hatred of Jews, certainly examples of it have not been condemned to obscurity. "Beginning in the late eighties," John Higham has written, "the first serious anti-Semitic demonstrations in American history occurred in parts of the lower South where Jewish supply merchants were common. In several parishes of Louisiana debt-ridden farmers stormed into town, wrecked Jewish stores, and threatened to kill any Jews who remained in the area. During the worst year, 1893, night-riders burned dozens of farmhouses belonging to Jewish landlords in southern Mississippi, and open threats drove a substantial number of Jewish businessmen from Louisiana."[12] Southern political history has, of course, reverberated with the voices of malevolence, like Tom Watson's; and his vitriol against "the libertine Jew," "the lascivious pervert," "the sodomite murderer," undoubtedly fueled the mob that lynched Leo Frank.[13] The bloodstained record of the Populists' vice-presidential candidate was not so offensive to Georgians as to disqualify Watson from representing them thereafter in the United States Senate. Mississippians elected the "Bilbonic plague," Theodore Bilbo, as governor and senator, even though his bigotry was so unsheathed that when the paladin of a Jewish defense agency protested, Bilbo addressed his reply on official Senate stationery with "My dear kike. . . . " On the floor of Congress, John Rankin, also from Mississippi, once called Walter Winchell a "little kike"; and none of his colleagues, Northern or Southern, rose to object. And of all the justifications for allying with the Soviet Union during the Second World War, Rankin's list of reasons was the oddest, beginning with "Stalin is a Gentile and Trotsky was a Jew."[14] Certainly the list of unashamed anti-Semites representing Southern constituencies could be extended.

But what is surprising is how short that list is, how sporadically anti-Semitism erupted in the Old South and the New. There was some anti-Semitism in the early phases of Mississippi whitecapping, for example, when notices appeared in 1892 in a few counties proclaiming: "This Jew place is not for sale or rent, but will be used hereafter as pasture." Yet William F. Holmes's article on the subject is striking for the paucity of evidence of anti-Semitism, unlike Negrophobia, that could be uncovered. In 1889 an agarian mob rode into Delhi, Louisiana, and, according to one newspaper, "demolished the stores of I. Hirsch, S. Blum & Company, Casper Weil, and Mr. Rosenfield." But Woodward denies that the incident reflected "widespread anti-Semitism. . . . Jewish supply merchants were quite common in the region in the period." The target was economic not ethnic. Louis Galambos's recent study of the agricultural press from 1880 to 1940 has located "only the slightest evidence of anti-Semitism. . . . Instead of attacking Jews . . . the Southern farmer made big business the target for his animosities, a choice indicating that, while he felt oppressed and was often confused about the source of his discontent, his reactions to a changing environment were not devoid of reason."[15]

Higham has noted the exclusiveness of clubs in Richmond, New Orleans, and elsewhere by the early twentieth century; yet he has also written that "most of the Klan's anti-Semitism was discharged against the shadowy, imaginary Jew who lived far away in the big cities. Klansmen felt a little guilty and ashamed at picking on the Jews whom they had known as good neighbors all their lives." About 1922, Edward Kahn has recalled, a young man inadvertently walked into the office of Atlanta's Federation of Jewish Charities, where he asked directions to the Klan office, then located in the same building. The secretary gave him the directions and went on with her work, when suddenly the young man realized where he was, walked back up to the receptionist, and apologized: "No offense intended, ma'am."[16]

Atlanta had not yet become "the city too busy to hate," but more generally Jews were able to serve as senators in the Old South and to hold a variety of offices since the Cause was Lost. The Southern political climate has been hospitable enough to permit association even with the pyrogenic demagogues whom Jews would normally distrust. One confidant of the fin de siècle Arkansas rabble-rouser Jeff Davis was Charles Jacobson— an assistant attorney general, a state senator, and an identifying Jew at a time of rampant racial bigotry that his mentor fomented. The treasurer of Huey Long's organization was Seymour Weiss, the guardian of the vaunted "deduct box"; and another Long sachem was Abe Shushan, who, like Weiss, earned a thirty-month prison sentence amidst the wave of convictions for corruption after Long's death. Though the notorious anti-Semite Gerald L. K. Smith was also part of the Kingfish's entourage (and was a Southerner by choice, having been born and raised in Wisconsin), Long himself was remarkably free of religious bigotry and once called it a mistake for Hitler to "mix" religion and politics—which utterly missed the point of Nazism, but in a reassuring way. And it is consistent with the central paradox to note that Tennessee's Cordell Hull—while secretary of state—was indifferent to the horrible fate of European Jews during the Holocaust. He did not sufficiently loathe Nazi racism to do much of anything about it, and yet he liked one particular Jew enough to marry her.

Even the worst outburst of anti-Semitism, the lynching of the president of the Atlanta lodge of the B'nai B'rith, can bear placement in an historical and comparative perspective. H. L. Mencken claimed in "The Sahara of the Bozart" that "the Leo Frank affair was no isolated phenomenon"; nevertheless, in a way it was unique.[17] Frank was the only Jew thus to lose his life in the region, though it hardly needs to be said that any victim of religious bigotry is one victim too many. Some Gentiles fared worse. Shortly after Frank was murdered, two Mormons were lynched; and in the decade between 1891 and 1901, twenty-two Italian immigrants were killed by Southern mobs. It does not diminish Frank's martyrdom to note that, over a decade earlier, at least forty-seven Jews had been killed in the pogrom in Kishinev. There is scattered autobiographical evidence—for example, from Bernard Baruch in South Carolina and Stanley Marcus in Texas, who encountered greater anti-Semitism when they went North—to lend credence to Herbert Stember's conclusion from attitude sampling that the South is less hostile to Jews than are other regions of the country. Moreover, the psychologist E. L. Hartley apparently discovered the existence of a generically prejudiced mind, in that his tests showed a high correlation between hostility to actual minority groups and hostility to Daniereans, Pireneans, and Wallonians, who are fictional.[18] Some Americans are primed to hate anyone. But given the recalcitrance of some forms of ethnic and racial animosities, the hostility toward Jews in the South has generally been mild, and more latent than blatant.

Southern anti-Semitism has generally been unencumbered by ideology and has lacked the Nazi compulsion to define Jewry as prepotent evil. Even from a Berlin devastated by Allied bombing, Hitler's last testament proclaimed his enmity to Jews. The Southern equivalent would undoubtedly be the suicide note left by Edmund Ruffin, in the wake of the defeat of the Confederacy, reaffirming "unmitigated hatred to . . . the perfidious, malignant and vile Yankee race."[19] He at least did not blame the victim. Anti-Semitism has instead been one aspect of the xenophobia that has hovered over the white South, a way of expressing anxiety at the shift from gemeinschaft to gesellschaft, a protest against the violation of the self-images of an agrarian order and its gods of the hearth. Thomas Wolfe's agent, for example, reported that the North Carolina novelist "had the villager's dread and dislike of urban Jews." (Nevertheless, "the great love affair of his entire life" was with a woman named Aline Bernstein, whom Wolfe called "my Jew.") W. J. Cash, whose *Mind of the South* was published in the same year as Percy's *Lanterns on the Levee*, explained that "the Jew, with his universal refusal to be assimilated, is everywhere the eternal Alien; and in the South, where any difference has always stood out with great vividness, he was especially so."[20]

The Jews have been resented as wanderers and interlopers who have often been forced, like Blanche DuBois, to depend "upon the kindness of strangers"; and in the South many of those strangers intensified their suspicion of outsiders with religious intolerance. When T. S. Eliot, lecturing at the University of Virginia in 1933, argued that the idea of a Christian society necessarily limited the number of "free-thinking Jews" to be included in the corporate body (a remark that was circumspectly dropped from the American edition of his lectures, published the following year), he was reformulating the opposition voiced earlier by a president of the University of Virginia, W. W. Thornton, who in 1890 told the editors of the *American Hebrew*: "All intelligent Christians deplore the fact that the historical evidences for Christianity have so little weight with your people." The educator added that anti-Semitism, which he too apparently did not loathe, could be explained (as Cash was later to do) by the "mere fact of difference."[21]

Given the religious origins of much of the historical derogation of Jews, given the importance of Protestantism in Southern society, the absence of violent or systematic hostility needs to be accounted for. Hodding Carter of the Pulitzer Prize–winning *Delta Democrat-Times* has wryly observed that "it takes perseverence to hate Jews and Negroes and Catholics all at the same time." (Carter himself left Hammond, Louisiana, for Greenville, Mississippi, on the advice of Will Percy and David Cohn and has recalled that "at almost every decisive period in my life, some Jew . . . has stood beside me and helped me forward.") Cash believed that hostility toward Catholics has in fact run deeper in the South than anti-Semitism. Demagogues like Alabama's primitive Tom Heflin, lacking Republican opposition, campaigned against the Pope instead; and Watson's weekly *Jeffersonian* conducted a vicious seven-year campaign against Roman Catholicism, once calling the Pope a "fat old dago." How widely the antagonism to papal influence suffused the outlook of Southern Protestantism can be gauged from the 1960 presidential campaign, when the Democrats' intercession with the Georgia judge who had sentenced Martin Luther King, Jr., to hard labor inspired King's father to switch his support from Nixon to Kennedy. In his pronouncement the Reverend Martin Luther King, Sr., explained his previous opposition was due to Kennedy's Catholicism, leading the Democratic candidate to remark privately: "Imagine Martin Luther King having a bigot for a father. Well, we all have fathers, don't we?"[22]

But if it makes sense that the Jew has been saved by the deflection of hatred elsewhere, there has been a more obvious target than the Catholic. "In most

Southern towns," Jonathan Daniels wrote in 1938, "except where many Jews
have recently come in, the direction of racial prejudice at the Negro frees the
Jew from prejudice altogether—or nearly altogether." The man whom
Daniels's own father served as secretary of the navy, Woodrow Wilson, is a
singular case in point. While the forthright militancy of Monroe Trotter
was so offensive to the president that he refused to permit further audiences
with that spokesman of Northern Negroes, the Virginia minister's son spoke
glowingly of the "Christian character" of the ardent Zionist Louis D.
Brandeis. And when an acquaintance regretted that a man as great as Brandeis
should be a Jew, Wilson gallantly replied that Brandeis would not have
been so great a man were he *not* a Jew—the sort of remark the segregationist
Democrat would not conceivably have made about, say, W. E. B. Du Bois.
When the president's friend Thomas Dixon, in a burst of emotion, shouted
across the screening room that the title of the film version of his novel
The Clansman should be altered to *The Birth of a Nation*, Dixon meant the
Aryan nation, but one in which blacks rather than Jews were to be degraded
and excluded.[23]

Dixon himself is an arresting case for those attuned to the complexities
and surprises that lurk in the interstices of American cultural and social
history. It is true that the modern Ku Klux Klan exploded from the nucleus
of the Knights of Mary Phagan who lynched Leo Frank. It is also probable
that the Klan was inspired by the D. W. Griffith film, that celluloid miracle
transmuted from the base metal of Dixon's fiction. With the royalties from
the novel and film, it is less well known, Dixon was able to purchase a
1400-acre estate in North Carolina, which he was forced to sell during the
depression to a Jew who converted it into a B'nai B'rith Youth Organization
"human-relations" camp. Of course it is tempting to stress the irony here
(the B'nai B'rith's Anti-Defamation League was also formed in the aftermath
of the Frank case), and even to find a confirmation of the promise God made
to Abraham after the binding of Isaac (and repeated every Rosh Hashanah)
from Gen. 22:17: "Thy seed shall possess the gates of their enemies." But
even though Thomas Dixon was undoubtedly the most racist litterateur in
American history, he was no enemy of Jews, whom he called "the greatest race
of people God has ever created." Warming to his subject, Dixon explained
hostility to the Jew "not because of his inferiority, but because of his genius.
We are afraid of him; we Gentiles who meet him in the arena of life get
licked and then make faces at him. The truth is, the Jew has achieved a noble
civilization—had his poets, prophets, and kings when our Germanic ancestors

were still in the woods cracking coconuts and hickory nuts with the mon-
keys."[24] The social Darwinism is quaint, the anthropology bizarre; and the
filiopietism has that distinctive Southern accent. Dixon undoubtedly also
knew that Jews were harmless. After a wave of synagogue bombings and
cemetery desecrations around 1960, a conference was organized in Jacksonville, Florida, for various Southern politicians and law-enforcement officials.
A list of violence-prone Southern whites was read aloud but, by a most
impolitic oversight, the name of Birmingham's commissioner of public
safety, Eugene C. Connor, was intoned. "Bull" Connor, who was in attendance, is reported to have blurted out an expletive and responded to the
accusation as follows: "Nigras, maybe, but Jews—why?"

Why indeed. Few in number and unobtrusive in manner, most Southern
Jews have seemed to want nothing more than to make a living; and their
history can perhaps most fully be categorized as a branch of business history.
The peddlers were ubiquitous; Jews with an eye for the main chance founded
stores like Garfinckel's in Washington, Thalhimer's in Richmond, Gold-
smith's in Memphis, Neiman-Marcus in Dallas, Sakowitz's in Houston,
Godchaux's in New Orleans, Cohen Brothers' in Jacksonville, Levy's in
Savannah, and Rich's in Atlanta (where Dr. King was arrested for trying to
integrate a lunch counter, for which he was sentenced harshly enough to
invite the Kennedys' personal and political concern). The label on one of
President Carter's suits reads: "Hart Schaffner & Marx, A. Cohen & Sons,
Americus, Ga." The traveler in the rural South can still observe how commonly the peddlers put down their packs to open stores and become pillars of
the local community, can still lose count of the dry-goods stores, hardware
stores, jewelry stores, clothing stores, and shoe stores that bear Jewish names.
But those names can be misleading, as an Anti-Defamation League representative once discovered after spotting a sign for Cohen's dry-goods store
in a Southern hamlet. He stopped by, but met only a man named Johnson,
since Cohen had sold the store eight years earlier to move to Jacksonville.
Johnson explained that "the sign's still *Cohen's* 'cause I bought the store with
Mr. Cohen's good will."[25] A Gentile preserving a Jew's name "for business
reasons" has a certain only-in-America charm about it; it is also another piece
in the characteristically Southern puzzle of individual acceptance, combined
wth general intolerance, of the outsider.

Aside from business success, Southern Jews were rarely conspicuous—
preferring to merge into the landscape, which their numbers made feasible.
They seemed in fact to partake, generation after generation, of virtually the

same values as their neighbors. Though her relatives were Jews, Lillian Hellman does not consider their religious and ethnic background—or her own—worthy of mention or reflection in her reminiscences; it apparently made no difference. And in her famous letter to the House Un-American Activities Committee in 1952, she mentioned her upbringing in "an old-fashioned American tradition," which for her meant "ideals of Christian honor." James K. Feibleman, a Tulane University philosopher, has recalled growing up in a New Orleans "where there was very little religious prejudice. . . . I was Jewish and that was that, but nobody seemed to care very much and nobody so far as I could see was very excited about it." In his memoirs, Kentucky's Arthur Krock, later Washington bureau chief of the *New York Times*, dismissed the subject entirely: "No religious instruction or attendance was ever required of me. . . . I was an early agnostic and have remained that way."[26] The novelist Hortense Calisher, whose father had been born in Richmond in 1861, remembers his "towering pride in his Jewishness *and* his Southernness." Her aunts found comfort "with Gentiles, having had them as close friends and neighbors, but this generation, except for one maverick, would not have married them. Their sons and daughters, including me, will do so entirely." Ludwig Lewisohn was even more adaptable, growing up in South Carolina as "an American, a Southerner, and a Christian." (His first book-length work, published in 1903, was a literary history of South Carolina entitled *Books We Have Made;* the pronoun suggests the intent of the young immigrant to use his study as his final citizenship papers.)[27] These feelings confirmed the impression of the Philadelphia rabbi and tireless publicist Isaac Leeser, who in 1850 came to New Orleans to help dedicate the synagogue building that Judah Touro had purchased. The religious receptivity of the city did not reassure him: "People came thither from all parts of the world to amass a fortune. . . . A degree of freedom in living was indulged in but little promotive of the growth of piety."[28]

Even for those Jews who maintained fidelity to institutional religion, adaptations to the Southern environment were wrought that suggest how eagerly many wanted to resemble their neighbors. In his Atlanta synagogue, at the dawn of the century, the New Orleans-born Rabbi David Marx abolished the wearing of skullcaps, inaugurated Sunday-morning services, minimized Hebrew in the liturgy, changed the age of confirmation to sixteen, and refused to perform the Bar Mitzvah even when parents and sons wanted the ceremony. Marx's primary responsibility was not, however, to innovate in Jewish ritual and liturgy but to improve and stabilize interfaith relations,

which meant making a good impression on the Gentiles.[29] One advertisement at the turn of the century read as follows: "Rabbi wanted by Congregation Temple Emanuel of Beaumont, Texas. He must be a good mixer. . . .
Salary $1,500." Good mixing meant not only the assurance of no divided
loyalties (and was therefore often a disparagement of Zionism before 1948)
but, more importantly, silence, if not explicit support, on the subject of the
region's racial mores—the central characteristic, in Ulrich B. Phillips' opinion,
of Southern history.[30]

No wonder that the Bull Connors of the region have often been baffled
that anti-Jewish feeling could be ascribed to them. No Jews who came to live
in the antebellum South were deeply affected by abolitionism; and their
ethical uneasiness over the peculiar institution can sometimes be demonstrated—but not abundantly. Many Southern Jews supported the Lost Cause
with converts' zeal. In the twentieth century, Will Percy's friend David Cohn
became an apologist for racial segregation, and it was largely due to Percy's
influence that James Feibleman in adolescence became "a full-fledged professional Southerner. I was prepared to explain that Northerners did not
understand the Negro question and ought not to presume to interfere."[31]
During the civil rights struggle, the Jew tended to fit the region's folk
definition of a moderate as "a white man without sidearms."

Having won the right to be equal (except where snobbery has held sway),
many Jews showed far less interest in the right to be different. Perhaps there is
more than a half-truth to a Lenny Bruce routine that might be paraphrased as
follows: If you live in New York or any other big city, you are Jewish. It
doesn't matter that you're Catholic. If you live in Macon, Georgia, you're
going to be goyish even if you're Jewish. Revisiting the Mississippi Delta,
Percy's friend David Cohn realized that the "Jews, by legend both intellectual
and shrewd, seem in this soft climate to have lost both these qualities. They
are distinguished neither by learning nor by riches."[32] One price paid for the
emulation of other Southerners has been the thinness of Jewish institutions,
which have had to negotiate an endless series of compromises and to make
quite meager demands on many adherents. A considerable proportion of
Southern Jews would have had no difficulty meeting the challenge that
angered Shammai; they could have summed up their knowledge of Judaism
while standing on one foot. The cultural price that was paid might best be
expressed, here as elsewhere, not by measuring but through metaphor. The
fact that the Jews who came South disproved a folk belief that they have
horns adds further meaning to the poignant scene in *The Glass Menagerie* in

which Laura shows the gentleman caller the unicorn in her collection. "Poor little fellow," Jim responds, "he must feel sort of lonesome." "Well," Laura smiles, "if he does he doesn't complain about it. He stays on a shelf with some horses that don't have horns and all of them seem to get along nicely together." But when Laura and Jim waltz, they bump into the table and the piece of glass is shattered. "Now it is just like all the other horses," Laura says. "Now he will feel more at home with the other horses, the ones that don't have horns."[33]

There was indeed an aura of make-believe in the attempts of Jews to be completely assimilated into Southern society. Since even the Jew who sought to become a professional Southerner had to do so through self-conscious effort, such an identity could not be fully and convincingly realized. The Jewish fear that the civil-rights movement might disrupt their own excellent relations with Christian neighbors suggests that those relations may have been less solid than had been acknowledged, that the equilibrium was more precarious than even the most defiantly Southern of Southern Jews would have liked to believe. It may not strain credulity to find an inadvertent symbolic touch in the choice of a Jew to play the role of Ashley Wilkes, the compleat antebellum Southern aristocrat, in *Gone with the Wind*—for Leslie Howard's is the least impressive performance, the least successful impersonation of an archetypal Southerner, in the film. The identity of the Southern Jew can thus be seen as problematic. For in their regrouping from pariahs to parvenus, Jews escaped the wrath of Russia's Black Hundreds without becoming fully accepted at Sutpen's Hundred either, much less at the homes of the gentry Sutpen displaced; and many of them have been completely at home neither in the borscht belt nor in the Bible Belt. A Jew whose family had lived in Savannah for generations once told Harry Golden: "Frankly, Ah don't have many relationships with mah Christian neighbors. Ah'm more comf'table with mah own. Ah puf-fer the Yudim."[34] And while this obviously bad mixer is an extreme case, he suggests the presence, if not the pervasiveness, of a double consciousness—based, however subtly, on the "mere fact of difference."

Nevertheless, Jews have shared something with Southerners which may distinguish both groups from other Americans. That common bond is the sixth sense, the sense of history, the disturbing weight of a collective past— for since that moment when the soldiers were told that they could keep their horses for the spring plowing, the memory of defeat infiltrated the Southern consciousness, causing so many dreams and ambitions to turn rancid, helping

Solomon Jacobs served as Grand Master of Virginia Masons from 1810 to 1812, and during the War of 1812 he was a private in the Nineteenth Regiment, Virginia Militia. He was president of the Beth Shalome Congregation in Richmond, Virginia, and a successful tobacco merchant, as well as city recorder and acting mayor. (Reproduced courtesy of the Valentine Museum, Richmond, Va., from *Richmond Portraits in an Exhibition of Makers of Richmond, 1737–1860* [Richmond, Va., 1949].)

to ensure the failure of many of the best Southern whites to break the cycle of poverty and misery and resentment, making of the past a nemesis. Percy's adopted son Walker Percy once explained with ungrammatical exactitude that Southern writing has been so resonant because "we got beat." That has surely deepened insight into the sadness and failure that are so frequently and so inescapably the stuff of human experience, for after the Civil War Southerners could no longer be simply considered the children of pride. The nursing of the Southern obsession with loss has shown that, while remembrance can be redemptive, forgetfulness is not necessarily worse. The obligation

A DISCOURSE

DELIVERED AT THE

SYNAGOGUE IN RICHMOND,

ON THE

First day of January, 1812,

A DAY DEVOTED TO

HUMILIATION & PRAYER,

In consequence of the loss of many

VALUABLE LIVES,

CAUSED BY THE BURNING OF

THE THEATRE,

On the 26th December, 1811.

By SAMUEL MORDECAI.

RICHMOND:
PRINTED BY JOHN O'LYNCH,
1812.

Title page of the speech delivered January 1, 1812, by Samuel Mordecai in Richmond, Virginia, as a result of the burning of the theatre and the consequent loss of life. (Source: American Jewish Historical Society.)

Pages from the 1836–62 circumcision record book of M. S. Polack of Baltimore, Maryland, which lists circumcisions performed by him in North Carolina and Virginia. (Source: American Jewish Historical Society.)

PROSPECTUS OF A MONTHLY MAGAZINE,

149.

TO BE PUBLISHED IN THE CITY OF RICHMOND,

DEVOTED TO

Hebrew and Miscellaneous Literature, Useful and Entertaining Knowledge,

AND TO BE ENTITLED

THE HEBREWS' MAGAZINE

AND JEWISH MISCELLANY.

It is designed to make it an exponent of the religion and laws of the Hebrew people: to advocate and encourage Hebrew education; to give historical sketches relative to our nation, their jurisprudence, habits, manners and customs; to solicit essays, moral tales and poetry, at the same time finding sufficient space for rabbinical and miscellaneous literature, the arts and sciences, and tasteful selections from the most popular publications of the day—with such interesting news as may be collected relative to the movements amongst our Jewish brethren in Europe, Asia, Africa and America.

A proper respect for the opinion of others, advocating different religious views, induces the publisher to assure them, that it is not designed to make the pages of this work a medium of attack on other religious denominations, or to *gain proselytes* to our own, but merely to *sustain* and *defend* the character of our religion *against* the assaults of others; but, should a controversy necessarily be forced upon us, the public may be assured it shall be conducted on our part in a friendly and respectful manner, with candor and moderation.

In proposing the establishment of this periodical, we do it from

a conviction that such a publication is much needed amongst us; that there is much latent talent possessed by our brethren, which, if developed, would greatly tend to elevate and ennoble the character of our people. Ignorance of our religion, literature and laws has produced for us, amongst other nations, an oppressive and hateful prejudice, which ought and can be removed; and confident that there is amongst us (where freedom of opinion and expression is guarantied to all) sufficient ability and means to effect so desirable a result, the projector and publisher will tender as a medium the pages of the proposed Magazine.

THE HEBREWS' MAGAZINE AND JEWISH MISCELLANY will be published monthly, as soon as 1,000 subscribers can be obtained; twelve numbers to complete the volume; and will contain about fifty large royal octavo pages each. It will be printed on good type, in the best style, on paper of fine quality, and will be furnished to subscribers at $5 per volume, payable in advance, or on the receipt of the first number.

All communications to be addressed to the Editor and Proprietor, Richmond, Va.

T. K. LYON.

RICHMOND, VA., 23d *Shebath,* 5602.
2d *Feb.* 1842.

Advertisement for *The Hebrews' Magazine and Jewish Miscellany*, to begin publication in Richmond, Virginia, in 1842. (Source: American Jewish Historical Society.)

Charleston, S. C. May 20th, 1844.

THE Citizens of Charleston, without distinction of Party, and with unexampled unanimity, have at a Public Meeting declared their decided wishes in favor of the IMMEDIATE ANNEXATION OF TEXAS TO THE UNION, and for the Ratification of the Treaty for that purpose, now before the Senate of the United States. At this meeting, the following Resolution was adopted :—

> "**Resolved,** *That a Committee of Vigilance and Public Safety, to consist of 27 Members, be appointed by the Chair, whose duty it shall be to correspond with similar Committees, and to take all steps necessary, to bring this important question fairly before the People, and unite their efforts for its success."*

The undersigned in behalf of the Committee appointed to carry the views of the meeting into effect, in discharge of this duty, beg leave to address you.

The importance of this Great American measure, cannot be over-estimated. To the whole Union it is of vast consequence, while to the South and West it is of vital import. We have every reason to fear that the ratification of the Treaty is in imminent peril of being defeated for party ends. Its success must be secured mainly, if not entirely, by the prompt and decided expression of the opinions of the People in its favor. It would seem advisable then that the People should be thoroughly informed, and their opinions be drawn out and expressed promptly and continuously, while this measure is pending, and that they be laid before Congress without delay. Permit us to suggest that the agitation of this matter be not relaxed, and that measures should be adopted not only for that purpose, but in case of its rejection, for such other and further measures as will be required to avert the loss of this " golden opportunity" for recovering so essential a part of the Valley of the Mississippi.

One measure has occurred to us as worthy of grave consideration. Under the Treaty of 1803, Texas was a part of Louisiana, and under the stipulation of that Treaty, was entitled to be admitted into this Union as a State, if they demand it. Should not a law of Congress be passed to permit such a proceeding? And would you not deem it advisable to obtain such an expression of opinion in your district, as would probably influence the vote of your Representative in Congress in favor of such a law? In our opinion it is desirable—if the Treaty be rejected.

If you have any suggestions, as to other modes of proceeding to be adopted, in the event of the rejection of the Treaty, or in any other aspect of the case, we will be pleased to receive them, and to confer and co-operate with you, in any proper measures to secure this great National advantage. To provide for concert and joint action, if necessary, Committees of Correspondence should be appointed in every quarter, composed of men of trust, who will give strict attention to it, and that a free and constant interchange of opinions be promoted through their agency.

You will oblige us by an early communication, informing us particularly, as to the state of public opinion in your section of the country, on this deeply interesting question.

Very respectfully, your obedient servants,

C. G. MEMMINGER.
HENRY BAILEY,
W. C. GATEWOOD.
M. C. MORDECAI.

Circular calling for the immediate annexation of Texas by the United States, distributed in Charleston, South Carolina, in 1844. Note that one of the signatures is that of M. C. Mordecai, a prominent member of the Charleston Jewish community. (Source: American Jewish Historical Society.)

DIGEST OF CASES

DECIDED BY THE

SUPREME COURT OF THE STATE OF ALABAMA,

FROM

MINOR TO VII. ALABAMA REPORTS INCLUSIVE,

WITH A

TABLE OF TITLES.

By P. PHILLIPS,

COUNSELLOR AT LAW..

For digesting of former law into method and order, three things are requisite; judgment to know them, art to dispose them, and diligence to omit none of them.

PREFACE TO IV. REPORTS.

MOBILE.

1846.

Title page of volume one of Philip Phillips, *Digest of Cases Decided by the Supreme Court of the State of Alabama.* A prominent attorney, Phillips served in the state legislature in 1844 and 1852 and was elected to the U.S. House of Representatives in 1853. His volume on *The Statutory Jurisdiction and Practice of the Supreme Court* went through five editions. (Source: American Jewish Historical Society.)

Daguerreotype of Capt. Jonas Phillips Levy, taken in Wilmington, North Carolina, November 12, 1861. Levy served with the United States Navy during the Mexican War and helped to establish the first synagogue in Washington, D.C. (Source: American Jewish Historical Society.)

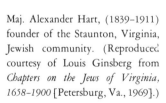

Maj. Alexander Hart, (1839–1911) founder of the Staunton, Virginia, Jewish community. (Reproduced courtesy of Louis Ginsberg from *Chapters on the Jews of Virginia, 1658–1900* [Petersburg, Va., 1969].)

Two-dollar bill of the Confederate States of America, carrying Judah P. Benjamin's portrait. (Source: American Jewish Historical Society.)

Hebrew Confederate Soldiers Cemetery, Richmond, Virginia. (Reproduced courtesy of Louis Ginsberg from *Chapters on the Jews of Virginia, 1658–1900* [Petersburg, Va., 1969].)

Bust made in Rome of Gen. Robert E. Lee by the prominent Southern-Jewish sculptor Moses Jacob Ezekiel, a native Virginian. (Source: American Jewish Historical Society.)

The Jewish South.

DEVOTED TO THE INTERESTS OF JUDAISM.

| Vol. I. | RICHMOND, VA., FRIDAY, AUGUST 25, 1893. | No. 1. |

BEN-BEOR.

A STORY OF THE ANTI-MESSIAH IN TWO DIVISIONS.

PART I.—Lunar Intaglios. The Man in the Moon, a counterpart of Wallace's "Ben Hur." PART II.—Historical Phantasmagoria, The Wandering Gentile, a companion romance to Sue's "Wandering Jew."

Here's a book for every Jew to read; to be passed from sire to son and from mother to daughter. The critic had this book for more than a year before reading it; he did indeed, soon after obtaining it make an attempt, but after going over a chapter or two concluded that the hallucinations of the author were hardly worthy of a further perusal. His attention having been recently called to the book by a lady of literary taste he returned to it with a suspicion of disappointment which, however, has not been confirmed. The work speaks for itself in such tones of strength that the Jewish reader may, with confidence, request any of his christian brethren to examine its contents without fear of the results.

By the over-zealous Jewish student it might be objected that too much has been conceded to the founder of Christianity, to whom, as well as to such followers as Luther and Calvin, he has been extremely liberal in his praise; but writing from so broad a platform as that occupied by the author it is probably best that he should make as many concessions as possible without injury to the cause he advocates. The Jew is at times handled with suspicious severity, but this treatment is generally based upon such occasional acts as merit reproof; in the end he receives ample justice at the hands of the author.

Balaam, the hero of the book, is represented as the carnal personification of hatred to the Jews, against whom he swears, in early life, undying hatred because the ideal woman whom he loves is friendly to the race and rejects his suit. After allowing his animosity full sway

and inventing many schemes that shall bring misery and unhappiness to this gifted people, he at length gives up life on this sphere and is transferred to the moon; there he follows the same tactics, but being expelled from lunar regions by Elijah, he is sent back to mundane scenes where he again takes up his career of undying hatred to the chosen people and is present at the destruction of the temple, the methods for which are arranged by him. Disappointed in his attempt to annihilate the followers of Judaism, he follows the scattered remnants from place to place, with bitterest malice inciting persecution and employing the most hideous methods of torture to gratify his unnatural antipathy.

The story of the middle ages, including the inquisition and the crusades, is told in terse and instructive style. The reader is by this time fully prepared to find that Balaam under an assumed name is the instigator of the inquisition as well as one of the main inquisitors; he is also the author of the blood-accusation for the Passover sacrifice, and the accuser who first charges the Jews with having poisoned the wells when the black-death pestilence raged with such fierceness throughout southern Europe. While it would otherwise never appear reasonable to the calm thinker that such monstrous charges should find credence, the author constructs his story with such logical cleverness that it seems quite consistent for such a character to be able to dominate during a period of superstition and bigotry.

The author further shows how the rise of civilization and the freedom of the Jews, go hand in hand on their destination and with a pen that rivals the genius of a Raphael, pictures to the mind scenes of bloodshed and brutality that accompany every false accusation.

Throughout the work there are presented leading characters of Jewish, Christian, Moslem and pro-

fane history, and by frequently quoting from their writings and forcibly introducing the best thoughts of the greatest writers, the interest of the reader is readily retained.

The book has many faults, some of them quite serious, but they may be readily forgiven by the Jewish reader in consideration of the eminently worthy object the author had in view and for the masterly way in which he has portrayed the iniustice of potentates, creeds and reformers to a people who through suffering and persecution have borne the banner of morality and truth out of the darkness of barbarism into the light of civilization.

Plate IV

Title page of the first issue of *The Jewish South,* published in Richmond, Virginia, intermittently from 1893–1902. (Photo courtesy of American Jewish Archives, Cincinnati, Ohio.)

Rabbi Bernard C. Ehrenreich with the 1904 Confirmation Class of Temple Beth Or, Montgomery, Alabama. (Photo courtesy of Mrs. Rosemary E. Krensky.)

Rabbi Bernard C. Ehrenreich (1876–1955) served the Montgomery, Alabama, Congregation Temple Beth Or from 1906 to 1921. (Photo courtesy of Mrs. Rosemary E. Krensky.)

Rabbi Irving Lehrman of Temple Emanu-El, Miami Beach, Florida, addressing a 1974 convention of B'nai B'rith. (Photo courtesy of Rabbi Lehrman.)

to transcend despair was perhaps best understood by Faulkner, probably the only American-born novelist of this century to whom Northrup Frye's statement applies, that his readers have grown up inside his work "without ever being aware of a circumference." The sonorous faith Faulkner expressed in Stockholm that "man will not merely endure, he will prevail" was not grounded in complacency or thoughtlessness or the compulsive optimism that has afflicted the American spirit; it was not merely a ceremonious expression of consolation intended to raise the threshold of pain, nor was it a cosmetic to disguise the scar tissue left by suffering.

But that faith does find partial corroboration in the history of the Jewish people, in which martyrdom and defeats have been commemorated but in which the past has also been rendered usable and borne as an ironic solace. (In the 1973 war, the Israeli army's impenetrable code for the various positions on the front was based upon the geography of Poland's Jewish communities that had been destroyed during the Holocaust.) The rather benign response to Jews in the South may be due to their commitment to family cohesiveness and the loyalty to ancestry that their neighbors could not help but notice. More importantly, Jews posed no genuine threat to the stability of Southern society and traditions, since they were not only white in color but few in number. Even as the cultural contradictions linger, perhaps the paradox this essay has also explored can be resolved by acknowledging how peripheral Jews have been, for even the archetype of the alien and the Christ-killer could not have had the same weight and urgency as the fear of the power of blackness. The "Dutch man of warre, that sold . . . twenty negars" to John Rolfe and the Virginians in 1619 was certainly more fateful for American and Southern history than was the ship from which twenty-four Jews disembarked in Nieuw Amsterdam in 1654. For Jews, the ubiquity of Gentiles could never be minimized or forgotten; but for Southerners, it has been relations with blacks that have mattered economically, socially, morally. Not casting so long a symbolic shadow, Jews could be recognized (and liked or disliked) as individuals.

But perhaps also Southerners saw in Jews an adaptability, an elasticity, a sense of how to bend in order not to break, that offered wry lessons in survival. Perhaps Southerners detected an indomitable spirit beneath the ingratiation, saw in their "solitary" presence in the region, as McCaslin Edmonds did, "a sort of courage."[35] Such qualities are part of the puzzle of history that stretches back to the first mention of Hebrews that archeologists have been able to uncover from the detritus of the secular past. It is a pharoah's victory column, over three thousand years old; and it contains the only mention of Israel in ancient Egyptian writing. The inscription announces that "Israel is laid waste" and will never rise again.[36]

Friend or Foe?
Southern Blacks View the Jew
9.
1880-1935

Arnold Shankman

Among the hundreds of thousands of Jews fleeing Czarist persecution during the last decades of the nineteenth century were Nathan and Mollie Blatt. In 1893, Nathan, a young man of twenty-nine years, left Russia first, promising to send for Mollie and their newborn son Jake as soon as he could save enough money to pay for their steamship tickets. Unlike most Jewish immigrants, he did not settle in one of the industrial cities of the North but chose instead "to walk the highways and byways [of South Carolina,] selling out of his pack that he carried on his back." Dixie suited the immigrant peddler who had driven horses in a Russian farming community, and he opened a dry-goods store in the tiny hamlet of Blackville, South Carolina. Early in 1895 he was able to send for Mollie and Jake. The New World was full of surprises for the bashful, sensitive twenty-four-year-old woman from Russia. When she arrived in Charleston, Mollie for the first time saw a Negro. It had never before occurred to her "that people of black color existed." The sight of one "terrified" her. For several months after she came to Blackville she was afraid even of the Negro washerwoman who came to her house every week to pick up the dirty laundry. "My mother," recollected Solomon Blatt, the veteran South Carolina legislator, "would put the clothes on the back porch and lock the door until the washerwoman had come and gone." But it was not long before Mollie Blatt was able to rid herself of her irrational fear of blacks.[1]

The writer wishes to express appreciation to the National Endowment for the Humanities for financial assistance for research costs. He also benefitted from the advice of Professors Morris U. Schappes of New York, Harvey Klehr of Emory University, and Mark K. Bauman of Atlanta Junior College.

Until more research is done on Southern-Jewish history we will not be able to determine whether or not Mollie Blatt's reaction to her initial encounter with blacks was typical. In fact, it is remarkable how little we know about Dixie's Jews. It has only been in recent years that more than a handful of historians have turned their attention to this much neglected subject, and despite the appearance in the 1960s and 1970s of several important books on Southern Jews, much remains to be done. Of the scholars now considering this subject in their writings, only Philip Foner, Lawrence Levine, and Eugene Levy have examined Afro-American primary sources.[2] It is important that we not rely exclusively on materials written by whites to uncover the history of Southern Jews.

One method is to examine the image of the Jew that appeared in Southern black newspapers, periodicals, memoirs, and other primary sources between the years 1880 and 1935. Almost nothing has been published on the way Afro-Americans regarded Jews during this fifty-five year period. There were no sociologists to conduct in-depth interviews on stereotypes held by Negroes; in fact, it was generally assumed that black attitudes on most subjects were unimportant. So prevalent was the belief that Negro history was irrelevant, that historical societies on both sides of the Mason-Dixon line rarely bothered to preserve black newspapers or other primary documents. Though nearly every large or medium-sized city in the South had one or more black journals, only a tiny handful survive, mainly in broken files. An examination of these files, however, indicates that on the whole blacks viewed Jews more as friends than as foes. Unlike other immigrant groups in the South, Jews did not compete with blacks for jobs. Blacks also believed that Jews were more willing than other newcomers to the South to raise their voices against racism and to treat the Negro as a man and not as a "boy."[3]

Dixie's Jewish population has never been large, but blacks and Jews have frequently come into contact with each other. After the Civil War, Jews controlled the dry-goods stores of the South to a remarkable extent. In virtually every important Southern town, one or more Jewish peddlers leased a store and began to sell notions, farm equipment, clothing, and groceries to the local population. In 1913 Timothy Thomas Fortune, who grew up in Florida during Reconstruction, recalled that after the Civil War "the Jews invaded the Southern States . . . with their merchandise in packs on their backs and began to open stores in the cities, towns, and crossroads as fast as their wholesale Jewish merchant connections in Baltimore, Philadelphia, and New York could ship the goods they ordered."[4] So completely did Jews appear to dominate the Southern retail trade that a sociologist studying Indianola, Mississippi, during the 1930s alleged that one could not purchase a pair of socks locally on a Jewish holiday.[5]

A South African touring the South around 1915 noted the large number of Jewish-owned stores he passed. What particularly impressed him was that these businesses "were crammed with Negroes."[6] Two decades later, in 1937, John Dollard, a sociologist, made a similar observation. He attributed the success of Jewish merchants in Indianola to their ability to win the Negro trade. Whereas gentile whites greeted blacks brusquely with "well boy, what do you want?" Jews were wont to address Negroes as "Mr." or "Mrs." and to ask, "What can I do for you?" The Jews, Dollard noted, put business before caste principles. Moreover, he declared, Jews did not "follow a strict one-price policy"; rather "they bargain with the Negroes and the Negroes like this."[7]

But did they? What did blacks actually think about Jews? Prior to Appomattox, many blacks had never seen a Jew. A few Negroes had been the slaves of Jews, and urban slaves in Charleston, Mobile, Savannah, Richmond, Louisville, Macon, and New Orleans doubtless encountered Jewish merchants from time to time. Plantation slaves, on the other hand, probably seldom came in contact with Jews. But even those slaves who did not personally see Jews knew something about the Children of Israel. Negroes were told about the Bible, and many, like Booker T. Washington, found "the most fascinating portion of that book . . . the story of the manner in which Moses led the Children of Israel out of the house of bondage, through the wilderness, into the promised land." According to Washington, "The Negro slaves were always looking forward to a time when a Moses should arise from somewhere who would lead them, as he led the ancient Hebrews out of the house of bondage."[8]

Even after emancipation, blacks continued to show a great interest in the Jews of ancient times. The famed educator Horace Mann Bond grew up in Alabama and Georgia. The only talk about Jews in his home was "about biblical Jews; and what with prayers before each meal and Scripture reading morning and night, and three church services on Sunday and daily chapel at school, one did hear a great deal about the People of Israel." As late as 1935, Kelly Miller, a Negro Howard University professor writing in a Virginia newspaper, argued that "the Negro takes to the Hebrew Scriptures as [a] duck to water." No part of the Bible was more interesting to him than some of the stories of the Old Testament. "Noah and the Ark, Daniel in the

Lion's Den, the Hebrew Children in the Fiery Furnace, Jonah and the Whale," Miller concluded, "are absorbed and relished as if they were an indigenous part of Negro folklore."[9]

Over and over again the freedmen would be told to liken their status to that of the Jews. Addressing a rally of Negroes in Mississippi in 1876, Pinckney B. S. Pinchback, who had briefly served as governor of Louisiana, told his audience that whenever they were discouraged, they should think of the Jews. "Like you they were once slaves," he reminded his listeners, "and after they were emancipated they met with persecutions." Generation after generation they fought their oppressors, and "backed by principles they believed were right," they finally emerged victorious. Once despised, they were now "leaders of education and princes of the commercial world," and one of their number, Benjamin Disraeli, had become prime minister of England. "What an example for you, my people, whose advantages are so great," Pinchback optimistically concluded. These sentiments were hardly unique. During the dark days following the end of Reconstruction, many blacks sought solace in the Holy Scriptures. "Colored people should not become discouraged," mused the *Richmond Planet*. "Read your Bibles and you will see that the plight of the Children of Israel at one time was much worse than ours seem[s] to be."[10] After all, one black minister observed, when freed from slavery in Egypt, the ancient Israelites were as degraded and ignorant as the ex-slaves in 1865. It had taken forty years before the Hebrews were ready for settlement in the Holy Land, and now they were acknowledged world leaders. Therefore, the preacher concluded, blacks too might hope eventually to become respected citizens.[11]

Eastern-European Jews doubtless would have argued that they had never achieved the status of respected citizens in their homelands, and after 1880 they flocked to the United States in great numbers. Some Americans objected to this influx of Jewish refugees, but almost without exception, Southern blacks welcomed the Jews. Booker T. Washington, who rarely had a good word for those emigrating from Europe, was careful to differentiate Jews from Gentiles. When he traveled through Europe, he dismissed many would-be European immigrants as beggars, anarchists, or superstitious peasants; Jews, on the other hand, were admired for their ability to withstand the "wear and tear of centuries of persecution" and rise "up to a position of power and preeminence" in Western civilization. Once in the United States, Washington stated, the Jew retained many of his customs, but he made an earnest effort to learn English and to adjust to "the manners of the new country of which he is soon to become, if he is not already, a citizen."[12]

It was understandable to blacks that Jews would want to flock to the United States, the golden land of opportunity. Still, they were amazed to learn that in parts of Europe and North Africa, the Children of Israel had fewer opportunities and were economically worse off than American Negroes. "African people everywhere have trouble-a-plenty," declared the *Norfolk Journal and Guide*, "but the Jews seem to be the trouble bearers of Christendom."[13] That the Hebrews were often able to dominate business affairs and the professions in the very countries that most severely persecuted them persuaded blacks that "they must be the children of the Lord." The Jews knew, Booker T. Washington enviously declared, "how to make their disadvantages their opportunities, and so get the best of the rest of the world, no matter how things are arranged."[14]

Blacks were convinced that, whatever their status elsewhere, the Israelites were thriving in the South.[15] For proof of the success of the Jews in the business world, a black needed only to read the advertisements in Afro-American journals. Virtually every issue of all Negro newspapers featured ads from firms clearly owned by Jews. In Little Rock, Arkansas, Negroes were wooed by M. Stern Dry Goods, Kaufman's Cheap Store, Cohn Dry Goods and Clothing, Stern's Ladies Wear, Ottenheimer's Dry Goods, and Gershenes' Whiskey and Cigars. In Richmond, leading advertisers over the years included Isaac Straus Liquor and Tobacco Company, Salomon's Wine and Liquors, G. Kaplan, Optician, and Julius Meyer's Dry Goods. Carolina blacks were urged to patronize Rosenbaum Dry Goods in New Bern, North Carolina, H. Kaminski Dry Goods in Georgetown, South Carolina, and I. S. Leevey Clothing and J. F. Eisemann's tailor shop in Columbia, South Carolina. Atlantans could shop for wearing apparel at Rich's, Louis Stern's, Eiseman Brothers, Hirsch's, Kaplan and Shimoff's, or Clearn's. For groceries they could go to B. Hirsowitz or I. L. Goldstein, and all of their pharmaceutical needs could be met either at Jacobs' Drug Stores or at Cronheim Pharmacy. Should they need a rifle, Greenblatt Brothers advertised first-quality weapons for as little as $3.90. Nowhere were Jewish firms more eager to win the black trade than in Savannah. Rarely did an issue of a Negro paper appear in that city with fewer than six or eight Jewish advertisers; usually the number was considerably higher. Jewish merchants may have been less numerous in Norfolk than in Savannah, but they often disguised this by taking out full-page ads in the *Journal and Guide*.[16] If one adds to the above advertisements from less obviously Jewish firms, one can readily understand why the *Columbia* (S.C.) *Southern Indicator* encouraged Negro readers to "follow the Jew [and] do 'beezness.'"[17]

Enterprising Negroes watched the success of individual Jewish merchants with awe and amazement. Booker T. Washington knew of a Jewish emigrant from Europe who had passed through Alabama in 1890 with all of his possessions in a single satchel. About sixteen miles from Tuskegee he noted an absence of stores in what seemed to him a prosperous cotton-growing region. He rented land, built a store, and within four years he owned a lucrative business grossing $50,000 per year, and he also had acquired hundreds of acres of land. Washington and other Negro leaders agreed with the editor of the *Savannah Tribune* that members of their race should emulate "the saving and economical qualities of the Jews."[18]

It was commonly believed that if Negroes properly observed the Jewish merchants of the South, they too could learn how to prosper in business. "Those of us that have tried," boasted the owner of Wood's Haberdashery in Columbia, South Carolina, "have made the Jews sit up and take notice." What Woods had learned from the Jewish merchants was not to give up easily. On occasion Jewish business ventures failed, but the merchants did not let this discourage them or persuade them to lose faith in themselves; rather they opened a new store in a different location and hoped for better luck.[19]

Moreover, the Jew was thrifty. "The average colored man complains that he does not have capital enough to run his business," one black editor noted, but "the average Jew starts his business on the money the Negro throws away." According to a popular joke of the 1920s, when God created the first men, He asked each what he wanted. When He approached the Negro, the black man said he wanted a million dollars. Then God came to the Jew, who merely requested "the address of the Negro you gave the million dollars."[20]

Joking aside, blacks were told that they should learn from the parsimonious habits of the Jew, keep their overhead low, and undersell the competition. According to the *Atlanta Independent*, Negro consumers, learning that "the Jew store sells for two or three cents less, . . . will go to the Jew store because he can get the same thing for less money." If the Negro merchant allowed "his goods to drop in quality and use[d] inferior help," added D. A. Hart, editor of the *Nashville Globe*, he would have no one but himself to blame if "his customers . . . go to the Jew."[21]

To the Negro merchant who complained that he could not profitably sell his goods as cheaply as the Jew, the *Savannah Tribune* offered some advice. It would be best, the *Tribune* suggested, if every member of the black merchant's family worked in the business. The Jew, his wife, and his children all worked together and were thus able to keep their store open as long as there were potential customers. According to one typical story about Jewish tradesmen, a Jewish woman once noticed black customers approach her store just after she had closed for the day. Coatless, she ran after the potential patrons and "persuaded them to buy." This she could do, for Jews were not too proud to live in a black neighborhood. Negro entrepreneurs, the *Tribune* complained, insisted upon living in a good house in another section of town and wasted much of their profit on transportation and mortgage payments. Moreover, when he made a few dollars, a black bought his wife a new dress and treated his children to a box of candy; the Jew dressed plainly and put his profits into his children's bank acccounts. [22]

Even when prices were the same, Jews continued to outsell their Negro rivals. This was because, in the words of the *Savannah Tribune* "so long as you are doing business from [the]m, the Hebrews would go to any length to satisfy a customer." Thus, though often "unlearned and almost unlettered," they catered to the most sophisticated Negroes. In Washington, D.C., Kelly Miller, who wrote for black newspapers in the South, daily saw evidence that "the Negro professional classes, the graduates of Howard University, and of the city high schools are perfectly satisfied to be catered to by these Jewish merchants and dealers." These storeowners seemed to welcome criticism from patrons. Negro businessmen, on the other hand, supposedly resented suggestions from their clientele. [23]

The Jacobs Drugstore chain of Atlanta demonstrated how Jews sought to meet the needs of their Negro customers. The Jacobs stores pledged "courteous treatment to ALL," but it was impossible to serve Negroes at soda fountains in stores patronized by both races. Jacobs attempted to solve this problem by opening a drugstore in a black neighborhood that would cater exclusively to Negroes. At this store blacks were the only ones allowed to sit at the soda fountain. Admittedly this was a slight gesture, racist by modern standards, but it was all that Jacobs could do in a segregated society. Atlanta Negroes were aware of this, and many gladly purchased their drugs at the Jacobs pharmacies. [24]

Serving blacks at soda fountains was one way to meet the needs of Negroes. Another was to allow black patrons to examine ready-made clothing without forcing them, as Gentiles did, to purchase every garment they tried on. Jewish merchants quickly learned that "respectable" whites in Dixie would never purchase goods that might have been worn by blacks. Hebrew peddlers in rural areas, mindful of local prejudices, were careful to sell ready-made goods only to blacks. Thus, white farmers had no basis for objecting to blacks trying on dresses or suits that the peddler carried in his wagon. In urban areas those Jews who sold clothing to Negroes normally sacrificed their white clientele. This was certainly appreciated by blacks, who were understandably annoyed at having to purchase, but not being able to return, clothing that did not fit.[25]

A more important way to help blacks was to provide them with jobs and to teach them the skills that they would need to open their own businesses. As early as the 1900s, when few white shopkeepers employed Negroes, black help was visible in such Jewish stores as Louis Adler's Shoe Store and at Kaufman's Clothes Store in Lexington, Kentucky. W. S. Madden, a Negro educated at Tuskegee, told a black gathering how a Jew had helped him when he arrived jobless in Oklahoma in 1907. Work was virtually impossible to find in the state then, for times were bad. A Jewish tailor, however, agreed to hire Madden as a journeyman and to pay him the impressive salary of $12 per week. Unemployed whites angrily demanded that the Jew fire his black employee and replace him with a white. The tailor refused, responding that Madden was competent, efficient, punctual, and reliable; moreover, he did not drink. The grateful employee remained at the job for three months and, when economic conditions improved, was able to go into business for himself.[26]

This was not a unique incident. Even Kelly Miller, who had ambivalent feelings about Jewish businessmen, admitted that if Negroes ever became their "own merchant[s]" it would be due to "Jewish tutelage." Working for a Jew as a clerical helper, Miller insisted, was better training than studying at a business school or working for a white Christian, who would never give "such intimate instruction." He also noted that Jewish businessmen and entrepreneurs had promoted the cultural renaissance of Harlem. In New York and elsewhere, "the Jew who controls the theaters, amusements, and largely the channels of literary publication of the nation, has given the Negro his chance."[27]

It was never suggested that Jews hired Negroes solely for altruistic reasons. The black salesman in the Jewish-owned store, a Savannah weekly acknowledged, was expected to be "a great drawing card for Negro trade." Thus, it is not surprising that black leaders were upset when confronted with evidence that black clerks did not necessarily attract black customers.

In 1928 a Jewish merchant named Bernstein opened a department store, The Fair, in Washington, D.C., which catered to the city's Negro community and employed seventy-five black salesladies. Though Bernstein stocked the store with quality merchandise, he went bankrupt by 1931, and the Negro women were jobless. To be sure, the Great Depression was partially responsible for the store's failure, but according to Ben Davis, a Negro editor in Atlanta, Washington blacks avoided the store, not because they thought its goods were shoddy or its prices were too high, but because they preferred to shop at places where whites would wait on them. "Th[is] enterprising Jew is . . . bankrupt because he tried to help a race of people who would not help themselves." The lesson was clear: Jews would only employ blacks if Negroes demanded that this be done and if blacks then patronized those stores.[28]

But if Jewish merchants were seen as potential employers and teachers of enterprising blacks, they were also portrayed as crafty exploiters and sharp traders. They were the type of people who might sell a Negro some property on the installment plan, pocket the money, flee, and force the luckless black to toil on his land as a sharecropper or tenant.[29] Kelly Miller might praise Jews for their willingness to train blacks, but he still thought that they looked "upon the Negro as an easy field" for their "cheap, shoddy goods, which by artistic arrangement and handling," they made "look attractive." Miller wondered if the Jewish talent for business was "inborn or acquired." He suspected that in ancient times "Jewish servant women borrowed earrings and finger rings of their Egyptian mistresses, presumably to set up their husbands in the jewelry business." Over the centuries Jews have learned how to conduct business affairs "more successfully than any other variety of the human family . . . the Jew seems to deem it his mission to cater to Christian needs and necessities. They violate their own Sabbath, gathering shekels, to supply Christians with their requirements for Sunday. Christmas and Easter furnish their superlative opportunity. When the Jews take a holiday, the Gentiles suffer for lack of their accustomed supply of creature comforts."[30]

The *Atlanta Independent* echoed Miller's sentiments that some Jews kept their businesses open on both Saturday and Sunday. Particularly offensive was the fact "the cheap Jew" operated dance halls, movie theaters, and other entertainment emporiums on Sunday. Why, the paper asked, should the Hebrew "desecrate our Sabbath and insult our religion by conducting places of amusement that interfere with the sanctity of our Sabbath?" These

places of amusement allegedly catered "to the Negro underworld" and promoted the "foolishness of social equality." Two decades earlier Roy Stannard
Baker, a prominent white social critic, had noted that in Atlanta "many of
the saloons for Negroes were kept by foreigners, usually Jews."[31]

Operating saloons and dance halls was considered disreputable, and
Southern blacks criticized Jews for engaging in such enterprises. In similar
fashion blacks were quick to denounce Jewish businessmen whenever they
mistreated or exploited them. As early as 1881 a New Orleans black editor
had castigated the "despicable" Israelite vendors at Spanish Fort, a fashionable
Louisiana lake resort, for refusing to sell refreshments to Negroes: "The Jews,
of all other people, should be the last to discriminate." Those who were prejudiced against blacks merited nothing but scorn. Two decades later another
black newspaper happily reported the fate of a Jewish peddler in Brunswick,
Georgia, who had dismissed Negroes "as being a worthless set." Upon hearing reports of these comments, Brunswick blacks staged a meeting, denounced their detractor, and refused to purchase his wares. "This," exulted
the *Baltimore Afro-American*, "is the right way to treat our enemies. Make
them feel our power." Southern Negroes paid close attention to the way
Jews treated them, and black newspapers occasionally printed stories about
Jews falsely accusing blacks of shoplifting, evicting black tenants when white
neighbors protested, and even physically assaulting Negro customers.[32]
Although Negroes did not boycott Jewish department stores in Savannah or
Atlanta, as had occurred in Harlem during the 1930s, Southern Negro news-
papers dutifully reported what was going on in the North.

What is surprising is the fact that despite frequent contacts between black
and Jew in the South, stories about Jews mistreating blacks were infrequent.
When it was pointed out that Jews charged high prices for poor quality
goods, blacks readily indicated that this practice was not a uniquely Jewish
trait. Jews were favorably compared with Greek, Italian, and German storekeepers. "Not only Jewish people thrive from [unfair] . . . practice[s]" a
Chicago paper–approvingly quoted in the *Savannah Tribune*–admitted,
"Gentiles [als]o mercilessly grind human flesh through their money-making
machines [to] reap full harvests." Even Kelly Miller concluded "that the
Jewish merchant is a blessing rather than a bane to the gullible Negro
purchaser. If he were withdrawn, the white Gentile dealer would exploit
him no less ruthlessly and with much less geniality."[33]

This view of the Jewish businessman helped soften the image of the
Jew as an unprincipled merchant. More important was the recognition that

"some of our truest and staunchest friends are numbered among the members of the Hebrew race." Joel and Arthur Spingarn, Julius Rosenwald, Henry Moskowitz, Lillian Wald, Abraham Flexner, and Jacob Billikopf donated their time, talent, and fortunes to improve the quality of medical care and education available to Southern blacks.[34] Rabbis Stephen S. Wise and Joseph Silverman of New York and Emil Hirsch of Chicago were quick to condemn lynchings and other manifestations of racial discrimination. In 1927 the Social Justice Commission of the Central Conference of American Rabbis passed resolutions supporting the rights of Pullman porters to organize and insisting that labor conditions be compatible with good health. In 1927 Rabbi George Solomon of Savannah's Congregation Mickve Israel was lauded in the black press as "one of the most liberal minded clergy of the city and [one] deeply concerned in civic affairs." Similar words could have been used in the 1930s for Rabbi David Marx of Atlanta, who was a prominent member of the Commission on Interracial Cooperation, a pioneer civil-rights group in the South.[35] Many agreed with Booker T. Washington that Jews consistently demonstrated "a sympathy and support . . . for the work I have had to do for my own people."[36]

This support was very much appreciated, and during the 1930s, when Northern blacks were becoming increasingly critical of Jews, their Southern counterparts insisted that "there is no Jew hated among us. . . . there are many things we must hate before we get to so lovable a people as the Jew." An Alabama black who had lived in eight states claimed that "the anti-Jewish feeling that exists among my people is small and insignificant." When the black-owned American Mutual Savings Bank contributed to a Jewish charity drive in 1926, the *Louisville News* lavished praise on the bank and doubted that "American Mutual ever made a better investment."[37]

Only one article has been found that called Jews "despicable" and people with "obnoxious habits," and this was published on July 23, 1881. Far more common were newspaper editorials that praised Jews as good, gentle and law abiding.[38] Negro preachers and editors frequently contrasted the alleged shortcomings of blacks with the supposed virtues of Jews in their sermons and editorials. Most important was the fact that Jews were proud of their heritage and were always willing to stick together whenever one of their number was in need, unlike blacks, who were "ashamed of being black." "The most exalted Jew," claimed newspaper columnist Frank Crosswaith, "will gladly unite with his less fortunate kinsman to oppose injustice of any sort aimed at Jews." When trouble struck, a Norfolk editor added, "Jews d[id] not disown and run away from Jews." Rather they came together and "assist [ed] one another in all reasonable ways."[39]

The B'nai B'rith was often cited as an example of the way Jews helped each other. The popular Jewish fraternal order fostered business cooperation, provided insurance benefits and other assistance to Jewish widows, sponsored the construction and maintenance of orphanages, dispensed sick benefits, and collected funds to help immigrants. What blacks needed, insisted one editor, was to establish their own counterparts to B'nai B'rith. In unity there was strength, and the *Savannah Tribune* admired the way that American Jews had learned the value of "group protection [in] . . . combatting collectively attacks which are heaped upon them."[40]

Credit for the "race pride" of the Jew belonged to the Jewish religion, which "idealizes marriage and the home." Jewish children "grow up in an atmosphere of reverence and respect for parents, teachers, rabbis, and all proper authority." They were taught to revere their heritage. By teaching that "Jewish history" represented "the highest possibilities of the human family," the Jew made certain that his child would never be ashamed of his origin.[41] Moreover, T. Thomas Fortune marveled, the Jewish child was encouraged to learn and to chase after honors in scholarship. In the Jewish home "education is considered the handmaid of religion." "They want to know everything there is to be known on a given subject," marveled an envious black writer for the *Savannah Tribune*. "They often work hard all day and study half the night, while the colored man frolics."[42]

Education inspired Jews to be hard workers and to reject idleness. "You have never heard of Jews begging anybody for anything," declared B. C. Baskerville. "They have sense enough to invest their money productively." Jews were not drunkards or beggars or residents of almshouses, added the *Richmond Reformer*. "Success seems to attend their pathway . . . [they] are our most progressive citizens." Blacks should emulate the Jew. "What he has done we can do. . . . When we add money, character, intelligence, and industry to our stock in trade, we will have friends to come to our assistance." Reverend T. Jefferson Goodall, minister of Savannah's First African Baptist Church similarly traced the success of the Jews to their good habits. They abided not only by "the common law but the laws of health and nature also. . . . They furnish a fitting example for life along these lines."[43]

Another reason for blacks to view Jews sympathetically was the continuous existence of anti-Semitism. "The Jew, our faithful ally," noted one clergyman, "has come in for his share of humiliation too." Hotels denied admission to potential guests with Jewish surnames, colleges imposed quotas on Jewish applicants, employment agencies often turned away Jewish job seekers, and even the army once was accused of failing to promote Jewish soldiers. All of this was duly noted in the black press.[44] A Virginia editor who accepted the stereotype of the Jew as a shrewd businessman noted that even though Southern Jews could vote and move about freely, they were not fully accepted by their neighbors. "In many of our Southern States . . . the Jews are considered undesirable citizens, mainly because of their racial clannishness and their ability to overreach every other kind of trader." In 1889 the *New Orleans Weekly Pelican* reported the pillaging of Jewish stores in Delhi, Louisiana, "by an armed mob." "The cause of the disturbance," the *Pelican* concluded, "has been traced to business rivalry." A more subtle form of anti-Semitism was encountered by the famed black writer Charles Waddell Chesnutt, when he grew up in North Carolina. In 1880 he commenced the study of German and French with a private tutor, Professor E. M. Neufeld, who had attended classes at Oxford and at the University of Paris. Whites in Fayetteville, North Carolina, were unimpressed with Neufeld's erudition; they were prejudiced against him because he was Jewish and a foreigner. So moved was Chesnutt by this bigotry that he hoped his professor would some day be able to hurt those who had mistreated him.[45]

Some Jews experienced even more serious manifestations of Southern hostility, which caught the attention of black editors. The most famous incident was the lynching of Leo M. Frank for the alleged murder of Mary Phagan, one of his employees. Ten years after Frank was murdered, Joseph Needleman, a young Jewish traveling salesman, was mutilated by a mob in Martin County, North Carolina, for supposedly mistreating a young girl. "Relatives of the girl and others took him from the jail," sympathetically related the *Chicago Defender*, "and subjected him to horrible treatment [castration]. The youth lingered between life and death for some days." Needleman survived, however, and later instituted an unsuccessful suit in federal court against members of the mob.[46]

Of greatest interest to blacks, however, was the mistreatment of David Weinberg, a forty-four year old tailor in Miami. Weinberg was considered a "dangerous" radical by his neighbors, since it was alleged that he was a Communist and that he was associating with Negroes. One night three men enticed him to leave his house, beat and gagged him, disrobed him, and then tarred and feathered him. Then "they tied him in a white hooded garment and tossed him from an automobile at a downtown street intersection." Weinberg was treated at a local hospital, but his ordeal was not yet over. He "was removed to the city jail on the charge that he had been too friendly with Negroes of the town." The tailor "denied the charges and was later released after his attorney had filed habeas corpus proceedings."[47]

But to be pernicious, discrimination need not take so violent a form. In rural Bryan County, Georgia, Jews were regularly eliminated from grand and petit juries. Even in the more cosmopolitan Richmond, Virginia, the local YMCA accepted Jews as members but not as lodgers. This prompted the *Richmond Planet* to comment, "It may not be too much to say that in some sections of the country the antipathy to Jews in the hotels is almost as marked as it is to Negroes." J. A. Rogers, a syndicated columnist in black newspapers, concluded that Jews "have certainly not been admitted to the sacred circles of Aryan or Caucasian or whatever term it is that the 'pale faces' have used to designate themselves."[48] Echoing Rogers's sentiments, another columnist, Frank Crosswaith, noted that "Jews, like the Negroes fac[e] a more or less hostile majority except that the Negroes meets this hostility in a more naked and brutal form since because of his color, he is unable to escape as easily as the Jew."[49]

Blacks could not change their color to avoid prejudice, but they could emulate the Jew by using the courts and economic pressure to secure a square deal. For example, one Negro paper noted, the Jews of Bryan County, Georgia, had not tolerated second-class citizenship. They took their case to court and persuaded the state supreme court to rule that they were entitled to serve on juries. The *Savannah Tribune* welcomed the decision and hoped it would spur Negroes to sue for their rights as well. A Richmond, Virginia, journal once offended that city's Jews, "and they of right withdrew their patronage from the paper" until it changed its editorial policy. The same paper "delight[ed] in attacking the Negro," and the *Richmond Reformer* suggested that if anything should be learned from the Jews, it was that "we must have manhood to retaliate." Retaliation could tumble even the mightiest; Jews had forced as powerful a man as Henry Ford to apologize for his "attacks upon their race." "When someone injures a Jew, observed the writer of "Colorful News Movies," a syndicated black news column, he's going to look right square into the muzzle of a gun loaded with serious consequences. It wouldn't hurt if we were more like the Jews."[50]

On occasion Jews and blacks cooperated to fight a common foe and blacks welcomed and expected such assistance. "We want their sympathy and it is their duty to give it," declared Dr. H. R. Butler, a Negro minister. "They should line up . . . always to lighten the burdens of the oppressed." Working together, marveled the *Norfolk Journal and Guide*, "it is quite remarkable how much success the Jew and Negro and the foreign-born have forced from the reluctant grasp of restraining laws and hostile public opinion." But eternal vigilance was necessary, the *Journal and Guide* added, and if men and women "had to fight for what they have got, . . . [so too will] they have to fight to hold on to it."[51]

Blacks recognized that Jews were not acting out of pure altruism in allying with them, for by helping the blacks, the Jew fought his own battle for justice. When Jewish groups joined the NAACP in protesting efforts to force a black woman to sell a house in a white neighborhood, the *Savannah Tribune* suspected that the Jews were interested in the matter "because of the effect the case will have on similar" lawsuits involving Jews. The *Norfolk Journal and Guide* analyzed Jewish assistance: "in many ways he [the Jew] sympathizes with and helps us. He gets his pound of flesh for doing it, but that is his due and the due of everyone who takes as well as gives." Less charitable was the *Atlanta Independent*, which insisted that "the Jew never gives his time and talent for his health," that rich Jews owned, directed, and controlled the major civil rights organizations, and that the NAACP was really affiliated with the Democrats and sought to defeat the Republican party at the polls.[52]

Other than the *Independent*, no paper has been located that cast suspicions on the motivation of the NAACP. Several journals, however, did object that oppression of Jews seemed more important to many than persecution of Negroes. Black writers were outraged that tens of thousands would assemble to weep for Jewish victims of pogroms or Nazi outrages but that these same people remained indifferent to the persecution of Southern blacks. Hitler, cautioned a Texas paper, "might tell us to wash our own dirty linen before telling him that his is soiled." There was also resentment that politicians avidly courted Jews but invariably ignored Negroes. Harry Byrd, for example, denounced those Virginia hotels that barred Jews, while he did nothing for blacks and was, in fact, in the words of a Richmond editor, "one of the chief exponents of racial prejudice and discrimination against the Negro citizens of Virginia, whom he also represents in the Senate of the U.S."[53]

Perhaps the prevailing sentiment of Southern blacks was best expressed by the *Norfolk Journal and Guide* on September 30, 1916: "The Jews are victims of petty prejudices in this country and in that account deserve sympathy, and they have ours. They certainly deserve more tolerant treatment at the hands of Christian Americans. But the real sufferers from race prejudice are the tens of millions of black[s]."

Not surprisingly, nothing upset blacks more than to discover that some

Jews in the South had adopted the same "philosophies pursued by other white groups," and that "to curry favor with the ruling classes," they had joined the Negro haters. In *Black Boy*, Richard Wright recalls that when he worked for an optical company in Memphis, one of the employees, a Jew named Don, expressed a "frantic desire to demonstrate racial solidarity with the whites against Negroes." Similarly, Isador Raynor and Isaac Strauss in Maryland promoted the disfranchisement of blacks during the early years of the twentieth century. This may explain also why in 1931 Joseph Berman, a Jewish alderman in Atlanta, introduced a segregation ordinance before the Atlanta City Council, which provided that "persons of different races shall not live within a radius of fifteen blocks of a school for either white persons or Negroes." Curiously, Berman's district was largely populated by blacks.[54]

There was apparently justification for believing that some Southern Jews had accepted the prejudices of their neighbors. Samuel Rosenberg, who lived in Virginia, admitted that Southern Jews from rabbis to merchants regard the Negro "as a second or third class being . . . treat Negroes as inferiors and are raising their children to do the same." While studying race relations in Indianola, Mississippi, during the 1930s, the distinguished anthropologist Hortense Powdermaker, who was Jewish, met with the sisterhood of the Reform temple of Greenville, the town nearest Indianola with a Jewish congregation. Greenville was a typical Mississippi delta community. Professor Powdermaker distributed questionnaires to those present at a sisterhood luncheon to determine attitudes on the race question. "The data from the questionnaire confirmed my impression of no difference between the attitudes of Jews and Protestants towards Negroes. Conversations with a few Jews who had moved from the North to Greenville indicated that some had become more Southern than the Southerners . . . in order to be accepted by the community."[55]

Similar findings were reported by Charles Rubin, a Polish immigrant growing up in Georgia, and Baruch Charney Vladeck, an editor for the *Jewish Daily Forward* in New York City and a labor leader. Rubin was shocked to see white youths throwing rocks at blacks. In Atlanta, he recalled: "I heard the term 'nigger' used by Jewish sons of immigrant parents with the same venom and contempt as the term 'Zhid' was used in the old country." Vladeck, traveling through the South, saw whites in Norfolk mistreat blacks. A group of Russian-Jewish immigrants silently viewed the scene. Stunned at the passivity of the Jews, Vladeck berated them, shouting, "How can you stand watching such outrages without trying to protect the innocent people? Why this is exactly what you fled from only a few years since."[56]

Blacks also remembered such incidents. In 1916, Horace Mann Bond and his parents moved to Atlanta. Shortly after their arrival young Bond passed by a small grocery store, and the young son of the owner began to chant, "nigger, nigger, nigger, nigger." Bond, himself but twelve years old at the time, had never before been called "nigger," and without any further ado, he retorted, "You Christ killer." Upon hearing this the Jewish boy burst into tears, and Bond left the scene, ashamed of what he had said. Nearly fifty years after the incident took place Bond recollected: "We moved to Atlanta one year after the lynching [of Leo Frank]. I now think that, somehow, the word I used hung immanent in the Atlanta air; and, somehow, it had entered my mind, and remained there like a knife, waiting only for opportunity for release. But of course the thought that Christ had been killed, and by the Jews, and that this little boy was such a one, may have had a more ancient basis in my twelve-year-old mind than I can now bring myself to admit."[57]

Bond was correct, for many Negroes were taught that Jews had had a role in the death of Jesus. One of the slave spirituals included the following lines:

The Jews killed poor Jesus, an' laid him in a tomb.
He 'rose, he 'rose, an' went to heaven in a cloud.

Another spiritual spoke about how "de Jews and de Romans had him [Jesus] hung." Decades after emancipation, Jews continued to be represented as the betrayers and slayers of Jesus. Richard Wright remembered that, during the 1910s, when he was growing up in Elaine, Arkansas, "All of us black people who lived in the neighborhood hated Jews . . . because we had been taught at home and in Sunday school that Jews were 'Christ killers.' With the Jews thus singled out for us, we made them fair game for ridicule." Among the chants local children learned was the following:

Bloody Christ killers
Never trust a Jew.
Bloody Christ killers
What won't a Jew do?[58]

There is little available in print to verify the accuracy of Wright's contention that black ministers taught their congregations to blame Jews for the crucifixion of Jesus. Some Negro clergymen did apparently believe that the Jews had a role in His death. Dr. J. H. Butler thought that "some of their people [had a part] in the crucifixion." He softened this statement somewhat by reminding people "that not all of the Jews of that day took part in that awful tragedy." The Reverend S. N. Vass of Raleigh, North Carolina, was silent on the role of Jews in the death of Jesus, but he believed that descendants of the old Hebrew Nation "are scattered over the earth to-day because they ceased to hold the whole Bible as their platform and chart."[59]

Charles Johnson and E. Franklin Frazier advised Hortense Powdermaker "not to reveal my Jewish background to Negroes or whites in a Bible Belt Community." The two black sociologists explained that to both groups "the Jews were still 'Christ killers,'" and they suggested that Ms. Powdermaker temporarily become a Christian. She followed this advice, and for the duration of her stay in Indianola, she pretended to be a Methodist.[60]

Blacks did consider Jews to be different from other whites. Socially, Jews and Christian whites seldom mixed, and, according to a writer for *The Voice of the Negro*, "Only now and then does a Jew cross the line and marry into another race." Miscegenation was uncommon among Jewish storekeepers living "right in the middle of a strictly colored neighborhood." Richard Bowling, a black Baptist minister in Virginia, commented about the Jewish businessman: "He will run his store on the first floor, live on the second floor himself, and in some cases rent out a possible third floor to some family of Negroes. Six days out of seven he, his wife, and his children will see more of colored people than . . . even their fellow Jews. Howbeit, they all remain Jews. Neither does colored blood filter into their family nor does any of the Jewish blood filter into the veins of Negroes. They are in the Negro world but not of it." Southern blacks, declared the *Voice of the Negro*, admired a people whose actions disputed "the Anglo-Saxon's argument that every other race is fairly crazy to marry into his race. Other races have more self-respect than the white man imagines."[61] Jews were admired as being too proud of their heritage and achievements to desire assimilation.

To Southern blacks, Jews had always been and would remain a people apart. This may explain why from 1880 to 1935 they were so fascinated with the Children of Israel. Every aspect of Jewish life interested Negroes. None, however, was more carefully studied than the way Jews earned their livelihood. Influenced by Booker T. Washington, Southern Negroes to an extraordinary degree admired the Hebrew shopkeeper and peddler. However menial peddling may have been to white Southerners, blacks respected the man with the pack on his back, for he escaped what Barry Supple has called the "*real* degradation of toiling for others." If he owned a store, however small, he was the boss. If he chose, he could close his shop to observe his holidays. Moreover, to blacks—who were very conscious of the necessity of sending their wives and teenage children out to work to supplement the family income—there was a certain dignity to the Jewish family. When Jewish women and children worked, they did so in the family store, not in the kitchens or laundry rooms of rich white folks.[62]

Similarly, of great significance is the fact that blacks and Jews seldom competed for jobs. As already noted, relatively few blacks became business-men. Virtually no Jews in the South were farm laborers or menial workers. "To put a Jew in the field cultivating [sugar]cane and corn alongside of a negro or a common white man, I don't believe in doing," asserted Joseph Weill of New Iberia, Louisiana. "There is no chance for a Jew in that capacity," he cautioned, "to improv[e] himself or his condition." Nor were opportunities better for Jews to work as common laborers in Southern cities. Visiting Atlanta, David M. Bressler, secretary of the Jewish Immigrants' Information Bureau, noted that Negroes, paid only $.75 to $1.00 a day, monopolized this work. "There is no earthly chance to compete with them, even if they were so inclined." Competition for jobs is a major factor in explaining the development of black prejudice against Chinese, Japanese, and Mexicans in the 1880-1935 period. It seems reasonable to conclude that the absence of this competition is important in accounting for the more favorable stereotype blacks had of Jews.[63]

Thus the evidence indicates that the image of Jews held by Southern blacks was positive. To be sure, Jews were occasionally criticized for their alleged greed, obnoxious habits, and indifference to the problems of Negroes. And there were those who still blamed the Children of Israel for killing the Messiah or for "getting Negro money while the Negro church is getting Jew religion."[64] More common though was praise for the "patience, per-severance, pluck, education and wealth" of the Jew.[65] The Jew was the merchant who said "mister," the Northern philanthropist who built schools and hospitals, the fellow sufferer in a society whose highest rungs were reserved for white Gentiles. The Jew was, declared T. Thomas Fortune, the man on the make, the one who "has not lost faith in himself," the person to imitate. Though there were obstacles in the path of the Jew, Southern blacks were certain he would eventually rise to the top, and when he made it, it would somehow be easier for Negroes to advance. Blacks watched and applauded the progress of the Jew, hoping they too could develop what the *Atlanta Independent* described as "a racial consciousness, a cohesion that binds them together."[66] By no means did Jews and Southern blacks have a model relationship, but life in the South during these years was hardly ideal.

10. Jewish Values in the Southern Milieu

Abraham D. Lavender

With the rise to national prominence of Jimmy Carter, much attention has been directed to the South and to "southern" values. While values such as honesty, openness, friendliness, and unpretentiousness have often been emphasized by some writers as characterizing the South, values such as racism, religious intolerance, and a disdain for "culture" and education have often been emphasized by other writers.[1] The Southern and small-town background of Jimmy Carter, combined with the emphasis on his "born-again" Christianity, made Carter particularly perplexing to American Jews—a group which is mostly Northern, urban, well educated, politically liberal, and justifiably nervous about "Christian Crusades." And yet there are close to half a million Southern Jews—many with Northern origins but some with long roots in the South, most living in urban areas but some scattered in small Southern towns, most more liberal than their Southern Gentile neighbors even though less liberal than Northern Jews. Interestingly enough, these Southern Jews do not have the trepidation about Carter's religion that non-Southern Jews have.[2]

Only a small amount of research has been done on the interaction between the Southern and Jewish subcultures, despite much writing about both the Southern subculture and the Jewish subculture.[3] The purpose of this paper is to suggest some values basic to each of these groups, to examine how the two have interacted in the past and how this has affected individuals who are members of both, and to suggest questions for further research concerning the future of this interaction.

Writing about the South has varied from historical and sociological studies such as those of W. J. Cash and Lewis Killian, to objective and subjective "participant observation" and impressionistic works of native sons and daughters such as Willie Morris, to novels such as those of William Faulkner and Thomas Wolfe.[4] The results have been mixed, but there are several characteristics of the South that are emphasized by most of these writers—the Anglo-Saxon background, the fundamentalist Protestantism, and the ever-present "white-black" problem.

The Anglo-Saxon background of the South is one of its strongest characteristics. The United States, throughout the colonial and national period, was heavily formed by the power and predominance of Anglo-Saxon values, and it "was in this atmosphere that the South developed." But as the remainder of the nation continued to grow and absorb other peoples and other values, the South remained basically Anglo-Saxon in composition and values. With a few exceptions, non-British settlers in the South—particularly French Protestants and German Protestants—were absorbed into the Anglo-Saxon culture. The South today remains the region of the country with the highest percentage of native-born, Anglo-Saxon, Protestant residents—the "most homogeneous section of the country, that region where, except for the distinct separation of the white and black races, there has been greatest assimilation of all persons into the political, social, and cultural pattern of the existing dominant group."[5]

It was this Anglo-Saxon, Nordic, North European, Celtic, Teutonic culture that provided the impetus for spreading to other parts of the world the religious values of Puritanism and Calvinism, the social values of the Protestant Ethic and social Darwinism, and the emphasis on rationalism. And it was in the United States that the frontier spirit and the overwhelming presence of the racial issue were added, and—especially for Southerners—were to join with these other values to mold the Southern way of life and the Southern value system.

The fundamentalist and absolutist morality of Puritanism and Calvinism is also a major characteristic of the South. As Lillian Smith has said, "Nothing was too small to be the concern of these moralists." "By the time we were five years old we had learned, without hearing the words, that masturbation is wrong and segregation is right, and each had become a dread taboo that must never be broken, for we believed God, whom we feared and tried desperately to love, had made the rules."[6] It was a religious belief that affected also their economic behavior—"They were self-reliant individualists and hardy fighters, sustained in their Calvinistic conviction that they had been called by the Lord to subdue the earth."[7] This belief permeates the life of the South—if not religiously, then socially and culturally—partly because of the teaching that this belief is "the only right way" but also because of the power and numerical predominance of those who accept this belief. As

Lillian Smith, among others, has explained, "We cannot understand the church's role as a teacher of southern children without realizing the strength of religion in the lives of everybody, rich and poor. . . . Church was our town—come together not to kneel and worship but to see each other." One may disagree with Lillian Smith that social reasons were more important than spiritual reasons for church attendance, but it is a fact as Smith has stated, "Few societies in modern Christendom can compare with the American South for proportion of religious affiliation or intensity of religious conviction."[8] Not all writers believe that it has always been that way, or that intense. Alston and Flynt argue that this pervasiveness is a relatively new phenomenon, that there was more intellectual openness and social involvement in the past than has been recognized. Nevertheless, even these writers state that Protestantism in the Bible Belt has usually concerned itself with "such issues as the morality of dancing" while "American society has been grappling with the problems of war, race, and justice," that it has "concealed the issues of God and man so successfully as to enable men to live in the midst of injustice and oppression without thought of revolution."[9]

As Anglo-Saxonism and fundamentalist Protestantism combined to intensify each other, so these resulting intensified values spread to influence nonfundamentalists and to affect the entire region. Attitudes toward education are perhaps indicative of this interaction, for just as education "was low on the list of priorities held by Southern churches, being absolute anathema in the eyes of some,"[10] so these attitudes sometimes were expanded to the point that education was discouraged (or at least was not encouraged) by the middle and upper-middle classes. It is partly due to the fear of pretension, the fear that the child will think he knows more and is better than others. As Anson has perceptively explained, "You don't want to do anything that will make you too different than anyone else in town. You see it here. A kid can be smart but he doesn't want to seem too intellectual, and he especially doesn't want to seem like a grind. Being too intellectual is identified with pretension and if there is one thing a Southerner can't stand, it's pretension."[11] It is easier to be accepted as a success in other ways—for example, sports, politics, and business. In these areas also, one must always be on guard that he is not perceived as being "better" or "stuck up," but education—at least formal higher eduaton—remains an area with fewer rewards and more dangers.

The Southern value system emphasizes lack of pretention, honesty in relations with others, loyalty to one's family and friends, and self-confidence in one's worth and one's values. But it is also a system which often allows that loyalty to shut oneself off from those who aren't family or friends and to have strong feelings against one's enemies; a system where confidence in one's values as absolute leads one to provincialism and intolerance. As William Workman says, "Despite a reputation for quick temper, the Southerner is amiable, friendly, and tolerant of all save those who would interfere with his family life. Southerners will wrangle among themselves . . . but they will draw together in quick resentment against the non-Southerner who proposes to alter their conduct by compulsion of word or deed."[12]

The Southern subculture is much concerned with good manners and with hospitality—a concern with "helpfulness, courtesy, and amicable relations" where even nonacceptances are "covered by gentility, good manners, and smiles" and where "to call a southerner inhospitable is comparable to calling him un-Christian." But this is a value system which is more likely to label disagreement as lack of loyalty and lack of manners, and where criticism of the status quo is more likely to be labeled as lack of appreciation for hospitality. The South is a land where the past matters, where memories of things long past and persons long dead are meaningful, but where the past is often worshipped without giving alternatives or change a chance. It is a system which, at least until recently, could probably still be summarized by W. J. Cash's description of it as "ninety-nine per cent pure Anglo-Saxon," which was "extraordinarily on the alert to ward off the possibility that at some future date [this purity] might be contaminated by the introduction of other blood-streams than those of the old original stock." The South has been a subculture where "any differences [have] always stood out with great vividness."[13] This differentness has been particularly obvious and harmful for the black, but it has also been harmful—to a lesser degree—for other "outsiders": the Catholic, the Jew, the "foreigner," and others.

Into this Southern subculture, where all differences have stood out with vividness, we now place the Jewish subculture. Jews have long been in the South. The first Jewish settlement of considerable size in the South was in Georgia in 1733. This particular community had dissipated by 1740, and "Jewish life in Georgia would rise and fall once or twice more before permanency was achieved in 1790." Meanwhile, other Southern Jewish communities—particularly the one in Charleston—were established, but throughout the colonial period the number of Southern Jews remained small, and they were largely of the "more relaxed and casual" Sephardic orientation.[14] In the middle decades of the 1800s increasing numbers of German-

Jewish immigrants settled in small communities in the South. In the 1900s—
and particularly as the children of the east-European migration began to
attain middle-class status and to spread throughout the United States, largely
following World War II—the Southern-Jewish community increased. The
size has always remained small, however, with Southern Jews comprising
less than one percent of all Southerners. In most Southern states, Jews
comprise about 0.25 to 0.5 percent of the population; Florida is the
exception—there, 3.7 percent of the population is Jewish.

In some ways these subcultures are similar. Jews also know that an attachment to a land is important, that tradition may be a major factor in preserving
group values, and that values such as group loyalty and a "feeling of belonging to a group" and "pride in . . . having a tradition worthy of being passed
on to others"[15] are characteristic of subcultures. There are some similarities
in the practice of these subcultures—although resulting from different
causes—that make for conflict between the two. Just as Southerners are fearful
of outside influences—but from a position of dominance and a desire to
preserve their society (although we must recognize that some of the effects of
having been subjugated during the Civil War and the Reconstruction still
remain)—so many Jews have a distrust of all outsiders as a result of hundreds
of years of Crusades, pogroms, forced conversions, and inquisitions at the
hands of Christian Europeans. The Sephardic experience has been different;
most Sephardim have not lived in the either/or (i.e., either assimilation to
Christianity or life largely enclosed in the ghetto) world of Christian Europe,
as have the Ashkenazim. Nevertheless, about 97 percent of American Jews are
from an Ashkenazic background and have been molded by this distrust.[16]

Despite their similarities, however, there are major ways in which Judaism
differs from Anglo-Saxon–influenced fundamentalist Protestant ways.
Judaism teaches that man is just a little lower than the angels rather than that
man is born in sin. Hence, the Jew has a more optimistic and less ascetic view
of human nature. For example, the social Darwinist idea of man's inherent
laziness is not accepted, and neither is the belief that strong law and order
is necessary to limit man's evil impulses. Judaism is a this-world oriented
religion, and this orientation has influenced it to stress the importance of
attaining social justice in this world rather than of accepting this world and
preparing for the next world. *Zedakah* ("charity," but really meaning "social
justice" rather than "giving alms") has been a major concept of Judaism.
The more optimistic conception of human nature, the orientation toward
this world, and the emphasis on social justice—along with the Jew's own

practical experience as a marginal man and an outsider—have all been suggested as having influenced the Jew to be liberal on political, economic, and social matters regardless of whether he is directly benefited. He has been influenced to favor a big government in areas of social justice and to hesitate to align himself with the political right even in those few cases where the right is philo-Semitic. Jews have consistently voted liberal and have participated in social and cultural causes far beyond their representation in the population.

Judaism has accepted much of the work-ethic aspect of the Protestant Ethic and American Jews have shown rapid upward mobility, but the social-Darwinist reverse idea that not making it is a result of laziness has not been accepted. Partly because of a strong commitment to helping others and a strong sense of belonging to the family and the community, the laissez-faire individualism and independence that customarily accompany the Protestant Ethic has also not been accepted by Judaism. Judaism has traditionally given its highest status to the scholar, and it continues to put much emphasis on learning. The Jewish family is child-centered, and this orientation—partly because it is combined with a higher concept of human nature—has led to a belief in the child as a person "whose opinion has been taken seriously, whose wishes have helped determine the actions of adults around him and the nature of his environment."[17] This approach, mixed with the love of learning and a certain amount of the Protestant Ethic, creates a subculture in which parents strongly encourage their children to become "my son, the doctor," in which the parents sacrifice and even suffer so that the children can improve themselves rapidly (it was not unusual for newly arrived poor immigrants to work extra jobs so that their children could go to good colleges and could even join the best fraternities and sororities), and in which parents receive much self-reward and pleasure (*nachus*) from their children's accomplishments.[18] These values—as well as experiences and acquaintances in various parts of the world—have encouraged the Jew to highly value cosmopolitanism over provincialism, and formal education and culture over their opposites.

Judaism also has absolute values, and a moral system similar to—although not as ascetic as—that of Christianity. In many ways, traditional Judaism is as fundamentalistic as fundamentalist Protestantism. "The doctrines of Orthodoxy . . . are more precise [than Conservative and Reform Judaism] and are by definition beyond compromise or even the appearance of compromise. . . . It is fair to say that the entire belief structure of American

Orthodoxy still finds verbal expression within the bounds of a rather narrow fundamentalism."[19]

But, American Jews—and particularly Southern Jews—have been much less affected by Jewish fundamentalism than American Protestants—particularly Southern Protestants—have been affected by Protestant fundamentalism. Consequently, there is more likelihood that the Jew will be flexible in his interpretations and applications of the specific moral rules and to think in "it depends" rather than in "either/or" terms. Because Jews "do not consider their bodily appetites as sinful, their behavior in matters of sex, drink, and food is affected accordingly. . . . Jewish proscriptions are generally against the excessive use of bodily appetites, not against their use at all."[20] For example, Jews are more likely than non-Jews to be liberal toward moderate use of alcohol and drugs such as marijuana, but are less likely to become alcoholics or drug addicts. The same principle holds in the area of sexual morality. For example, a recent National Opinion Research Center poll summarized by Alston indicated that 76 percent of white Protestants thought that extramarital sex was "always wrong" and 2 percent thought it was "not wrong at all," while only 22 percent said "almost always or only sometimes wrong"—that is "it depends." For white Baptists—by far the largest single religious group in the South—the corresponding figures were 82 percent "wrong," 1 percent "not wrong," and 17 percent "it depends." For Jews, however, the corresponding figures were 24 percent "wrong," 7 percent "not wrong," and 69 percent "it depends." That this attitude extends not only to behavior which is common, but also to rarer "victimless behavior" is indicated by the figures for attitudes toward homosexuality. Here there is even more of a contrast between the either/or and the it-depends ideologies for Protestants and Jews. The figures for Protestants on attitudes concerning homosexuality were 79 percent "wrong," 8 percent "not wrong," and 13 percent "it depends." For Baptists, the figures were 88 percent "wrong," 5 percent "not wrong," and 7 percent "it depends." For Jews, the figures were 32 percent "wrong," 38 percent "not wrong," and 30 percent "it depends."[21] And yet most research suggests that Jews are more likely than non-Jews to marry, more likely to value having children, and less likely to divorce. But, of course, what is community spirit, social justice, liberalism, and practicality to some is rabble-rousing, socialism, communism, permissiveness, and immorality to others.

With a mixture of such values, some conflict and marginality for Jews is inevitable. To the Jew, much of what has been described here as "Southern" is actually "Gentile," even though there are some major differences between

Southern Protestants and New England Protestants in such things as the latter's greater interest in passionate introspection and humanist education. However, since attempting to enter the modern world in the last few centuries, Jews have found that "the various societies, together with their traditions and memories, are still Christian—at least as far as the Jews are concerned. However secular these societies have been from one perspective, they have not been secular in the sense of being neutral between Christianity and Judaism, Christians and Jews."[22] As a result of this, there has probably been a tendency from the Jewish perspective to give too much homogeneity to Protestantism—and particularly to Christianity, for many "ethnic" Catholics are much closer to Jews than they are to Protestants on many issues. Nevertheless, just as the South is a more intense and more absolutist version of Gentile and Christian America, so the problems faced by Jews in the South have been intensified, and this has affected the interaction of the two subcultures.

There are a few issues on which Jews and Southerners agree. Southerners are more likely than non-Southerners to be pro-Israel. Even more than other Southerners, Southern Baptists and other fundamentalists support Israel "almost mystically because their own interpretations of the Bible include a Second Coming of Jesus Christ in the land of the Chosen People, Jews"[23] But this is not translated into an acceptance of Jews as Jews, into a policy which allows diversity. A 1966 study by the Anti-Defamation League, for instance, showed that 97 percent of Southern Baptists agreed with the statement that "Belief in Jesus Christ as Saviour is absolutely necessary for salvation" and 80 percent agreed with the statement that "The Jews can never be forgiven for what they did to Jesus until they accept Him as the True Savior."[24] Hence, the same religionists who support Israel also have an absolutist belief-system which teaches that Christianity is the only true religion, and that it is the duty of a "good Christian" to convert the "nonbelievers" (including Jews) to Christianity. The result has been an unrelenting pressure on Jews to convert. This started early, and continues, with ebbs and flows, today. Few Jews in the South (and elsewhere too, but especially in the South) have not been approached time after time by a would-be proselytizer trying to save souls, often with an intensity and tenacity approaching harassment. A story in a weekly newspaper in 1976, for example, tells of the effort over a twenty-year period to convert a Jewish man in a small Southern town. He was a good man, "but Jewish." Whenever this Jewish man "heard of anyone in our town who was in any kind of trouble, he tried to help. . . . And he went to synagogue regularly." For twenty years, his fishing buddies (a next-door neighbor, who wrote the article, and two ministers) took advantage of every opportunity to "slip in a witness" to Jesus. As the author states, "Since he was my next-door neighbor, I'd drop by and visit him whenever he got sick. And I'd always ask for permission to pray, but he wouldn't let me. . . . 'No, your belief is different,' he answered. 'I don't want to hear any more about Jesus'." But the buddies continued until finally, when he was hospitalized and his buddies were still trying to get him "to realize that as a man of integrity he couldn't refuse the claims of Christ," he converted.[25] This is an extreme case, but—as Eli Evans has said—"That was the shame, the oppressive burden of Christian history. Some Jews in the South crumble under it and others try to ignore it; some slink and hide, others despair, but most absorb it and block it out, and survive. All of us in the South had to face it in one way or another."[26]

If the difference between Anglo-Saxon and Jewish values, and the difference between Christianity and Judaism, has made the life of the Jew in the South precarious or at least uncomfortable, the race issue has made it almost unbearable at times. Alfred Hero notes that discouraging pressures on all white racial moderates and liberals have been virtually overwhelming, but that they have usually been even more compelling for Jews than for Gentiles of such persuasion, and he concludes that the responses have varied from intimidation to outspokenness. Responses range from that of the anonymous "Jewish Southerner" who wrote in the era of heightened racial tension that there were many Jews who "realize, as I do, that any white Southerner, Christian or Jew, must do all he can to help maintain segregation," to that of the "vast majority" of Southern Jews, who are "tending toward thoughts sympathetic to the Negro."[27]

The Southern Jew is not the only Southerner who has been marginal in the South—the Catholic, the black, and the liberal native WASP have also been marginal and ambivalent. C. Vann Woodward talks about the paradoxes and ironies in the South, and one reads of W. J. Cash's "love-hate intensity" of feeling, his "dedicated concern," his "personal anguish." A Louisiana legislator who fought vigorously for segregationist measures in the 1960s had changed by 1972 because "I did not want to leave my children with the legacy that their daddy was a bigot and a racist." Willie Morris writes that the longer he lives in New York the more Southern he seems to become, "the more obsessed with the old warring impulses of one's sensibility to be both Southern and American . . . we love it and we hate it, and we cannot turn our backs upon it"[28]

But if the white Southerner is sometimes torn between being a Southerner and an American, so much more is the Southern Jew torn between being an American Southerner and a Jew. Eli Evans perhaps expressed this most succinctly: "I am not certain what it means to be both a Jew and a Southerner–to have inherited the Jewish longing for a homeland while being raised with the Southerner's sense of home. The conflict is deep in me–the Jew's involvement in history, his deep roots in the drama of man's struggle to understand deity and creation. But I respond to the Southerner's commitment to place, his loyalty to the land, to his own tortured history, to the strange bond beyond color that Southern blacks and whites discover when they come to know one another."[29]

The Jew in the South is a person in the middle–marginal, more liberal than the Southern Gentile but less liberal than the Northern Jew. He has rarely converted to Christianity, and his Judaism has been influenced very little by Christianity. Indeed, if anything, he has probably recognized even more the historical contrasts within himself between Judaism and the Anglo-Saxon–influenced version of Protestant Christianity. At the same time, a lack of Jewish mates, particularly in the small towns, has encouraged a high rate of intermarriage and the loss of one's children through assimilation. Hero has suggested that he is probably closer to the Southern Gentile on the issue of race relations in the South, but probably closer to the Northern Jew on issues which are not as salient and intimidating to his everyday life in the South. Theodore Lowi's study indicates that Jews who live in the South for a long time have "customs, aspirations, and general life-styles" which differ from those of recent Northern Jewish migrants to the South (and which presumably differ even more from those of Northern Jews).[30] The Southern Jew, for example, is likely to put less importance on expensive Bar Mitzvahs and on economic status symbols in general, is likely to be less assertive and more casual in his interpersonal relationships, and is more likely to have intimate Christian friends and to interact in a Christian atmosphere without fear of assimilation. At least until recently, his educational and occupational goals were relatively more likely to lead to business (or law) than to academia and the liberal professions.

But just as the Southern Jew does not necessarily view himself as any less Southern because he has some Jewish values, so he does not necessarily view himself as any less Jewish because he has been influenced by and has reacted to some Southern values. Much of what is perceived as Jewish actually has European or non-Jewish origins, and many Jewish values are a reaction, either positively or negatively, to the past and present environment. The Northern Jew's definition of Jewishness is a modification of the Jewish culture, just as the Southern Jew's is a modification in a different way.

The South is often described as if it were monolithic, but of course it is not. There is a difference between the South of the Atlantic Seaboard and the South of the Gulf, between the provincial and fundamentalist rural South and the cosmopolitanism of the big cities. Despite the nonmonolithic character of the South, and despite many scores of thousands of individual exceptions, the Anglo-Saxon–fundamentalist–Protestant values have been pervasive enough and exclusive enough to mold the overall character of the religion.

There is a "New South"–the latest in several "new" Souths since the Civil War, largely the result of the shift from agriculture to industry–but even when the term refers only to this newest "New South," it has different meanings. Sometimes it means a land where millions of previously disenfranchised people now vote, a land more just in its treatment of blacks, a land which "will solve the racial problem long before the North does," a land more accepting of diversity and outsiders, and a land determinedly moving toward lessening the three Ps: provincialism, prejudice, and poverty. It is a South which has gained much attention with the rise to national prominence of Jimmy Carter. But this newest New South is still the South of the economically conservative laissez-faireism of the oil industry, the anti-unionism of the textile industry, and the primacy of large defense installations–a land which now represents the new ideological heart of the Republican party, the new center of the battleground for the preservation of "individual initiative and free enterprise and the battle against the 'drift toward socialism.'"[31]

Whether these differences in the New South are sufficient, whether the new influence of blacks will be sufficient, to affect the overall values of the region–including the historic Southern attitude toward Catholics and Jews and other outsiders who are different, and who are increasingly moving to the South–is a question still to be answered. Allied with liberal and moderate whites–who only a decade ago were referred to as "Communists" because they were in favor of racial equality and antipoverty measures–Southern blacks can be a permanent new force for change on many issues. The extent to which Southern Jews and Southern blacks will be allies in this New South is another question to be answered, but there is no question that both blacks and Jews will be more comfortable in a less absolutist and more tolerant South.

11.

Ethnicity in the South Observations on the Acculturation of Southern Jews

John Shelton Reed

We seldom think of ethnic diversity as a characteristic of the American South. In a recent presidential address to the Southern Historical Association, George Tindall characterized his region as "the biggest single WASP nest this side of the Atlantic," and certainly the region's non-British ethnic groups (disregarding its blacks, as usual) have been small—as Southern chambers of commerce used to remind us. But they haven't been *few*. Tindall quoted a South Carolina historian, writing in 1809: "So many and so various have been the sources from which Carolina has derived her population that a considerable period must elapse, before the people amalgamate into a mass possessing a uniform nation character."[1] And, although a considerable period *has* elapsed, Tindall could still produce an impressive catalog of ethnic enclaves scattered around the South.

These Southern ethnic groups have not been totally ignored by social scientists,[2] but we have yet to realize the contribution that the study of such groups could make to our general understanding of ethnic-group relations. That realization will come, I suspect, only when we introduce an explicit comparative emphasis and ask how these groups have differed from similar groups elsewhere in the United States. There are hints, here and there in the literature, that ethnicity has somehow worked out differently in the South. For instance, Tindall speculates that the South is "perhaps, the one part of the country where the melting pot really worked, because so few ingredients were added after independence. Over the years all those Southerners with names like Kruttschnitt, Kolb, DeBardeleben, Huger, Lanneau, Toledano, Moise, Jastremski, or Cheros got melted down and poured back

This article is a revised version of one that appeared in *Ethnicity*, vol. 5, no. 3 (Copyright © 1978 by *Ethnicity*) and is published here with permission.

out in the mold of good old boys and girls, if not of the gentry. Who, for example, could be more WASPish than Scarlett O'Hara, in more ways than one?"[3]

Whether Tindall's hunch is correct or not, a more important point is that we might want to test our generalizations about American ethnic groups in the Southern context. The ties that bind Southerners, like those that hold ethnic groups together, are primordial, and "Southernness" may interact and compete with ethnic identification and ethnic culture in ways that "Americanness" does not.[4] If the Southern result has been different, we may learn something important about the South *and* about American ethnic groups. At the very least, ethnic identification in the South has produced some colorful hybrids—like the Irish of Savannah, who celebrate St. Patrick's Day with a breakfast including green grits. All of this suggests an ambitious program of research, but is only a preface to a modest effort to use secondary analysis of national sample surveys to study some aspects of the acculturation of Southern Jews.

My first encounter with the phrase "Shalom, Y'all" was when I saw it on a ceramic plaque outside an Armenian merchant's shop in the Old City of Jerusalem. That shopkeeper evidently knows something we often overlook—that a lot of Jews live in the South. In fact, nearly half a million do—giving the South a Jewish population larger than that of all but five nations in the world. But if Southern Jews are not exactly few, they are certainly far between: out of every 1000 Americans, about 260 live in the South and about 30 are Jewish, but only 2 are Jews who live in the South—and one of those lives in Florida, which hardly counts.[5]

This may be one reason why the literature on Southern Jews is thin. It appears that to study Southern Jews, you have to *intend* to study them; most students of American Jewry have neglected the 7 percent who are Southerners, and most students of the South ignore the fraction of 1 percent of the Southern population who are Jewish. Even if one sets out specifically to study Southern Jews, the task is not an easy one; and there are some daunting methodological problems involved in locating a representative sample to study. Thus, what literature we have was characterized a few years back as "a handful of biographies, autobiographies, and historical works (mostly of dubious quality), and the results of interviews in several southern Jewish communities."[6] Until recently we have lacked even a simple demographic description of Southern Jewry as a whole, and discussions

of the attitudes, values, and behaviors of Southern Jews have rested on informed surmise or extrapolations from studies of a few, perhaps atypical,
communities.

The ways in which those attitudes, values, and behaviors have been
influenced by the Southern environment is not clear. Lewis M. Killian
observes that many Southerners, black and white, see Southern Jews as at
least potentially "different," particularly with regard to their racial attitudes.
On the other hand, most social scientists who have studied them emphasize,
usually disapprovingly, their acculturation. As Dinnerstein and Palsson
summarize the literature: "Except for different religious practices, [Southern]
Jews made every effort to become absorbed into the activities of their adopted
home. Their life-style closely resembled that of their gentile neighbors."[7]
Almost certainly, either extreme view is an oversimplification. The point is,
however, that we have no basis for assuming much of anything about what
Southern Jews believe, in the aggregate, or about how they behave.

In order to examine those questions directly, I constructed a sample of
166 Southern Jews by pooling data from fifty-six Gallup Polls conducted
between November 1968 and November 1972.[8] While any conclusions based
on these data must obviously be very tentative, at least the shortcomings of
this method are rather different from those inherent in previous studies of
Southern Jews. The great advantage of this pooled sample is that it appears to
be geographically representative of the total population of Southern Jews,
and there are reasons to suppose that it is representative in other respects as
well. Although the sample size is still quite small, it is comparable to those
employed in many community studies.

Demographic Characteristics

When the results of the National Jewish Population Study are published,
we will have a demographic description of Southern Jewry far superior to
anything this small sample can give us.[9] In the meantime, however, it may be
worthwhile to summarize the description which emerges from these data.
Disregarding the Floridians, Southern Jews are predominantly an urban
population (roughly two-thirds live in cities larger than 250,000); are well
educated (a majority have at least some college education); are concentrated
in professional, managerial, and executive occupations (about half of the

heads of households are in these categories, perhaps one in eight is a skilled or unskilled worker, and the balance are clerical or sales workers or are retired); and are, in consequence, economically well-off (median reported income was between $10,00 and $11,000). Compared to non-Southern American Jews, they seem, on the average, to be somewhat better educated, although the two groups have virtually the same occupational and age distributions. The Southernness of Southern Jews may be reflected in their median income (which is lower than that for non-Southern Jews), and in the fact that a somewhat larger minority—perhaps one in eight—live in rural areas and towns under 50,000 population. The Jews of Florida, on the average, are older and have lower incomes than either non-Southern Jews or other Southern Jews, and their educational distribution looks about like that for the former group. [10]

One implication of these data is that the attitudes and behavior of Southern Jews should not be compared to those of the white Southern population as a whole, but rather to those of middle-class, urban Southern whites—the group they might reasonably be expected to resemble.

Voting Behavior

Most of the Gallup Polls which were pooled to yield this sample asked how their respondents voted in the 1968 presidential election. Of the 166 in the sample, 79 were asked that question, had voted in 1968, and recalled how they voted. While we cannot, with these data, explore in any depth Southern Jewry's political views, this single indicator has much to commend it as a measure of general political orientation. A vote for Hubert Humphrey can probably be taken without much error to indicate center-to-left views; a vote for Richard Nixon, center-to-right views; and (in the South) a vote for George Wallace of Alabama was highly correlated with a whole array of culturally conservative attitudes (including—but by no means limited to—support for racial segregation), which one student of the Wallace movement has labeled the "traditional [Southern] value of orientation." [11]

Certainly the 1968 election was one in which the voting behavior of white Southerners generally differed greatly from that of most American Jews. Jewish voters went for Humphrey, the Democrat, by nearly four to one over Nixon, and virtually ignored the Wallace candidacy. White Southern voters, on the other hand, gave Nixon twice as many votes as Humphrey (who got only one vote in five), and gave Wallace nearly as many votes as

Nixon. Even among college-educated white Southerners, Wallace took one vote in five and Humphrey only one in four.[12] Few population groups in the country were more clearly on opposite sides in that election than American Jews and Southern whites. How did Southern Jews, who belong to both groups, resolve these cross-pressures?

There are some reasons, in principle, to suppose that Southern Jews will look pretty much like their non-Southern coreligionists—that is, unlike their fellow white Southerners: "For all studies of Jewish political opinion agree that the *social-class* factors which strongly divide non-Jews on political lines . . . have little effect on the views or party choices of Jews." Herbert Hyman has also suggested that "To use an old-fashioned term, the membership characteristic 'Jewish' is '*prepotent*'—it overrides class membership."[13] Perhaps if being Jewish can wash out the effects of social class—that powerful predictor of political behavior—it can override the effects of region as well.

On the other hand, as we have seen, some of the literature on Southern Jews has pointed to their acculturation to the folkways of the white South. George Maddox implies as much when he notes "surface indications that Jews have been fairly well integrated into predominantly Gentile communities within the region," while observing that "this acceptance depends on continuous public manifestations of accommodation by Jews, whatever their private opinions, to the regional culture, especially in regard to race relationships." Lewis Killian argues that the marginality of Southern Jews "has placed a high premium on conformity to the regional mores," and that, whatever the level of anti-Semitism in the South, "there has been *enough* latent anti-Semitism . . . to make good Southerners out of many Jews."[14] Whether this alleged conformity to Southern ways is internalized or is only a sort of protective coloration, this view suggests that the political views Southern Jews express (including those they express to Gallup Poll interviewers) should resemble the views of their white neighbors.

Obviously, we should not expect either extreme outcome—complete similarity to non-Southern Jews or to other Southern whites. There are good reasons to suppose that the degree of acculturation varies considerably from one community to another. Even within specific Southern towns, Lowi has argued, degree of acculturation varies, and serves as a basis for stratification within the Jewish community.[15] Moreover, Southern Jews should not be compared to the aggregate of Southern whites, but rather to other Southern whites with similar demographic and economic characteristics.

In fact, Southern Jewish voters did show a level of support for Hubert Humphrey intermediate between that of non-Southern Jews and that of middle class Southern whites generally. Although in this respect Southern Jews look somewhat more like other American Jews than like other middle-class Southerners, the effect of region is by no means obliterated among Jews; it is substantial and at least as great as the regional effect found among middle-class voters in general. Put another way, the difference between Jews and other middle-class white voters generally is no larger in the South than elsewhere in the United States—and not much smaller either. The effect of region is simply superimposed on the larger effect of religion—or vice versa.

This generalization does not hold, however, when we look at support for George Wallace. Although Southern Jews were twice as likely as non-Southern Jews to vote against Humphrey in 1968, their votes went to Nixon, not to the Wallace third party. Wallace received 37 percent of the votes of Southern whites and about half that proportion of the middle-class white vote, but he received only a miniscule proportion of the votes of Jewish Southerners. In this respect, Southern Jews resembled non-Southern Jews (and non-Southern middle-class voters generally). Being Jewish, therefore, washed out the observed regional difference in support for Wallace; only in the South was there a difference between Jews and the total category of white middle-class voters.

To judge by this single indicator, then, Southern Jews, in the aggregate, do show the effects of their regional environment. If a Nixon vote in 1968 can be taken to indicate conservatism, they are more conservative than non-Southern Jews—to about the same extent that middle-class white Southerners in general are more conservative than non-Southern middle-class whites. But their acculturation has not been so great as to blot out their differences from Southern Gentiles, nor did it lure them into the Wallace camp in any significant number.

Attendance at Religious Services

One of the persisting differences between Southern and non-Southern white Protestants has been that the former are more likely to belong to a church and to attend its services. Many observers of the South have commented on the subtle and not-so-subtle pressures to adhere at least nominally to some church, almost without regard to which one.[16]

Just how this pressure is experienced by Southern Jews is not clear, but they may feel more obliged than non-Southern Jews to define themselves as *something*, religiously, by active membership in a religious congregation.

There is, in addition, the effect of living as a very small minority in a population composed almost entirely of evangelical Protestants. Although this situation—and the sometimes-documented anti-Jewish sentiment of many Southern Protestants—may make Jewish religious life more difficult, it may also increase the need for it among those who continue to define themselves as Jewish.

Perhaps it is not surprising then to find that the Southern Jews in our sample (excluding those from Florida, who look in this respect like non-Southern Jews) are relatively likely to answer affirmatively when asked by a Gallup interviewer: "Did you, yourself, happen to attend church [*sic*] in the last seven days?" Of the 61 respondents not from Florida who were asked the question, 35 percent said they had, compared to an average figure for the total U.S. Jewish population of 19–20 percent. This regional difference is at least as large as that reported elsewhere for white Protestants.[17] In both South and non-South—perhaps especially in the latter—Jews are somewhat less likely than white Protestants to report attendance. Here again, the effects of region and religion are simply superimposed. "Acculturation," however, has a novel twist in this instance: by being more "Southern"—that is, by participating in organized religious activities—Southern Jews are at the same time more "Jewish." I suspect this is just one of many paradoxical features of Jewish life in the South.

Limitations and a Suggestion

The limitations of these data are painfully obvious. Some of the problems are with the sample—not the least of which is simply its size (particularly when Floridians are excluded), which effectively precludes analysis of variations within the Southern-Jewish population. Certainly there must be such variations. Presumably Jews in large Southern cities, with large Jewish populations, display different patterns of accommodation than Jews who live isolated in small towns with one, two, or half-a-dozen Jewish families and no Jewish communal or congregational life to speak of. A larger sample would let us paint a more detailed picture.

Another shortcoming, again an obvious one, is that we have no way of distinguishing recent migrants to the South from longtime residents. Indeed, we cannot even estimate at present what proportion each is of the population. This factor probably exaggerates the apparent differences between Jewish and non-Jewish Southerners (and the similarity between Southern and non-Southern Jews), but there is no way to estimate the magnitude of the exaggeration.

Finally, it would be delightful if it were possible to inquire about a wider range of "acculturation" variables, using better measures than those provided by the Gallup Poll (which was conducted for entirely different purposes). The nature of the polling operation that produced the sample leads to "lowest-common-denominator" variables, and there is nothing to be done about that.

Maybe, however, this preliminary (and inexpensive) venture in secondary analysis will serve to suggest that there are some interesting, important, and unanswered questions about Jews in the South, questions deserving the attention that could be given them by "primary" analysis—by research, that is, undertaken specifically to answer them.

12.   Southern Jews and Public Policy

Alfred O. Hero, Jr.

This paper represents an effort to review current relevance of, and to update conclusions from, an empirical study of the attitudes and behavior of Southern Jews toward race relations and foreign policy conducted in the early 1960s. The original research was part of a larger study of Southern behavior toward foreign affairs that involved some 1100 interviews, extensive secondary analyses of data of major national survey and polling agencies, content analyses of over fifty Southern newspapers, and examination of linkages between votes of Southern congressmen and constituent opinion in their districts.[1] Of the 194 Jewish interviewees, 138 lived in one of ten sample communities chosen to be broadly representative of the diverse "Souths," while the remaining 56 were selected from elsewhere in the region on the basis of either their influence in the international domain or their influential roles within their own areas of the South. Southern Florida, suburbs of the District of Columbia, and Texas were purposely excepted as probably atypical of Southern Jewry in respect to the particular issues in which we were primarily interested.

The Early Sixties

Southern Jews, even when compared with other Southerners of comparable education, socioeconomic status, and roles in the same communities, were significantly more liberal, egalitarian, and desegregationist in respect to blacks, were generally more cosmopolitan, and were more amenable to multilateral international cooperation.

For instance, Jews were more likely than comparable non-Jews to vote Democratic rather than Republican, to prefer more liberal over more conservative candidates in either party, and to accept as descriptive of themselves the term *liberal* rather than *conservative*.

Even when education was equivalent, Southern Jews were significantly more likely to read analytical material of liberal, cosmopolitan bents, especially periodicals, dealing with public affairs—e.g., the Sunday *New York Times, Harpers,* the *Saturday Review,* the *Atlantic,* the *New Republic,* and the *Reporter* (now defunct).

Though not widely so viewed by their neighbors (Jews were frequently quiet concerning controversial social and political issues on which they felt most of their neighbors disagreed with them), Jews more than other white Southerners accepted desegregation as inevitable (if not necessarily desirable); felt blacks should receive equal access to jobs, promotion, and political activity; and supported the efforts of the federal executive and courts in these regards in the South. Even when they were anxious about, or criticized, racially liberal stances of national Jewish organizations and of articulate Northern Jews in respect to race relations in the South, their criticism focused more on tactical concerns—especially fear of generating anti-Semitism and difficulties with their own Gentile neighbors—than on the substance of the views expressed. The typical Southern Jew of that period was among those one might term "quiet moderates" on race. There were very few outspoken Jewish racists of the Citizen's Council variety, but many paternalists who preferred segregation and the "Southern way of life" felt there should be mutual obligations between blacks and whites, but considered change toward equality inevitable. They would not aid in the desegregation process, but they would not commit much time, energy, prestige, or whatever to fighting it either. Moreover, Jews were a disproportionately large fraction of the desegregationist white-liberal minority of the period, far in excess of the slightly more than 0.5 percent they represented of the total white Southern population or even of the the larger percentage they were of the Southern middle and upper-middle classes.

Racial attitudes of Jews were associated with most of the same factors that characterized those of other Southern whites, plus some others particular to Jews. Those educated outside the South—particularly at elite universities—and at the more intellectually stimulating Southern institutions were generally more liberal than products of more typical Southern colleges. College-educated Jews generally—and especially those in such liberal professions as law, education, and architecture—were more liberal on most issues than those who did not go to college, particularly businessmen.

Jews in the more dynamic, modern cities were more liberal than Jews in more traditionalist communities—particularly those Black Belt communities in which the local population contained only a handful of Jewish families, with black majorities. Locally raised Jews whose families had resided in such communities for several generations tended to hold racial views approaching those of other whites in similar educational, occupational, and social roles. Individuals of Jewish ancestry whose families had resided in such traditional Deep-South rural and small-town settings for as long as three generations were frequently so assimilated into white Protestant society as to harbor views on most aspects of public policy—including race relations—scarcely distinguishable from those of the white middle class generally. Local Jews who held less conservative opinions were more apt to keep them to themselves than were their counterparts in urban, or less conservative, locales—particularly those in which white thinking was more diverse.

In some traditional "old South" communities such as Charleston, New Orleans, Mobile, and Savannah there were Jewish families tracing their origins into the antebellum, and even the prerevolutionary, South who still considered themselves to be Jewish, and who maintained genteel traditions of an elite of several generations of local prestige and leadership—including a gracious way of life, reading of thoughtful literature, and tolerance of differences of opinion on controversial questions. Though many of these people were not particularly active in public affairs, their views on public issues, including race, tended to be less conservative than those of comparable members of Protestant or Catholic (in southern parts of Louisiana, Mississippi, and Alabama) "old families." Seldom, however, were they identified with militantly liberal (or radical) activities, black or white.

Like other middle-class white migrants to the region, many Northern Jews who had moved South had apparently come from the less intellectually oriented, less socially conscious, less cosmopolitan, and more conservative (and perhaps more materialist) elements of Northern Jewry. A number probably moved South to take advantage of cheap labor, right-to-work laws, inexpensive household servants, etc. Nevertheless, they too were more egalitarian racially and were otherwise less conservative than non-Jewish white migrants from the North—and more so especially than the general white middle class of Southern upbringing.

Thus, Jewish thinking on race relations, as on other public issues, tended to parallel that of middle-class and upper-middle class whites in the same communities. If their white Gentile peers were relatively conservative, so were the local Jews. If the former were more liberal or progressive, the latter tended to be so also. Nonetheless, typically the Jews were at least somewhat less conservative than their local Gentile counterparts.

In the early sixties, however, Jewish racial liberals tended to be quieter and generally more circumspect in making evident their nonconformist views than were like-minded Gentiles. Although this generalization was more apt to reflect the behavior of those in smaller, more conservative settings (e.g., Natchez) than those in Atlanta, Nashville, or New Orleans, it nevertheless applied to some extent even in metropolitan settings. Pressures from within the Jewish community on would-be proponents of controversially liberal views seemed as influential in muzzling the racially liberal Jewish minority as the apparent pressures, or concrete experiences, they received from local Gentile conservatives. The more intense the emotions and the more controversial the issue in the local community, the quieter the Jewish liberals. Often their Gentile peers felt local Jews were as conservative as they, even when the private thinking of those Jews was distinctly more liberal. Fear of generating anti-Semitism and the desire to continue to live in prosperity and harmony with their local Gentile peers seemed the principal causes of this silence.

Racially liberal views among Jews, as among whites generally, were typically correlated with relatively liberal (or at least less conservative) views on most other public issues—social welfare; federal-government participation in the economy and in society generally; economic, technical, and charitable aid to less-developed countries; intercultural exchanges; immigration; negotiations and compromises with the Communist powers; liberalized international trade; shifts in emphasis from military means to other forms of multilateral cooperation in world affairs; and so on. On the other hand, the few Jews who agreed with white supremacists that blacks were constitutionally inferior, and who were active members of Citizens' Councils, and the like, either were indifferent to international questions, held isolationist or "fortress America" views, or favored unilateral—primarily military—intervention abroad. Most of the few convinced Jewish racists, like their Gentile peers, would have sharply reduced (or terminated) foreign nonmilitary aid and other cooperation with Asia, Africa, and Latin America, withdrawn from the United Nations if China were admitted, and adopted a tougher line toward Communist regimes abroad.

It was therefore not surprising that Southern Jews were, on the average, clearly more internationalist, or multilateralist, in their foreign-policy views than were their white non-Jewish peers concerning the international issues on which they were questioned in the early sixties. Moreover, traces of traditional Jewish cosmopolitanism, liberalism, and respect for intellectual and analytical endeavor—however attenuated they might be among the small

Jewish merchant and (to a lesser extent) the professional class in small Deep-South communities—continued to exert some influence on the international views of even racially conservative Jews.

Most Jewish racial segregationists who had some contact with a rabbi or another Jew of cosmopolitan inclinations, were at least vaguely aware of support given to international cooperation by national (and international) Jewish organizations, and read the international content of at least a weekly news magazine. They were more inclined to manifest some interest in world developments and to expose themselves to world affairs through the press, including television, than were Gentiles adhering to similar white-supremacy views. Jewish segregationists were likewise more likely to have voted for Kennedy against Nixon and Johnson against Goldwater in the presidential elections of that period. Even several Jewish clothing manufacturers who were in competition with foreign imports and were not above using racism to discourage unionization of their plants were rather apologetic, even sheepish, protectionists, in contrast with most local Gentile manufacturers of comparable goods vulnerable to liberalized trade in the Kennedy Round of multilateral tariff negotiations of that period.

The polls of that period indicate, however, that compared with Northern Jews, Southern Jews were considerably more conservative on race relations and at least somewhat more conservative on most other issues as well. The less patent the connection between the issue and black-white relations in the South, the more closely did Southern-Jewish opinions approach Northern-Jewish norms. However, the Northern-urban-Jewish leftist, socialist, or radical minority had little counterpart in the South. The Southern experience and milieu of earthy pragmatism, close interpersonal relations, distrust of abstractions, and caution about abrupt or far-reaching social change had influenced Jews considerably, as it had other Southerners.

Some Hypotheses On the Latter Seventies

The following hypotheses derived from demographic trends over the last decade and a half, projections from our systematic data of the early 1960s, and impressions from recent contacts and experiences in the South—in a number of instances with Jews of the next generation from those interviewed earlier. Unfortunately, there is no recent comparable systematic study of Southern Jewish views on public issues.

The views of Southern Jews on public questions seem generally more nearly congruent with those of their Northern coreligionists than before. In comparison with those of the preceding generation, a larger proportion of Southern Jews today were raised outside the region, are college educated, are in the liberal professions, and reside in urban settings rather than in more traditional, agrarian-based, smaller communities—all factors correlated with more cosmopolitan, liberal, and generally informed thinking on most regional, national, and international issues. Moreover, fifteen years ago young Jews harbored more liberal opinions than their parents and other seniors—views that were also more liberal than those their seniors had held when they were young.

Perhaps even more important, the pressures, especially on Jews, to conform to, and to remain publicly uncritical of, racial segregation have been greatly attenuated. Not only are they freer to express themselves and to behave more in line with their private views in respect to race per se, but gradual acceptance (however grudging) of racial change among Southern whites as a whole has removed a major deterrent to flexibility and freedom of thought, of discussion, and of overt behavior pertinent to controversial issues generally throughout the region. Jews have become more candid in expressing views atypical of those prevailing locally concerning social, political, and other public matters.

These changes since nearly a generation ago have, of course, affected Gentile whites as well. Consistent regional differences in prevailing opinion on many public issues between Southern and non-Southern whites in the direction of more conservative thinking on the part of Southerners continue to be reflected in survey data.[2] However, on most issues of national and international significance—race relations, civil liberties, governmental involvement in and regulation of the economy, and foreign policy—the magnitudes of differences between the regions have declined over the last two decades. The growing impacts of national media; rapid transportation; travel and geographic mobility; industrialization and urbanization; integration of the South into the national economy, society, and body politic; and more widely available and substantively improved public education have all influenced many of the values and attitudes of most major segments of the Southern population in the direction of those of their Northern counterparts.

Nevertheless, a number of indicators suggest that when contrasted with white Gentiles differences in the direction of more liberal, cosmopolitan

Jewish thinking continue to prevail, even when other relevant demographic and social factors are held constant. Jewish names are still much more numerous on subscription lists to such cosmopolitan periodicals as the Sunday *New York Times, Foreign Affairs,* the *Atlantic,* and the *New Republic* than their relative numbers in the regional affluent classes would suggest. Jews are likewise still disproportionately numerous among members and other supporters of such organizations and activities as the Urban League, Human Relations Council, Committee on Foreign Relations, Great Decisions discussion group, League of Women Voters, and other liberal civil-rights, civil-liberties, and public-policy bodies (as they are among board members and attenders of art museums, symphony orchestras, operas, serious local theaters, and other cultural activities). At least as much as in the past, Jews today are more apt than Gentiles of comparable status to attend intellectually elite universities and colleges, both outside and within the region. Southern Jews remain much more apt than Gentiles, particularly those with similarly comfortable incomes, to vote for center-to-left Democrats rather than for center-to-right Republicans in national elections.

Unfortunately, Southern ethnic groups other than blacks and white Protestants continue to receive little or no systematic study by social scientists from within or outside the region. Fruitful research on such groups as Jews, Cajuns, and Cubans (not just those in Miami)—from masters' theses through Ph.D. dissertations to more ambitious studies by matured political scientists, sociologists, cultural anthropologists, and social psychologists—would seem of relatively high priority. Moreover, such research could be readily executed by individuals at Southern institutions. Research on Southern ethnic groups could be at least as intellectually interesting, and as fundable, as a good deal of the less-imaginative research often done by social scientists, including graduate students, with the necessary training, motivation, and means.

The possibilities for manageable masters' and Ph.D. theses, for instance, would seem virtually limitless. Community studies in proximity to graduate students' universities—preferably done on both Jews and others of like status to permit comparability and analysis of interactions across ethnic lines—could shed much light on the values, attitudes, and behavior of this important and potentially more influential Southern minority since the "racial revolution" of the post–World War II period. Coordinated community studies by several graduate students supervised by mature social scientists at the same institution could produce comparative findings on Jews in several different types of Southern communities, from metropolitan areas to more traditional small towns, and in several disparate Southern subcultures. Such studies might probe not only attitudes and behavior in respect to important issues among Jews of different backgrounds and walks of life but also roles of Jewish minorities in significant aspects of local decision making and action.

13. Utilizing the Southern-Jewish Experience in Literature

Ronald L. Bern

In a recent column in *Hadassah Magazine,* book reviewer Gloria Goldreich noted that, "The French *histoire* suffices for both history and fictional tale, linguistically asserting that the two are inextricably bound. The strength of fiction is often rooted in the writer's understanding of the historic implications of his characters' emotional makeup, and novelists have often emerged as the most reliable historians of their eras."[1]

She was kind enough to add that as writers of *histoires,* I–along with such luminaries as E. L. Doctorow and Saul Bellow–embrace the twin traditions of literature and history. In so writing, Ms. Goldreich managed to connect our disciplines–that is, history and fiction–quite neatly, and in a way which I find wholly satisfying.

I believe her thesis is correct, but all the proof I have is personally experiential. By way of example, I mean that for me, the transcribed Southern "history" that lives freshest and clearest in my mind is that written by novelists like William Faulkner, Robert Penn Warren, Margaret Mitchell, and Mark Twain, and by historians like Bruce Catton who, quite frankly, write like novelists. I readily admit that their accounts may be fairly criticized as imperfect by scholars steeped in the events and the times they recorded, but I believe that one must approach criticism, of novelists or of historians, with a bit of caution. As Tolstoi wrote in his epilogue to *War and Peace,* "The subject of history is the life of peoples and of humanity. To catch and pin down in words–that is, to describe directly the life, not only of humanity, but even of a single people, appears to be impossible."[2]

The task, then, of writing *histoires*–whether one writes consciously to relate his point in time and place or simply to tell a story that reflects them– is an awesome one. Perhaps, as Tolstoi implied, it is even impossible to do so with a precision that will satisfy posterity.

Certainly I did not presume to do so in my novel *The Legacy.* I did, however, attempt to place my characters in a real setting of time and events, based upon my own experiences to a considerable degree. And in so doing, I recalled the events, the people, the places, the times, the joys and sorrows, the victories and defeats that I myself remember.

I do not claim for myself the historian's ability to cast all of these forces in perfect perspective. This imposes too much of a burden of scholarship, and it also invites a kind of historical scrutiny that few novelists would survive. I make this point as a qualification, for I have, indeed, looked subjectively backwards in time to my own experiences in fashioning a novel about the Jewish experience in the South.

More properly, I should call it *a* Jewish experience. For my work does not record all Southern Jewish experience, or for that matter, even a typical Jewish experience. It is only my experience, my times, my life that provides the soil in which my novel is rooted.

Quite honestly, the concept of a typical Jewish experience exceeds the limits of my imagination. Leo Frank's was not typical, any more than was my colleague Eli Evans's, whose father was mayor of the North Carolina city in which he grew up. Most of us neither were lynched nor were we children of privilege brought up in cities in which our fathers were mayors. Most of us lived lives of rich diversity, of broadly differing experiences, sometimes dictated by forces and influences well beyond our control—a diversity illustrated on its outer limits, perhaps, by Leo Frank and Eli Evans. And every one of these lives is perfectly valid, perhaps yielding the potential stuff of a novel as yet unwritten.

I grew up in a small town in the South Carolina Piedmont, the son of first-generation–American parents. My father was born in Augusta, Georgia. My mother was born in Anderson, South Carolina, the daughter of Russian immigrants who had been part of the wave of *Ostjuden* who streamed westward to America about the turn of the century, leaving the societal and spiritual givens of the shtetl for the confusing, frightening Lower East Side of New York. Unlike most of their peers, neither of my grandfathers found a home on the Lower East Side.

My mother's father, whom I knew best, particularly yearned for a place where he could breathe clean, free air; where he could, by dint of his own remarkable intelligence and will, find a place for his young wife and children and, perhaps, even build an empire. He hated the freezing cold of New York's winters, just as he had hated the winters in Russia. It was warmer in the South, he was told. The South was open. There were opportunities there. The South was a place to grow, if only a Jew had the courage to strike out into the unknown. If only he had the strength to make yet another exodus to a strange land, having so recently come to this one.

When he bought his train ticket, my grandfather had no destination in mind. He simply placed money on the counter and said, "South," as far South as the money would take him. It took him to Greenville, South Carolina, and when he got off the train, he was disappointed. It was a larger town than he had wanted. It was crowded and bustling. So he put another dollar on the counter. And another railroad clerk heard the word "South" and understood. This time the train ride was much shorter: thirty-two miles to Anderson, South Carolina.

When my grandfather stepped down from the train, he was a new Southern Jew, in a strange place of rabbit hunters, gentlemen farmers, hard drinkers, and Southern Baptists. But it was a place in which he sensed he could build. He began as a peddler, drifted into the livestock business, and thirty years later, as the town teetered on the brink of bankruptcy in the depths of the Depression, the City Council turned to him for help. That help was immediately forthcoming in the form of a $60,000 cash loan to the city.

Interestingly, the board of directors of the local country club came to him with a similar plea. They were losing the mortgage on the club, they explained, and begged him to help. He told them that he felt every town should have a country club, and he bought it and held it for its members until after the Depression. The image is ironic, perhaps even absurd. This little Russian Jew now the owner of a graceful colonial mansion, of tennis courts and a golf course and a grand ballroom. What is more ironic, however, is that although he owned it, he never visited it. The club's bylaws forbade a Jewish presence on the grounds.

Eventually, the directors offered my grandfather a lifetime membership, out of a sense of guilt, perhaps, or of the absurdity of the situation. However, when he pressed them, he was told that the bylaws would not be amended, that his membership would be voted as a special exception. When he pressed them further, he was told that his own children would not be eligible for membership. Of course he did not join.

A paradox? Of course.

A set piece of the strange collocation of Jewish and traditionally Southern cultures? Perhaps.

This was the place where I was born and raised.

I entered grammar school in Anderson, South Carolina, in 1942, an unfortunate accident of timing. As in many small towns across the country—and perhaps most particularly, across the South—there was a swelling resentment in my town against the Jews at that exact moment in time.

Despite its grace and manners, the South has long operated on a kind of scapegoat psychology in times of trouble. In the past, the Eastern liberal press or the Supreme Court or the blacks or the Republicans or the Yankees had served well when the ignorant white Southerner looked around for a source on which to blame his troubles. But the Second World War was different. Good white Christian boys were dying thousands of miles from home in a war the isolationist South never wanted, and the reasons why were unclear; a convenient point of blame was illusive.

Father Charles Coughlin had been shaping the consciousness of some of these people for years with his radio rantings about the Jews. Copies of Henry Ford's *Dearborn Independent* had been read there, serving to dust off and bring back to life the old "Protocols of The Elders of Zion," that historically anti-Semitic document—forged and published in Russia in 1905—which described a supposed Jewish plot for world domination. Then came the war, the questions, and, only very slowly, a gathering coalescence of understanding as to whose fault the war really was, and on whose hands the stain of their innocent blood really spread. For a time, it was unarticulated. Then the local newspaper editors decided to give it a basis in published fact. And in a series of virulent columns, our newspaper placed the blame for the war squarely and exclusively on the Jews.

The results were predictable. Significant parts of the populace were inflamed by the columns, which continued despite the urgent pleas of the local Jewry. Not that any Jewish man was beaten or hanged. Not that mass rallies were held against us in public. Not that the Ku Klux Klan burned any of our houses. But much of the town turned a cold, wholly unaccustomed face toward its Jews, who had always been welcome there before. A sense of hostility grew; a sense of estrangement dogged the steps of the Jewish citizens.

The adults were relatively subtle in their actions. But the children, less restrained than their parents, acted out on the school grounds what they heard at home, and the only Jewish boy in the local elementary school system was, unfortunately, me.

When the first child called me a "dirty Jew," I did not understand what he meant. I had been raised in a gentle tradition of love and acceptance, and the words were foreign to me. When I asked my father that afternoon what the boy had meant, there was a look of faraway resignation in his eyes, a look of pain that I had never seen there before. He explained it to me, all of it, trying to simplify the entire skein of our history, of our persecution and suffering in a way that a six-year-old child might understand.

All I really understood was the inevitable conclusion: if the situation persisted, I could deal with it in one of two ways: I could walk away, or I could fight. I asked him what he had done as a small boy in Augusta, Georgia, and he said he had fought. And so the die was cast for another little Jewish boy in another small Southern town.

I fought almost daily, struggling to preserve my sense of dignity, and I won. But it was not over in a week. Or even in the several months before Bernard Baruch personally intervened to force an end to the hate-filled columns in the local newspaper. It went on for several years. I hated the fighting, but I continued to win, always; perhaps because I became so terribly experienced at using my fists, or perhaps because I sensed that I could not afford to lose, because in losing I had no place to fall back to—not unlike Israel, with only the sea at her back and enemies on all sides.

Ultimately, it was over. The convulsion of anti-Semitism died, and I had fought my way into a kind of grudging acceptance—perhaps even admiration—among my peers. But the scars remained, and in a way, they became, thirty years later, the first foundations for my novel *The Legacy*.

I wish to emphasize the word novel here, because it is, by any literary definition, precisely that. But by the same token, it does draw heavily on my own experiences for whatever power it has and for its combined sense of loneliness and outrage.

The protagonist is David Harris, who grows up as that paradoxically curious combination: Deep-South Southerner and Jew. David is shaped by the primary forces in his life—the fighting, not unlike my own, balanced with others that are more positive.

There is Isaac Shulman, his grandfather, the son of a brooding rabbi of a tiny Russian village. The old man is powerful both intellectually and in his will, and he sees in the boy a chance to leave a monument to himself. Because the boy, unlike his own sons, is perceived by the old man to possess his will to win and his determination. And so Isaac Shulman fills the boy with a sense of his heritage, with the meaning and the importance of being a Jew.

There are his parents. Ben—tough, proud, unbending and yet compassionate. Rachel—warm, strong, loving, brokenhearted at her son's loneliness and his struggle, yet powerless to intervene.

There is the South itself, which, for all of its repression and violence, is still

David's place. A place in which he grows—always struggling to relate the influences and the values in his life, to maintain his own heritage and still to find a place for himself in his own culture.

Ultimately, David grows to manhood and falls deeply in love with a non-Jewish girl, an eventuality which forces him to come to grips with many of the paradoxes which shaped him. His view is neither clear nor objective. He perceives that if he marries her, he will somehow be turning his back on his family, on Jewish history, on Masada, the Warsaw Ghetto, Buchenwald, and even his great-grandfather, the ancient rabbi of the Russian village whose ghostly presence filled his childhood. If he leaves her, however, he will be forsaking his hard-won sense of place in society, his almost arrogant individualism, and, of course, the girl he loves.

This is the novel's final conflict, but symbolically, it is a conflict which is threaded through the novel from its first pages to its last. And all of it, to me, is the Southern Jewish experience—the loneliness, the fighting, the rejection, the conflict, but also the love, the warmth, the ultimate winning of a sense of belonging and of place.

The Jews of *The Legacy* and of my own experience are essentially different Jews from those whose huddling instincts have kept them together in the cultural comforts of the large cities. They are Jews who in no way lend themselves to any kind of stereotyping: Jews who are tough, proud, individualistic. Jews who will not be forced into social or emotional molds.

New York Times reviewer Seymour Epstein understood this. When he reviewed *The Legacy*, he noted that, "The Shulmans are not a weak-eyed, weak-kneed bunch cringing in some dry goods store, but brawny athletes, men of the soil, who meet the ancient curse with the roughest fists in town."[3] Former South Carolinian Bob Talbert, now a top columnist for the *Detroit Free Press*, called it, "one of the most accurate views of the macho, bigoted South of the '30s, '40s and '50s that I have ever read."[4]

And yet, my novel is not an indictment of the South. There is much of love in *The Legacy*, including love of Gentiles for Jews and Jews for Gentiles, and particularly, love of Jews for the Southern places in which they choose to make their homes.

Perhaps the reviewer in *The Jewish Post* of New York understood my characters best of all: "Not products of the northeastern urban ghetto, not predictable in their reactions, they are instead men who have cast off the huddling instinct, who have removed themselves from the old comforts of the ghetto, who are—in a cultural sense—very much alone. Yet they refuse to surrender one whit of their dignity, their faith, or their consciousness of the central importance of Jewishness in their lives."[5]

Is theirs a foreign experience in the South, or one which is unique? I have heard it so argued, but I doubt it very seriously. I believe that such a conclusion is drawn on the basis of memories that yearn to put differences behind us, memories that prefer the narcotic of moonlight and magnolias to a sure perception of all that has gone before us and a consciousness that it can happen again.

I do not, I repeat, claim to be a reliable historian of my era. I do claim, however, to have captured between hard covers both the substance and the shadows of one real Southern Jewish experience.

14. Southern-Jewish History Alive and Unfolding

Eli N. Evans

When I first went South to interview people for my book, I didn't know what to expect. One of my early introductions occurred in a talk with a man from Anniston, Alabama, a Mr. Sterne from an old German-Jewish family. "What was Friday night like in Anniston, Alabama?" I asked.

And he answered, "Oh, it was memorable. First," and he lifted his hands up, "Mama blessed the lights and then we settled down to our favorite Friday night meal—crawfish soup, fried chicken, baked ham and hoppin' John (black-eyed peas and rice) and sweet-potato pie." I knew then I had fallen down the rabbit hole, into the complex world of the Southern-Jewish mind and experience. For those of you who have wandered into this world for the first time, I welcome you to the maze.

I have some wonderful memories from my travels in the South. One of the first persons I went to see was Thomas Jefferson Tobias down in Charleston, South Carolina. His great-great-grandfather so admired Thomas Jefferson that he rode by horseback all the way from Charleston to Monticello to shake Jefferson's hand. In each succeeding generation, there was a child named Thomas Jefferson Tobias. I asked Tom—and I was fortunate to interview him only two weeks before he died—"Why is it that of all the families from the Sephardic wave, your family is one of the few that has survived?"

And he answered, "We were lazy. The reason is that we lacked adventure and we were comfortable here; so everyone else went off to the Delta where the cotton was growing strong and high, and we stayed."

I remember meeting Gertrude Weil, down in North Carolina, a very remarkable woman then in her nineties, one of the original suffragettes and a founder of the League of Women Voters. I interviewed her in the very room in which she was born, if you can imagine such a thing. Entering her house

This article is based on an address delivered at the dinner session of the Conference on Southern-Jewish History.

was like going through velvet curtains into another world of old photographs and brocaded furniture. I asked her, "Miss Gertrude, who was the first president you ever remember hearing about?"

And she replied, "Well, I did remember talking to a man who remembered as a boy hearing about Thomas Jefferson." It's an extraordinary fact that this country is only two long lives old and therefore what we think of as history in America would be smiled at tolerantly in Israel, like a recent coin that the Israelis would throw back in the sand.

Whenever I traveled, I was always asked, "What are the differences between Jews in the North and Jews in the South?" Implicitly, that is one of the central questions confronting analysts of Southern-Jewish history.

From living in New York for the last few years I have one answer. I think being Jewish in the South is like being Gentile in New York. What I mean by that is that Jews in the South live as a minority in a majority culture. The schools close on Jewish holidays in New York; they don't in the South. The generation of my friends in New York played stickball in the streets of the East Side while I was picking blackberries in the backyard. They were upwardly mobile; we wanted roots.

In the North the seamstresses and the tailors worked to get their children up and out of the ghettos and to Long Island. In the South the fathers wanted to build businesses to keep their sons at home. The drama of Jews in the South revolves around the fathers who built their businesses for the sons who didn't want them. That painful day that I told my father that I wasn't going to go into the family business was an event that echoed time and again as I interviewed young people in my generation and is a fundamental drama of Jews in the South.

More than that, Jews in the South are different from Jews in the North in that we are part of Southern history. You know that story: in 1800 there were more Jews in the city of Charleston than in any other city in America, and from 1860 to 1865, between 3,000 and 10,000 Jews fought on the Confederate side in the Civil War.

A few years ago, Jacob R. Marcus asserted: "No Jew was ever the first person to go anywhere. There was always a cousin or an uncle ahead of him." I was listening and took Dr. Marcus's aphorism as a challenge. I vowed to myself, "I am going to find someone who was the first Jew in his community" and so I searched. I found almost no one. Finally I stumbled on a man in Scotland Neck, North Carolina, not the kind of place one would settle in for just ordinary reasons—a little crossroads of a town. I asked him,

"Mr. Goldstein, I have been looking everywhere for you; why is it that you settled here in Scotland Neck, North Carolina?"

"You really want to know?" he asked.

"Yes," I replied with growing excitement.

And he confessed, "The horse died."

What I found was that whereas historians and scholars of Southern history like W. J. Cash saw Jews as aliens in the Promised Land, we were indeed not aliens, but blood and bones part of Southern history.

I came to this subject personally and not as a historian. When I began my research, it was the first time that I had reached into the literature of Jews in the South. One question began to gnaw at me, and it's a question that ought to be primary in our minds. If there is such a rich history of Jews in the South—I think everyone who has studied it, who has read of it, who has immersed himself in it, would agree that the story is rich with humanity and irony—then why hasn't there been more written about it? Where are the poets and the playwrights, the artists and the novelists?

Ron Bern's fine novel *The Legacy* is only one of a handful of novels written in the last decade on the Southern Jewish experience. How many other books are there? Perhaps fifty, certainly less than a hundred through the years. Compared to the tremendous outpouring from the Northern centers of Jewish learning about Jewish life in America, it's almost negligible. Why is it then that there hasn't been much writing on the subject in comparison to Jewish writing on other aspects of the American-Jewish experience?

I think there are a number of reasons for it. One thought, which was suggested to me by Richard King, a Southern historian from Federal City College, is that there has been such a fascination in the South with black and white conflict that the varieties of the white experience have just been overwhelmed and overlooked. No one has concentrated on the Jewish or the Catholic experience, or on that of any other white minority group in the South.

Moreover, Jews in the South have the habit of low profile—an instinctive shyness. It's something that we grow up with, something internal. I remember that when I went to New York, I felt unimportant. I had always been conditioned throughout my life to believe that we were the Jews on the periphery, that it was New York, the world of our fathers, that was the center of Jewish life in America. Jews in the South were out here on the rim where it didn't matter.

For one thing, the Jewish community in New York is self-occupied. We were the country cousins and they were the city slickers. In New York, I didn't know anything about them. After their first questions on the South, I realized that they didn't know anything about us either.

Why did the Jews come to the South? Many came as peddlers looking for a better life, because the South was the place of opening opportunity after the Civil War. Many of them were failures in the North, and even if they became successful later, that's certainly the feeling of Northern Jews about Jews who came to the South. My grandfather was one of those peddlers. He had a dairy route in the North, he ran a little bakery for a while, and finally, as a last resort, he opened a three and nine cents store. That didn't work either, because Woolworth's was too strong. But time is changing the South's loser image. Now that the South is emerging as a major regional force in America, Jews in the South may be experiencing the end of our own sense of inferiority, the sense of inadequacy, the subconscious lack of confidence that has been in the Jews in the South all these years.

Now, at last, with growing interest in the Southern-Jewish experience, we can look more energetically at the gaps in our knowledge. What do we know really of the life of the peddlers in the South? Because it's not such an unhappy part of the Jewish experience, the amount of literature on the subject is sparse. We ought to research that. There are a lot of ex-peddlers around the South who are still alive. We ought to talk to them soon.

What do we really know about blacks and Jews, I mean the internal and psychological part of their relationships to each other? Just the little bit of interviewing I did in the black community (and I would suggest that approach to Jewish scholars—a broad approach in which you interview all kinds of people, not just Jews) revealed that Jews are molded by the ethos we grow up in—and our attitudes and psychology are shaped by that ethos.

Look at race and religion through the eyes of the participants. When the black man saw the peddler, he said to himself, "Here is a white man with an accent (not Southern), who doesn't own slaves, who will smile at me, and come to my door." I once talked to a black woman whose grandmother said she remembered that when the Jewish peddler came by in his wagon, she called him "the rolling store man"—a wonderful poetic phrase to describe the peddler who opened up his packs, she said, and released the smells of spices through the little shack that her grandmother lived in.

From the Jewish side, the peddlers were conditioned to be afraid of the muzhiks, the Russian peasants, who came storming into the shtetl to rape and pillage during the pogroms. They had no previous experience with blacks, no reason to fear them. They approached the ex-slaves openly as customers, and the two became linked economically.

They were linked in another way as well. Listen to the spirituals—"Go down, Moses, let my people go"; "Joshua fit the battle of Jericho"; and "Daniel in the lion's den." They were linked by the Old Testament feelings of blacks in the South, the story of the Israelites who struggled out of the land of bondage into the land of freedom. Moses and the children of Israel were very much a part of the black psyche, very connected.

What do we know about the history of Zionism in the South? It's a fascinating story, because the longing for Zion is wrapped up with Jewish identity, with feelings for Jews all over the world.

What do we know about growing up Jewish in the Bible Belt? Of relationships with Southern Baptists and Catholics? How do we weigh not only anti-Semitism but a place where philo-Semitism is in the air. How do children deal with the love-hate syndromes of Southern fundamentalists?

What do we know about Jews in politics? It's a special interest of mine, because my father served as mayor of our town for twelve years. The subject stretches back to Judah Benjamin and forward to today. In my own informal poll, as I went through the South, I found that there had been 150 Jews elected to public office in the South since World War II. That's a remarkable statistic. I don't know exactly what it means, but I think it's related to the fact that, for the emerging black vote, Jews were a moderate choice; for the most part, these were moderate Southern politicians.

And finally, what of the differences for Southern-Jewish women in their relationships with Jewish and non-Jewish boys; with college men and women who were Yankees and Southerners; and what are the special characteristics of Southern Jewish female attitudes toward home, job, family, and education?

We are seeing in America an end to the melting-pot theory as the central philosophy governing so much of American life. There is a search for roots going on. An Italian writer has said, "We learned to be Americans by learning to be ashamed of our grandparents." No more. There's an explosion of ethnicity, a curiosity about where we came from, a curiosity about where we are and where we are headed. Today we celebrate the validity of the Southern-Jewish experience—as a subject for academic research and for literature—with a pride in its history and in its struggle, in the unique Jewish perspective on Southern history, on the insights that history reveals about being Jewish in America. We celebrate the Southern-Jewish experience as a body of knowledge that is not finished but needs deeper probing, that requires growth and sustenance from our perspective as Southerners and as Jews, the conflict between the Southerner's commitment to his own place as his homeland and to the Jewish search for a home.

I would suggest that we ought to reactivate and reinvigorate the Southern Jewish Historical Society—not just for academics, not just for amateur historians and rabbis who have an interest, but for all of us who live in the South. Let's start a broad-based publication that can draw articles from the young sociologists who have a passing interest in this subject, both Jewish and non-Jewish, and for Southern historians and Jewish historians who are interested in it as an avocation or as part of their other work. Let's publish poems and essays and thoughts and oral histories; let's give prizes and awards for best books and best research papers. We know a great deal about the external history of the major Jewish communities in the South—New Orleans, Charleston, Richmond—but what of their internal histories? What of the psychological experiences of being Jewish in the South, the emotional experiences? What would anthropologists or psychologists or sociologists say about it? We must ask not only what Jews in the South did—who they married, how much property they had, what kind of wills they left, and did they own slaves or not—but also *how did they feel?* I repeat it: How did they feel? And today out in the small towns away from the major centers, who is telling them that their history is important, that they are a part of American-Jewish history and that what happened to them matters because it is part of the passing of American Jewish life. As one old man told me, "When the Jewish stores were here, all these towns were different, and then the chain stores came and now every little town looks alike." There is so much truth in that statement but I would like to know what happened to all those families out there.

When I was growing up, Southern-Jewish history was the province of the aristocratic Southern-Jewish families who wanted to show how deep their roots were. The rest of us were newcomers, and we were treated that way by both the old Jewish families and the old Gentile families in the South. There was a preoccupation with the Civil War among people who wanted to show that they had good claim to membership in the Daughters of the Confederacy. Yet most of the Jewish immigration to the South occurred *after* the Civil War. As Mrs. Goldberg of Richmond observed to me, "The immigrant generation had to be remade. Your generation is different." I am not so sure my generation is different, but I would like to know more about the fascinating story of what it meant to be the immigrant generation in the South and to be remade.

The black writer Alex Haley has written a new book called *Roots*. It's an extraordinary book which could have a profound effect on America if it truly succeeds in linking up blacks in this country to their African heritage. One of the stories that he tells is about a visit to the village of his forefathers in Gambia where he visits with the *Griot,* who was the living oral archive of his tribe. He sat for hours listening to this old man trace the fragment of the name of Haley's great-great-great grandfather, recounting the entire history of the tribe for many, many hours, all from his memory. The old man was an oral historian. It was the tradition of the tribe, which had no written history. From that man, Haley learned the story of his ancestor, who was dragged to the slave ship and grabbed two handfuls of earth from the beach at Gambia to take to that ship.

I would like to discuss briefly my own experience with oral history, how it was linked with my discovery of self and what I believe all of us must do.

The increasing mobility of Americans has left most families scattered across the country—the old people remain at "home" to float in memories and their offspring are off somewhere and phone in on anniversaries and holidays. The distance deprives the young of roots, of any feeling for family or attachment to place. It robs the old of a close relationship with grandchildren and of the roundness of life that should come from easy talk about the past in the natural warmth that connects the old to the very young.

For the last year, I have been working with the "Kin and Communities" program of the Smithsonian Institution, which is trying to do something about encouraging families to record their histories in this bicentennial year. Under the direction of Margaret Mead, the program has produced booklets to encourage families to hold reunions, to read family diaries, to look at scrapbooks, letters, and wills, and to record conversations with each other. Says Dr. Mead, "Interview your grandfather or write for your grandchild."

Historians are now calling this approach "New New Social History"—not about the great men and women of history nor about great moments but about ordinary people in everyday life. It is true that writing a family history will leave a legacy that will be useful for future historians searching for the texture in the lives of everyday people, but it can also have a profound impact on future members of your own family.

A few years ago, I chanced upon a yellowing typed manuscript, less than a hundred pages, that my grandmother Jennie Nachamson had dictated to one of her eight daughters during the last year of her life in 1939. The story told of the early days in Lithuania, the family debate to come to America, the first years in a Baltimore slum, and subsequently, of my grandparents' decision to gamble on the South. It was the story of raising a large Jewish family in the eastern North Carolina tobacco belt in the early 1900s, of running a small store and coping with the loneliness that plagued small-town Jews throughout the South. Jennie's story connected me with the life-force in my roots and personalized the pain of the immigrant struggle. And she stirred the Southerner in me by revealing the Jewish wellsprings, a genesis far deeper than the Confederate ancestry the old families in my hometown of Durham, North Carolina, used to brag about.

We had a large family—for Jennie and Eli produced not only eight consecutive daughters but finally a son, all of whom begat my twenty-seven first cousins. I interviewed my aunts about their childhoods and asked my artist aunt (there's one in every family) to do sketches of growing up; my mother was the oldest and therefore had custody of the family photograph albums. Together we picked out the best pictures (that her sisters had fought over for years) and gave all of it to a local printer, who offset and bound it like a book—Jennie's story, the interviews, the sketches, and the photographs—to give to every member of the family and to friends.

After that, my interest mushroomed into a three-year project in which I traveled through the South talking to old and young people, poring over dozens of other family histories, and finally writing a book combining Jennie's story with interviews of my mother and father, entwining our family with the history of Jews in the South.

It was one of the deepest and most fulfilling experiences in my life, and I recommend collecting your own family history to everyone. All of us hear stories about our families from our parents and older relatives, but collecting them in a systematic way as a reporter freed me to ask questions of my parents that I would never have asked as a son. Here's how to do it.

Talk to the family first and reach an understanding with the older generation that what you seek is not mere dates and events, but personality, feelings, memories, experiences—the stories and details to pass on to future generations of your family tree. It matters not whether the story of your family is a noble one, whether it is filled with success or failure. What matters is that it happened.

Prepare yourself by charting a family tree with as many dates and events as you can put down—when the family moved, marriages, children. Keep in mind that the chart will guide you in your questions, enabling you to calculate how old parents and grandparents were in the twenties, in the depression, where they lived during the wars.

Borrow or buy a tape recorder and about a half-dozen tapes (perhaps you can share the expense with several other families, a synagogue, or a civic group). Practice operating it; nothing is more disconcerting to someone talking than a listener who keeps fiddling with a tape recorder. Look them in the eye so they are not performing for the tape recorder but talking to you.

Set aside several weeks to do the interviews, for you should let your parents and grandparents (or yourselves) unravel memories at their own pace, not more than an hour or so a day. That way, they will look forward to the sessions and add their own energy to the project.

Ask them about their parents, the neighborhood they grew up in, the nicknames of friends, the games they played as children. Ask them to sing childhood songs, to recite bedtime stories they were told and the ones they told your parents. Don't forget pets, toys, and jokes.

What were winters like? Who were their favorite teachers? When did they see their first automobile and movie or hear their first radio and television show?

Ask about love—about the first time your mother met your father, the first time they kissed, and the evening he proposed. How did they spend Saturday nights and what were holidays like—Rosh Hashanah, Yom Kippur, Passover, or the Fourth of July? What holiday dishes do they remember eating? Did they keep kosher? Who built the local synagogue, and what were the rabbis like?

Don't be afraid of unpleasantness—funerals, illnesses, accidents, anti-Semitism, political fights in the town, the impact of war and depression are all a part of life. What is painful to one generation is insight for the next.

What gossip do they remember in town? Whom did they admire and whom did they despise? Did they vote for candidates for governor or mayor, and why? What did people think of Roosevelt and Truman?

Ask your mother or grandmother about growing up—the clothes she wore, how she fixed her hair, her first dance, what dances they did, and did she wear makeup? Ask your father or grandfather about fishing or hunting, about skinny-dipping, and whether he ever saw Babe Ruth play. Ask what the Great Depression was like for the family, what jobs he got, his bosses, and what he was doing when Pearl Harbor happened and when Franklin Roosevelt died? If you get stuck, open photograph albums and discuss the pictures.

Interviewing my parents and aunts made me feel less lonely somehow—no longer a particle of sand on the beach, but a part of all our family and of the immigrant generation who went before and struggled, wandered, settled, loved, married, and bore children. Talking about our family history provided me not only a bridge to the past but an anchor for the future. My grandmother always hoped one of the grandchildren would write her story, for she was aware of the drama of her voyage from the Old World to the New. What she didn't realize was that I could never have done it had she not sat down with my aunt in the summer of 1939 and told her own story in her own words. Neither can you predict the impact of interviewing your family or telling your own story to your children or grandchildren—but do it. It will be a contribution to history but that's incidental; it will leave a treasure for your family.

Southern Jewish history is alive and unfolding; the search is on not only for what happened but for what people felt, hoped, feared—Jews . . . in the South . . . Southern Jews, Jewish Southerners . . . interlaced and inter-mingled. . . A prism to reexperience Southern history, to explore and discover these new participants in the Southern drama, an exciting and vital part of the Jewish experience in America.

Notes
Contributors
Index

NOTES

1. Portrait of a Romantic Rebel
Bernard C. Ehrenreich (1876-1955)

Byron L. Sherwin

1. Sermon delivered by B. C. Ehrenreich in Montgomery, Alabama, quoted in "Pleads for Youth," *Montgomery Advertiser,* November 8, 1906.

2. Theodore Herzl is generally considered the founder of modern political Zionism.

3. Quoted in the *Jewish Gazette,* English Supplement (September 23, 1898), vol. 24, no. 38, p. 1. See also *Gan Ha-Dorot—Garden of the Generations,* ed. Rosemary Krensky (privately printed, n.d.), p. 83, in the library of the American Jewish Historical Society. *Gan Ha-Dorot* contains replications of the primary sources noted.

4. Quoted in the *Jewish Chautauqua Assembly Record* (July 17, 1900), p. 5. See also *Gan-Ha-Dorot,* p. 89.

5. Quoted in an article about a speech delivered by B. C. Ehrenreich, probably from *Jewish Chautauqua Assembly Record,* 1900. See also *Gan Ha-Dorot,* p. 83.

6. On the Kahl-Montgomery Congregation during the Civil War, see Bertram W. Korn, *American Jewry and the Civil War* (New York, 1970), pp. 49-50. On Philip Stein, see Philip Bregstone, *Chicago and its Jews* (Chicago, 1933), pp. 300, 308.

7. Sermon delivered by Ehrenreich, quoted in *Montgomery Advertiser,* November 8, 1906.

8. Ibid.

9. Letter of Governor Emmet O'Neal to Ehrenreich, dated September 20, 1913. See also *Gan Ha-Dorot,* p. 111.

10. From undated notes of Irma Ehrenreich. These notes were the basis of a speech she delivered to the Local Suffrage Association of Alabama. See also *Gan Ha-Dorot,* p. 107.

11. Jacob Weinstein, "Rabbi Ehrenreich—Doughty Battler for the Lord," *National Jewish Post,* April 1, 1955, p. 5. See also *Gan Ha-Dorot,* p. 130.

12. Quoted from Irma Ehrenreich's private papers (dates from approximately 1919). Irma Ehrenreich's papers are in the possession of her daughter, Rosemary Krensky, who made them available to me.

13. Undated notes of Irma Ehrenreich's speech to the Montgomery section of the Council of Jewish Women. Apparently she was quoting from the words of her husband, B. C. Ehrenreich. See also *Gan Ha-Dorot,* p. 110.

14. *The American Israelite* (Cincinnati), Februrary 1918. See also *Gan Ha-Dorot,* p. 115.

15. Michael Aaronsohn, *Broken Lights* (Cincinnati, 1946), p. 140.

16. The *American Israelite,* February 1918, from a letter to the editor by Mrs. E. Shohl.

17. From a letter from Ehrenreich to D. Louis Grossman, March 12, 1918, in the private papers of B. C. Ehrenreich in the possession of R. Krensky.

18. From a letter of Thomas Kilby to Ehrenreich, April 1921, in the private papers of B. C. Ehrenreich.

19. Notes from a copy of a speech delivered by Isidor Weil at the Standard Club of Chicago, April 21, 1921, from the Ehrenreich papers in the possession of R. Krensky.

20. Ibid.

21. By Bertha Loeb from an unidentifiable source. The text of this quote is noted in *Gan Ha-Dorot*, p. 125, where no source is provided.

2. Reflections on Southern Jewish Historiography

Stanley F. Chyet

1. See the letter by Rebecca Alexander (Mrs. Hyman) Samuel published in Jacob R. Marcus, ed., *American Jewry: Documents, Eighteenth Century* (Cincinnati, 1959), pp. 53–54.

2. Rabbi H. Bamstein, of Houston, responding to Nathan Cohn's Address of Welcome, in *Southern Rabbinical Association: Conference Papers and Sermon Delivered at the Fourth Annual Convention Held in Nashville, Tennessee, December 24, 25, and 26, 1906* (Nashville, 1907), p. 9.

3. Wilbur J. Cash, *The Mind of the South* (Garden City, N.Y., 1956), p. 105; the book first appeared in 1941.

4. Ludwig Lewisohn, *The Story of American Literature* (New York, 1937), pp. 77–79.

5. Willard Thorp, *A Southern Reader* (New York, 1955), p. vii; Cash, *Mind of the South*, pp. 300, 334. See also the childhood reminiscence the novelist William Styron assigns the narrator in "The Seduction of Leslie" (*Esquire*, September 1976, p. 131): ". . . there quickly flashed across my mind a vision of the homely yellow-brick temple . . . in my hometown in Virginia . . . the silent and shuttered synagogue with its frowning cast-iron portals and intaglio Star of David [represented] in its intimidating quietude . . . all that was isolate, mysterious and even supernatural about Jews and Jewry and their smoky, cabalistic religion." The narrator is not totally mystified by Jews themselves in "civil life," but "out of the glare of daylight . . . [they] disappeared into their domestic quarantine and the seclusion of their sinister and Asiatic worship"–a problem "for an eleven-year-old Presbyterian."

6. Quoted by Steven Hertzberg in "The Jewish Community of Atlanta from the End of the Civil War until the Eve of the Frank Case," *American Jewish Historical Quarterly* [*AJHQ*] 62 (1972–73):285.

7. C. Vann Woodward, *Origins of the New South, 1877–1913* (Baton Rouge, La., 1951), p. 311.

8. Cash, *Mind of the South*, p. 337.

9. See E. Milton Altfeld, *The Jew's Struggle for Religious and Civil Liberty in Maryland* (Baltimore, 1924); Henry Cohen, "Settlement of the Jews in Texas," *Publications of the American Jewish Historical Society* [*PAJHS*] 2 (1894):139–56; idem, "The Jews in Texas," *PAJHS* 4 (1896):9–19; Barnett Elzas, *The Jews of South Carolina: From the Earliest Times to the Present Day* (Philadelphia, 1905); Herbert T. Ezekiel and Gaston Lichtenstein, *The History*

of the Jews of Richmond, from 1769 to 1917 (Richmond, Va., 1917); Jacob Ezekiel, "The Jews of Richmond," *PAJHS* 4 (1896):21-27; J. H. Hollander, "The Civil Status of the Jews in Maryland, 1634-1776," *PAJHS* 2 (1894):33-44; Leon Hühner, "The Jews of Georgia in Colonial Times," *PAJHS* 10(1902):65-95; idem, "The Jews of Virginia from the Earliest Times to the Close of the Eighteenth Century," *PAJHS* 20 (1911):85-105. See also Hühner, "The Jews of North Carolina prior to 1800," *PAJHS* 29 (1925):137-48; Lewis N. Dembitz, "Jewish Beginnings in Kentucky," *PAJHS* 1 (1893):99-101; Alfred G. Moses, "A History of the Jews of Mobile," *PAJHS* 12 (1904): 113-25; idem, "The History of the Jews of Montgomery," *PAJHS* 13 (1905): 83-88; Abram Simon, "Notes of Jewish Interest in the District of Columbia," *PAJHS* 26 (1918):211-18.

10. See Bertram W. Korn, *American Jewry and the Civil War* (Philadelphia, 1951); idem, "Jews and Negro Slavery in the Old South, 1789-1865," *PAJHS* 50 (March 1961):151-201; idem, *The Early Jews of New Orleans* (Waltham, Mass., 1969); idem, *The Jews of Mobile, Alabama, 1763-1841* (Cincinnati, 1970); Jacob R. Marcus, *Early American Jewry: The Jews of Pennsylvania and the South, 1655-1790* (Philadelphia, 1953); Marcus, ed., *Memoirs of American Jews, 1775-1865*, 3 vols. (Philadelphia, 1955); Marcus, *The Colonial American Jew, 1492-1776*, 3 vols. (Detroit, 1970); Leonard Dinnerstein, *The Leo Frank Case* (New York, 1968); idem, "Southern Jewry and the Desegregation Crisis, 1954-1970," *AJHQ* 62 (1972-73):231-41; idem, "A Note on Southern Attitudes toward Jews," *Jewish Social Studies* 32 (1970):43-49; Dinnerstein and Mary D. Palsson, eds., *Jews in the South* (Baton Rouge, La., 1973); Leo Shpall, *The Jews in Louisiana* (New Orleans, 1936); idem, *The Sheftalls of Georgia* (Savannah, 1943); Malcolm Stern, *Americans of Jewish Descent: A Compendium of Genealogy* (Cincinnati, 1960); idem, "New Light on the Jewish Settlement of Savannah," *AJHQ* 52 (1962-63):169-99; idem, "The Sheftall Diaries: Vital Records of Savannah Jewry (1733-1808)," *AJHQ* 54 (1964-65):243-77; Isaac Fein, *The Making of an American Jewish Community: The History of Baltimore Jewry from 1773 to 1920* (Philadelphia, 1971); Charles Reznikoff and Uriah Z. Engelman, *The Jews of Charleston: A History of an American Jewish Community* (Philadelphia, 1950); Mark Elovitz, *A Century of Jewish Life in Dixie: The Birmingham Experience* (University, Ala., 1974); Fedora Frank, *Five Families and Eight Young Men (Nashville and her Jewry, 1850-1861)* (Nashville, 1962); Arnold Shankman, "A Temple Is Bombed–Atlanta, 1958," *American Jewish Archives [AJA]* 23 (1971):125-53; idem, "Atlanta Jewry–1900-1930," *AJA* 25 (1973):131-55; Janice Rothschild, *As But a Day: the First Hundred Years* (Atlanta, 1967); idem, "Pre-1867 Atlanta Jewry," *AJHQ* 62 (1972-73):242-49; Louis Ginsberg, *History of the Jews of Petersburg, 1789-1950* (Petersburg, Va., 1954); Elaine Maas, "The Jews of Houston: An Ethnographic Study" (Ph. D. dissertation, Rice University, 1973); Myron Berman, "Rabbi Edward Nathan Calisch and the Debate over Zionism in Richmond, Virginia," *AJHQ* 62 (1972-73):295-305.

Among other works: Julian B. Feibelman, *A Social and Economic Study of the New Orleans Jewish Community* (Philadelphia, 1941); Ben Kaplan, *The Eternal Stranger: A Study of Jewish Life in the Small Community* (New York, 1957); Harry Simonhoff, *Under Strange Skies* (New York, 1953); Abraham I. Shinedling, *West Virginia Jewry: Origins and History, 1850-1958*, 3 vols. (Philadelphia, 1963); James Lebeau, "Profile of a Southern Jewish Community: Waycross, Georgia," *AJHQ* 58 (1968-69):429-43; Theodore Lowi, "Southern Jews: The Two Communities," *Jewish Journal of Sociology* 6 (1964):103-17.

11. See Humboldt's essay reprinted in Leopold Von Ranke, *The Theory and Practice of History,* ed. G. G. Iggers and K. von Moltke (Indianapolis, 1973), p. 8.

12. Woodward, *Origins of the New South,* pp. 451–52; Cash, *Mind of the South,* pp. 333, 335.

13. Lowi, "Southern Jews," p. 114.

14. Rabbi Isidore Lewinthal of Nashville, in his presidential address, in *Southern Rabbinical Association: Conference Papers,* p. 24.

15. Henry W. Grady, "The New South," in Thorp, *Southern Reader,* p. 459.

16. Thorp, *Southern Reader,* p. vii.

17. Woodward, *Origins of the New South,* p. 317.

18. Humboldt in Ranke, *History,* p. 22.

19. Mark Pinsky, "South Toward Home," *Present Tense,* winter, 1976, p. 71, commenting on Eli Evans, *The Provincials: A Personal History of Jews in the South* (New York, 1973).

20. Elovitz, *Century of Jewish Life in Dixie,* p. 174, and see Allen Krause, "Rabbis and Negro Rights in the South, 1954–1967," *AJA* 21 (1969):20–47; Dinnerstein, "Southern Jewry and the Desegregation Crisis, 1954–1970," *AJHQ* 62 (1972–73): 231–41.

21. Harry Golden, *Our Southern Landsman* (New York, 1974), p. 100.

22. "Reverse Migration," *Time,* September 27, 1976, p. 50.

23. Lowi, "Southern Jews," p. 115. Golden, however, insists on the opposite: "Jewish identity in the South is based more on religion than ethnicity," yet he admits: "The attendance at the religious services . . . is not one iota greater than the attendance at religious services elsewhere, but the attendance in the recreational hall and banquet room [of the synagogue] is far beyond that of other Jewish communities."

24. *Time,* September 27, 1976, pp. 29, 30–31.

3. The Role of the Rabbi in the South

Malcolm H. Stern

1. The larger and more established Caribbean communities of Barbados and Curaçao did have rabbis; see I. S. and S. A. Emmanuel, *History of the Jews in the Netherlands Antilles* (Cincinnati, 1970), passim.

2. The exception was Congregation Rodeph Shalom of Philadelphia, whose origins as an Ashkenazic congregation can be traced back to 1795.

3. Albert M. Hyamson, *The Sephardim of England* (London, 1951), p. 159; Charles Reznikoff, *The Jews of Charleston* (Philadelphia, 1950), p. 15.

4. Isaac M. Fein, *The Making of an American Jewish Community* (Philadelphia, 1971), pp. 54 ff.

5. Quoted in Fein, *The Making of an American Jewish Community,* p. 54.

6. *Year Book of the Central Conference of American Rabbis 5690–1890/91* (Cincinnati, 1891), p. 4.

7. "Isaac Leeser," *The Universal Jewish Encyclopedia* (New York, 1939–43), 6:588; Bertram W. Korn, *Eventful Years and Experiences* (Cincinnati, 1954), pp. 156 ff.

8. Abraham J. Karp, "Simon Tuska Becomes a Rabbi," *Publications of the American Jewish Historical Society* 50 (December 1960):79–97.

9. Korn, *Eventful Years and Experiences,* pp. 196 ff.

10. Herbert T. Ezekiel and Gaston Lichtenstein, *The History of the Jews of Richmond from 1769–1917* (Richmond, 1917), p. 240.

11. Jacob S. Feldman, *The Early Migration and Settlement of Jews in Pittsburgh, 1754–1894* (Pittsburgh, 1959), p. 15.

12. James G. Heller, *Isaac M. Wise* (New York, 1965), chap. 27; statistics derived from a comparison of *The Graduates of the Hebrew Union College-Jewish Institute of Religion: A Centennial Register* (Cincinnati, 1976) and "Biographical Sketches of Rabbis and Cantors," in *American Jewish Year Book 5664 (1903–1904),* (Philadelphia, 1903), pp. 41–108.

13. Malcolm Stern, "Some Notes on the History of the Organized Jewish Community of Norfolk, Virginia," *Journal of the Southern Jewish Historical Society* 1 (November 1963): 12–36.

14. Communications to the author from Rabbi David Geffen of Wilmington, Delaware, and Rabbi Joel Geffen of New York, grandson and son of Tobias Geffen.

15. Quoted in David Philipson, *The Reform Movement in Judaism* (New York, 1931), p. 356.

16. "Maximilian Heller," *The Universal Jewish Encyclopedia,* 5:309.

17. Communications to the author from Mrs. Milton Krensky of Chicago, daughter of Rabbi Ehrenreich.

18. Bertram W. Korn, *American Jewry and the Civil War* (Philadelphia, 1951), chaps. 2–3.

4.   The Rabbi in Miami—A Case Hisory

Gladys Rosen

1. Kirkpatrick Sale, *Power Shift: The Rise of the Southern Rim and Its Challenge to the Eastern Establishment* (New York: Random House, 1975).

2. Daniel J. Elazar, *Community and Polity: The Organizational Dynamics of American Jewry* (Philadelphia: Jewish Publication Society, 1976), p. 140. In dealing with the implications of community size and community impact, Elazar notes that only in the South is the largest city not the regional center. Attributing this to the fact that Greater Miami is still a very new community, he goes on to his prediction regarding Miami's future role.

3. Fred Massarik, "Special Report No. 1, Miami," *National Jewish Population Study* (New York: Council of Jewish Federations and Welfare Funds, 1972), typescript, p. 26.

4. Kenneth D. Roseman, "Power in a Midwestern Jewish Community," in *Understanding American Judaism,* vol. 1, ed. Jacob Neusner (New York: Ktav Publishing House, 1975), p. 161.

5. Salo W. Baron, "The Image of the Rabbi Formerly and Today," in *Steeled by Adversity: Essays and Addresses on American Jewish Life,* ed. Jeanette Meisel Baron (Philadelphia: Jewish Publication Society, 1971), p. 147.

6. Arthur Hertzberg, "The American Jew and His Religion," in *Understanding American Judaism,* vol. 1, ed. Neusner, p. 19.

7. *Jewish Floridian*, October 12, 1945, p. 6. Quoted from the text of a congratulatory telegram from Rabbi Stephen S. Wise to Rabbi Irving Lehrman on the announcement of plans for the half-million-dollar synagogue expansion.

8. Interview with Nathan Perlmutter, October 18, 1976. This was Perlmutter's personal opinion based upon his experience in Florida during the period of the controversial civil rights activities of the fifties.

9. Quoted in Polly Redford, *Billion Dollar Sandbar: A Biography of Miami Beach* (New York: E. P. Dutton & Co., 1970), pp. 273, 274.

10. Interview with Rabbi Irving Lehrman, August 29, 1974.

11. Interview with Harry A. Levy, Vice-President of the Greater Miami Jewish Federation, August 29, 1974.

12. Elazar, *Community and Polity*, p. 268.

5. Rabbi in the South—A Personal View

Jack D. Spiro

1. Wilbur J. Cash, *The Mind of the South* (New York: Alfred A. Knopf, 1941).

2. Amos 9:7.

3. *The Union Prayerbook for Jewish Worship*, I (New York, The Central Conference of American Rabbis, 1959), p. 45.

6. Judah P. Benjamin

Richard S. Tedlow

1. Gary Wills, "Kissinger as Disraeli?" *Moment* (1, no. 2) (July–August, 1975): 14-20; Bernard Kalb and Marvin Kalb, *Kissinger* (New York, 1974), pp. 60-61 (Kissinger claims not to like this comparison, but the blurb on the Kalbs' book nonetheless proclaims him: "America's Metternich . . . "); Patrick Anderson, "The Only Power Kissinger Has Is the Confidence of the President," *New York Times Magazine*, June 1, 1969, pp. 11 ff. A reading of numerous recent articles on Kissinger has failed to reveal any mention of Benjamin.

2. Pierce Butler, *Judah P. Benjamin* (Philadelphia, 1907), p. 24. It is hard to say how accurate this characterization is. Some of Benjamin's ancestors were men of distinction. His grandfather and namesake was at one time president of the Jewish Congregation on St. Eustatius. In 1814 he was, according to one scholar, living in Christiansted, St. Croix, where he owned eight slaves. Philip Benjamin, Judah's father, appears, according to Rabbi Malcolm H. Stern, a leading genealogist, "to have moved about a great deal." In the 1810s, after the birth of Judah, he moved to North Carolina thanks to the encouragement of his wife's uncle. By 1823 the Benjamins had moved to Charleston, South Carolina, which was then the largest Jewish community in North America. Philip joined the Reform Society of Israelites "and had the distinction of being the only member expelled." I would like to thank

Rabbi Stern (letter to author, November 11, 1976) and Dr. Joseph G. Adler (comments at Conference on Southern Jewish History, October 24, 1976) for the above information.

3. Ibid., p. 28; Robert D. Meade, *Judah P. Benjamin, Confederate Statesman* (New York, 1943), pp. 20-30.

4. S. I. Neiman, *Judah Benjamin* (Indianapolis, 1963), p. 31.

5. Rollin G. Osterweis, *Judah P. Benjamin, Statesman of the Lost Cause* (New York, 1933), p. 46.

6. Butler, *Benjamin*, p. 36.

7. Meade, *Benjamin*, p. 124.

8. John B. Jones, *A Rebel War Clerk's Diary* (New York, 1935), 1:166.

9. Quoted in Meade, *Benjamin*, p. 154.

10. Ibid., pp. 115-17.

11. Ibid., pp. 219-29.

12. *Twenty Years of Congress* (Norwich, Ct., 1884) 2:22-23; Goldwin Smith, "New Light on the Jewish Question," *North American Review* 153, no. 2 (August 1891): 129-43.

13. Sylvan M. Dubow, "Identifying the Jewish Serviceman in the Civil War," *American Jewish Historical Quarterly* [*AJHQ*] 59, (1970): 357-62.

14. Bertram W. Korn, "American Judaeophobia," in Leonard Dinnerstein and Mary Dale Palsson, eds., *Jews in the South* (Baton Rouge, La., 1973), pp. 137-40; Henry S. Foote, *The War of the Rebellion* (New York, 1866), pp. 352-53; Edward A. Pollard, *The Lost Cause* (New York, 1866), p. 213.

15. Max J. Kohler, *Judah P. Benjamin: Statesman and Jurist* (Baltimore, 1905), pp. 70, 85.

16. Butler, *Benjamin*, pp. 62, 428-29.

17. Rembert W. Patrick, *Jefferson Davis and the Confederate Cabinet* (Baton Rouge, La., 1944), p. 157. Patrick is wrong, however, in thinking Benjamin "forgot" the Confederacy. See Meade, *Benjamin*, pp. 361-62.

18. Meade, *Benjamin*, p. 158; Martin Rywell, *Judah Benjamin, Unsung Rebel Prince* (Ashville, N.C., 1948).

19. "An Act to Authorize the State of Florida to Accept as a Gift from Certain Public-Spirited Citizens of Manatee County the Property Known as Gamble Mansion, . . . as an Historical Monument of the Flight and Escape of Judah P. Benjamin. . . . " typescript, Benjamin Papers, American Jewish Historical Society, Waltham, Mass.

20. Robert D. Abrahams, *Mr. Benjamin's Sword* (Philadelphia, 1948). There is another recent novel about Benjamin. It is Vina Delmar's *Beloved* (New York, 1956). Ms. Delmar's other works include *Bad Girl, Loose Ladies, Kept Woman, Women Live Too Long*, and *The Marriage Racket*.

21. Bertram W. Korn, *Eventful Years and Experiences* (Cincinnati, 1954) p. 93.

22. Bertram W. Korn, "Jews and Negro Slavery in the Old South, 1789-1865," *Publications of the American Jewish Historical Society*. 50 (March 1961): 201, Abraham J. Karp, "Discussion: The Jews and the Liberal Tradition in America," *AJHQ* 51, (September 1961): 24; Benjamin Kaplan, "Judah Philip Benjamin," in Dinnerstein and Palsson, *Jews in the South*, p. 84; Hans L. Trefousse, *Benjamin Franklin Wade* (New York, 1963), p. 109.

23. Korn, *Eventful Years*, pp. 94-95, 142.

24. Leonard Dinnerstein, "A Neglected Aspect of Southern Jewish History," *AJHQ* 61, (September 1971): 66.

25. Ibid., p. 64.

26. Benjamin quoted from Butler, *Benjamin*, pp. 7-8; Meade, *Benjamin*, pp. vii-ix.

27. There are numerous brief comparisons to Disraeli in the Benjamin literature. The only one of any substance is Burton J. Hendricks, *Statesmen of the Lost Cause* (Boston, 1939), pp. 154-57, and even this is of limited usefulness.

28. Kohler, *Statesman and Jurist*, p. 83.

29. Davis quoted from Korn, *Eventful Years*, p. 84.

30. Robert Blake, *Disraeli* (London, 1966), pp. 201-5.

31. Cecil Roth, *Benjamin Disraeli* (New York, 1952), p. 58.

32. Blake, *Disraeli*, pp. 183-283.

33. Quoted from Roth, *Disraeli*, pp. 68, 70-71.

34. Blake, *Disraeli*, pp. 10-11.

35. Smith was enraged by Disraeli's portrayal of him in *Lothair*. Blake, *Disraeli*, pp. 511, 519.

36. In his comments on papers delivered at the Conference on Southern Jewish History on October 24, 1967, Dr. Joseph G. Adler showed that suggestive insights can be achieved by comparing Benjamin to his close friend and fellow antebellum senator David Levy Yulee.

7.   Charles Jacobson of Arkansas

Raymond Arsenault

1. John Higham, *Strangers in the Land: Patterns of American Nativism, 1860-1925* (New York, 1963), p. 92. See also Leonard Dinnerstein, "A Neglected Aspect of Southern Jewish History," *American Jewish Historical Quarterly* [*AJHQ*] 61 (September 1971): 57-62; Dinnerstein, *The Leo Frank Case* (New York, 1968), pp. vii-ix, 62–106; Higham, *Strangers in the Land*, pp. 92-94, 160-61, 185-86; Higham, *Send These To Me: Jews and Other Immigrants in Urban America* (New York, 1975), pp. 162-76; Oscar Handlin, "American Views of the Jew at the Opening of the Twentieth Century," *Publications of the American Jewish Historical Society* [*PAJHS*] 40 (June 1951):323–44; Harry Golden, "Jew and Gentile in the New South," *Commentary* 20 (November 1955): 403-12; William F. Holmes, "Whitecapping: Anti-Semitism in the Populist Era," *AJHQ* 63 (March 1974):245-61.

2. See Rowland T. Berthoff, "Southern Attitudes Toward Immigration, 1865-1914," *Journal of Southern History* 17 (August 1951):328-60; Charlton Mosely, "Latent Klanism in Georgia, 1890–1915," *Georgia Historical Quarterly* 56 (fall 1972):365-86; Clarence Cason, *Ninety Degrees In The Shade* (Chapel Hill, N.C., 1935), pp. 89, 106; Seymour Martin Lipset and Earl Raab, *The Politics of Unreason: Right-Wing Extremism in America, 1790–1970* (New York, 1970), chap. 3; Peter Viereck, *The Unadjusted Man* (Boston, 1956); Victor C. Ferkiss, "Populist Influences on American Fascism," *Western Political Quarterly* 10 (1957):350-73; Oscar Handlin, "Reconsidering the Populists," *Agricultural History* 39 (April 1965):68-74; and the essays in Daniel Bell, ed., *The New American Right* (New York, 1955).

3. Higham, *Send These To Me*, pp. 162, 170, 176.

4. The economic, social, religious, and political activities of the Southern Jewish community

are described in impressive detail in Cyrus Adler et al., eds., *The American Jewish Year Book* [*AJYB*], Vols. 1-17 (Philadelphia, 1899-1916); see especially vol. 9 (1907-8), pp. 124ff.

5. Based on an examination of the annual lists of American Jews elected or appointed to public office compiled by *AJYB*, vols. 1-42 (1899-1940); see also Eli N. Evans, *The Provincials: A Personal History of Jews in the South* (New York, 1973), appendixes A and B.

6. Among the region's leading Jewish politicians were: William Winter, state legislator from Shreveport, La. (*AJYB 1905-1906*, 7:194); M. Henry Cohen, a municipal judge (elected) in Tampa, Fla. (*AJYB 1906-1907*, 8:185); Ernest R. Bernstein, mayor of Shreveport, La. (*AJYB 1907-1908*, 9:477); Israel Moses, state legislator from Natchez, Miss. (*AJYB 1908-1909*, 10:121); Phillip Stern, state solicitor of Alabama (appointed) *(AJYB 1909-1910*, 11:232); Bertrand Weil, state senator from Alexandria, La. (*AJYB 1909-1910*, 11:233); Benjamin Kowalski, mayor of Brownsville, Tex. (*AJYB 1910–1911*, 12:329); Abe Cohn, state legislator from Memphis, Tenn. (*AJYB 1911-1912*, 13:278); J. E. Kaufman, state legislator from Galveston, Tex. (*AJYB* 1911-1912, 13:283); Benjamin A. Banks, state legislator from Norfolk, Va. (*AJYB 1912-1913*, 14:274); Laz Schwarz, mayor of Mobile, Ala. (*AJYB 1912-1913*, 14:286); J. Isaac Friedman, state legislator from Natchez, La. (*AJYB 1913-1914*, 15:257); Harry Goldstein, state legislator from Fernandina, Fla. (*AJYB 1913-1914*, 15:258); A. Greenhut, mayor of Pensacola, Fla. (*AJYB 1913-1914*, 15:258); Simon Leopold, state legislator from Phoenix, La. (*AJYB 1913-1914*, 15:261); David B. Samuel, state legislator from Shreveport, La. (*AJYB 1913-1914*, 15:265); Isidore Shapiro, state legislator from Birmingham, Ala. (*AJYB 1914-1915*, 16:160); Henry Faber, mayor of Montgomery, Ala. (*AJYB 1916-1917*, 18:107); Joseph Fromberg, state legislator from Charleston, S.C. (*AJYB 1915-1916*, 17:215); Mordecai Moses, mayor of Montgomery, Ala. (*AJYB 1919-1920*, 21:206); Simon Bloom, mayor of Pine Bluff, Ark. (*AJYB 1913-1914*, 15:265); L. S. Ehrich, mayor of Georgetown, S.C. (Evans, *The Provincials*, p. 336); in addition, Benjamin Franklin Jonas served as a United States senator from Louisiana from 1879 to 1885 (*AJYB 1910–1911*, 12:228).

7. For an estimate of the size of the Southern Jewish population at the turn of the century, see *AJYB 1901-1902*, 3:129.

8. See Dinnerstein, *The Leo Frank Case*, pp. 84-162; C. Vann Woodward, *Tom Watson: Agrarian Rebel* (New York, 1938), pp. 435–49.

9. See Ferkiss, "Populist Influences on American Fascism," pp. 350-73; Ferkiss, "Ezra Pound and American Fascism," *Journal of Politics* 7 (May 1955):173-97; Lipset and Raab, *The Politics of Unreason*, chaps. 1, 3; Edward A. Shils, *The Torment of Secrecy* (Glencoe, Ill., 1956); Viereck, *The Unadjusted Man*; and Bell, ed., *The New American Right*. For a critique of this view, see C. Vann Woodward, "The Populist Heritage and the Intellectual," pp. 141-66 in *The Burden of Southern History*, rev. ed. (Baton Rouge, La., 1968); Norman Pollack, "The Myth of Populist Anti-Semitism," *American Historical Review* 48 (October 1962):76-80; Pollack, "Hofstadter on Populism: A Critique of 'The Age of Reform,'" *Journal of Southern History* 26 (November 1960):478-500; Pollack, "Fear of Man: Populism, Authoritarianism, and the Historian," *Agricultural History* 39 (April 1965):59-67; Paul S. Holbo, "Wheat or What? Populism and American Fascism," *Western Political Quarterly* 14 (September 1961):727-36; and Michael Paul Rogin, *The Intellectuals and McCarthy: The Radical Specter* (Cambridge, Mass., 1967).

10. See Rupert B. Vance, "A Karl Marx for Hill Billies," *Social Forces* 9 (December 1930): 180- 90; Charles Jacobson, *The Life Story of Jeff Davis: The Stormy Petrel of Arkansas Politics* (Little Rock, Ark., 1925); L. S. Dunaway, ed., *Jeff Davis, Governor and United States Senator: His Life and Speeches* (Little Rock, Ark., 1913); and C. Vann Woodward, *Origins of the New South, 1877-1913* (Baton Rouge, La., 1951), pp. 376-77.

11. Jacobson, *Life Story of Jeff Davis*, p. 59.

12. Vance, "A Karl Marx for Hill Billies," p. 184.

13. Davis's father, Lewis W. Davis, served as a Baptist preacher in Sevier County, Arkansas, from 1850 to 1864. From 1864 to 1865, he was a chaplain in the Confederate Army. Though he abandoned the ministry for a law career in 1866, he remained active as a Baptist lay leader until his death in 1906. During the 1870s and 1880s, he was a delegate to several denominational and ecumenical conventions and served as the chairman of both the Pope County Sunday School Association and the Russellville Auxiliary of the American Bible Society. Bayless Walker Price, "The Life of Jeff Davis" (M.A. thesis, University of Alabama, 1929), p. 1; Jacobson, *Life Story of Jeff Davis*, p. 13; *Russellville (Ark.) Democrat*, February 9 and July 27, 1882, February 21, 1884, January 28, 1886, September 28, 1887; Dunaway, *Jeff Davis*, p. 220.

14. Dunaway, *Jeff Davis*, p. 55.

15. *Arkadelphia Southern Standard*, November 21, 1901; *Arkansas Gazette* (Little Rock), April 8, 1902.

16. *Arkansas Gazette* (Little Rock), April 8, 1902.

17. U.S. Bureau of the Census, *Census of Religious Bodies: 1906* (Washington, D.C., 1910), table 4, p. 297, reported that there were 673 Jewish heads of household in Arkansas in 1906; *AJYB 1904-1905*, 6:307, estimated that there were 3,085 Jews living in Arkansas in 1904. For a description of the organized Jewish community in Arkansas in 1906, see *AJYB 1907-1908*, 9:127-30.

18. *The Universal Jewish Encyclopedia* (New York, 1939-43), 1:481, 7:139; *Encyclopaedia Judaica* (Jerusalem, 1972), 3:459; *Who's Who in American Jewry, 1926* (New York, 1927), pp. 620-21; *AJYB 1908-1909*, 10:118, 119, 121, *1909-1910*, 11:226, *1910-1911*, 12:332, *1913-1914*, 15:255, 260, *1914-1915*, 16:160, 164, *1917-1918*, 19:250.

19. Fay Hempstead, *Historical Review of Arkansas: Its Commerce, Industry, and Modern Affairs* (Chicago, 1911), *U.S. Census 1880*, manuscript returns, population schedules for Saint Francois Township, Saint Francois County, Missouri, vol. 29, microfilm reel 714, p. 427, and for the town of Morrilton, Conway County, Arkansas, vol. 3, microfilm reel 41, p. 294, located in the National Archives, Washington, D.C.

20. The family of Simon Jacobson, Jacob Jacobson's older brother, moved to Morrilton from Farmington sometime in the early 1880s. *U.S. Census 1880*, manuscript returns, population schedules for Saint Francois Township, Saint Francois County, Missouri, vol. 29, microfilm reel 714, p. 427. *The Arkansas State Gazeteer and Business Directory for 1888-89* (Chicago, 1888), lists S. Jacobson as the proprietor of a general store in Perryville, Perry County. The *Arkansas State Gazeteer and Business Directory for 1892-93* ([Chicago, 1892], p. 327) lists Simon Jacobson as the proprietor of a general store in Morrilton. Apparently Simon was Jacob Jacobson's senior business partner. See also Fay Williams, *Arkansans of the Years* (Little Rock, Ark., 1953), 3:165.

21. *U.S. Census 1900*, manuscript returns, population schedules for Conway County,

Arkansas, located in the National Archives, Washington, D.C.; *U.S. Census 1900, Supplementary Analysis* (Washington, D.C., 1900), p. 264, lists the black population of Conway County as 25.1 percent in 1880, 39.4 percent in 1890, and 38.5 percent in 1900. For a description of Conway County, see *Historical Reminiscences and Biographical Memoirs of Conway County, Arkansas* (Little Rock, Ark. 1890).

22. *U.S. Census 1890, Population,* pt. 1, vol. 8 (Washington, D.C., 1895), pp. 755, 611.

23. *U.S. Census 1890, Statistics of Churches*, vol. 7 (Washington, D.C., 1895), p. 236; U.S. Bureau of the Census, *Census of Religious Bodies: 1906*, pp. 296-98, reported that there were 1,379 Catholics in Conway County in 1906. The *Arkansas Gazette* (Little Rock), August 19, 1900, reported that there were 556 white Baptists in Conway County in 1900.

24. Williams, *Arkansans of the Years*, 3:165.

25. Hempstead, *Historical Review of Arkansas*, p. 702.

26. Williams, *Arkansans of the Years*, 3:165.

27. Ibid.; Hempstead, *Historical Review of Arkansas*, pp. 702-3; Jacobson, *Life Story of Jeff Davis*, pp. 18-19.

28. Williams, *Arkansans of the Years*, 3:165.

29. Hempstead, *Historical Review of Arkansas*, p. 703; Jacobson, *Life Story of Jeff Davis*, p. 21.

30. See Clifton Paisley, "The Political Wheelers and Arkansas' Election of 1888," *Arkansas Historical Quarterly* 25 (spring 1966): 3-21; James Harris Fain, "Political Disfranchisement of the Negro in Arkansas" (M.A. thesis, University of Arkansas, 1961); W. Scott Morgan, *The Red Light: Southern Politics and Election Methods* (Moravian Falls, N.C., 1904); J. Morgan Kousser, *The Shaping of Southern Politics: Suffrage Restriction and the Establishment of the One-Party South 1880-1910* (New Haven, 1974), pp. 123-26.

31. Williams, *Arkansans of the Years*, 3:165. Even by Arkansas standards, Conway County politics in the late 1880s and early 1890s was a rough-and-tumble affair. Ballot-box stuffing, extralegal disfranchisement, physical violence–even murder–were all part of the game. For example, in January 1889 the county witnessed the cold-blooded assassination of John M. Clayton, a Republican candidate for Congress and the brother of Powell Clayton, the leader of the Arkansas Republican party. Having been defeated by questionable means in the November 1888 election, John Clayton formally contested the seating of his Democratic opponent, Clifton R. Breckenridge. Unfortunately for the Republicans, Clayton was shot in the back by an unknown assailant while he was examining contested ballots in the village of Plumerville. A short time later, when a close friend of Clayton's journeyed to Morrilton to investigate the murder, he too was gunned down. Although both murders were committed in broad daylight in front of several witnesses, neither crime was ever solved–primarily because local Democratic officials refused to take the matter seriously. Such were the politics on which young Charles Jacobson was nurtured. Powell Clayton, *The Aftermath of the Civil War in Arkansas* (New York, 1915).

32. Hempstead, *Historical Review of Arkansas*, p. 703.

33. Ibid.; Jacobson, *Life Story of Jeff Davis*, pp. 24-27, 31-36.

34. Williams, *Arkansans of the Years*, 3:166. In 1894 Conway County was the only county in the district to vote in favor of saloon licenses. In Yell, Pope, and Johnson counties, a majority of the electorate voted anti-license. In Conway County, the vote was 1186 pro-license and 444 anti-license. *Biennial Report of the Secretary of State of Arkansas, 1895-96* (Little Rock, 1897), pp. 63-64.

35. Williams, *Arkansans of the Years*, 3:166.

36. The primary vote in Conway County for attorney general was Davis, 1222; Baker, 198; Watson, 153; Hicks, 130. *Arkansas Gazette* (Little Rock), June 17, 1898.

37. Hempstead, *Historical Review of Arkansas*, p. 703; Jacobson, *Life Story of Jeff Davis*, pp. 31-41; Williams, *Arkansans of the Years*, 3:166.

38. Williams, *Arkansans of the Years*, 3:166; Hempstead, *Historical Review of Arkansas*, p. 703; *Arkansas Gazette* (Little Rock), January 13, 1900, January 10, 1901.

39. Jacobson, *Life Story of Jeff Davis*, p. 157.

40. Ibid., pp. 42-49.

41. Ibid., pp. 54-65; Williams, *Arkansans of the Years*, 3:167; Dunaway, *Jeff Davis*, pp. 46-70.

42. Jacobson, *Life Story of Jeff Davis*, pp. 209, 213, 64.

43. Williams, *Arkansans of the Years*, 3:167-68; Hempstead, *Historical Review of Arkansas*, pp. 703-4; *Arkansas Gazette* (Little Rock), May 4 and June 6, 1901, July 8, 1903.

44. Jacobson, *Life Story of Jeff Davis*, pp. 179-80; Dunaway, *Jeff Davis*, p. 76.

45. Jacobson, *Life Story of Jeff Davis*, pp. 19-20, 120, 123. Jacobson described his situation as follows: "Having been confined to the office pretty closely by reason of the fact that the work had to be done, I figured that as long as the Governor was getting the office, it was my duty to see that it kept going" (p. 123).

46. Williams, *Arkansans of the Years*, 3:167-68.

47. For information on Davis's advisors, see Dallas T. Herndon, ed., *Centennial History of Arkansas* (Little Rock, 1922), 2:786-87, on Jeptha Evans; Ibid., 2:589, and Hal L. Norwood, *"Just a Book," Reminiscent of Changes in Customs, Interesting Trials, and Other Events* (Mena, Ark., 1938), pp. 59-61, on Hal Norwood; Jerry Wallace, *An Arkansas Judge: Being a Sketch of the Life and Public Service of Judge J. G. Wallace 1850-1927* (n.p., 1928), on J. G. Wallace; Hempstead, *Historical Review of Arkansas*, 2:1274-75, on Webb Covington; Ibid., 2:855-56, on John Page; L. S. Dunaway, *What a Preacher Saw Through a Key-Hole in Arkansas* (Little Rock, 1925), p. 33, Herndon, *Centennial History of Arkansas*, 2:273-74, and Hempstead, *Historical Review of Arkansas*, 2:913, on J. V. Bourland; and Alexis Schwitalia, *Who's Who in Little Rock, 1921* (Little Rock, 1921), p. 71, on Jesse Hart. For a description of the Davis machine, see Dunaway, *Jeff Davis*, pp. 223-25.

48. Jacobson, *Life Story of Jeff Davis*, pp. 96-97.

49. *Arkansas Gazette* (Little Rock), September 27, 1903.

50. Jacobson, *Life Story of Jeff Davis*, pp. 28, 36, 73, 155, 159, 163-64, 172.

51. Ibid., 130-36.

52. Ibid., p. 130; Williams, *Arkansans of the Years*, 3:169.

53. Williams, *Arkansans of the Years*, 3:169.

54. Jacobson, *Life Story of Jeff Davis*, 132, 141.

55. Ibid., pp. 142-43, 169.

56. Ibid., pp. 182-87; Williams, *Arkansans of the Years*, 3:169.

57. Hempstead, *Historical Review of Arkansas*, pp. 702, 704; Williams, *Arkansans of the Years*, 3:171.

58. *Arkansas Gazette* (Little Rock), March 1-April 11, 1910; Williams, *Arkansans of the Years*, 3:169; Hempstead, *Historical Review of Arkansas*, p. 704.

59. *Journal of the Senate of Arkansas, 1911* (Little Rock, 1911), includes an index of bills introduced. See also p. 234.

60. Ibid., pp. 273, 359, 234, 417, 424, 214; Williams, *Arkansans of the Years*, p. 169; *Arkansas Gazette* (Little Rock), March 28–29, 1912, September 11-12, 1912.

61. Williams, *Arkansans of the Years*, 3:169; *Journal of the Senate of Arkansas, 1911* (extraordinary session) (Little Rock, 1911), pp. 705-7, 715-19, 723-25, 734; *Journal of the House of Representatives of Arkansas, 1911* (extraordinary session) (Little Rock, 1911), pp. 81-83; *Biennial Report of the Secretary of State of Arkansas, 1913* (Little Rock, 1913), pp. 408-10; the Turner-Jacobson bill was Act no. 1 in the September 1912 referendum; *Dardanelle Post-Dispatch*, September 14, 1911, August 1 and September 12, 1912.

62. *Arkansas Gazette* (Little Rock), May 1-15, 1913; *Journal of the Senate of Arkansas, 1913* (Little Rock, 1913), pp. 4, 78, 226.

63. Williams, *Arkansans of the Years*, 3:170, 163. Jacobson died in Little Rock on July 14, 1957, following a lengthy illness; *Arkansas Gazette* (Little Rock), July 15, 1957 (obituary). See also *Arkansas Democrat* (Little Rock), July 17, 1957.

64. Dinnerstein, *The Leo Frank Case*, pp. 95-106; Woodward, *Tom Watson, Agrarian Rebel*, pp. 437-39.

65. Dinnerstein, *The Leo Frank Case*, p. 93; *Arkansas Gazette* (Little Rock), April 15, 1914; *Fort Smith Southwest American*, April 1914.

66. *AJYB*, vols. 17-21 (1915-20).

67. *AJYB*, 19:250; *The Universal Jewish Encyclopedia*, 1:481. Louis Joseph returned to public life as a Texarkana municipal judge in 1927.

68. *Arkansas Gazette* (Little Rock), 1891-1915; *Arkadelphia Southern Standard*, 1886-1905, 1907-11; *Dardanelle Post-Dispatch*, 1900, 1904-5, 1907-13; *Arkansas Sentinel* (Fayetteville), 1898–1910; *Russellville Courier–Democrat, 1891-1906*; *The Arkansas Methodist*, 1900-1904; *Little Rock Democrat*, 1900-1915; *The Helena Weekly World*, 1895-1902; *Morgan's Buzz Saw* (Hardy, Ark.), 1894-1900; *Pine Bluff Commercial*, 1888-1900; *Pine Bluff Daily Graphic*, 1896-1912; *Nevada County Pecayune*, 1888-92, 1906-14; *Mena Weekly Star*, 1896-1913; *Newport Weekly Independent*, 1901-14; *Drew County Advance*, 1894-1906, 1912-13; and *Sharp County Record*, 1888-1914, were among the newspapers consulted.

69. Williams, *Arkansans of the Years*, 3:165. For a modern version of this problem, see Evans, *The Provincials*, 120-39.

70. Williams, *Arkansans of the Years*, 3:171; for a biographical sketch of Rabbi Louis Wolsey, see *AJYB 1903-1904*, 5:106.

71. *Arkansas Gazette* (Little Rock), quoted in the *Fayetteville Arkansas Sentinel*, January 22, 1901. *AJYB 1907-1908*, 9:129. Williams, *Arkansans of the Years*, 3:171, notes that Jacobson later served two terms as president of the Concordia Club.

72. Hempstead, *Historical Review of Arkansas*, p. 704; Williams, *Arkansans of the Years*, 3:170-71; *AJYB 1907-1908*, 9:129; *The Universal Jewish Encyclopedia*, 7:139; the program, "70th Anniversary Services and the Dedication of the New Altar, Congregation B'nai Israel, Little Rock, Arkansas, [March 5-6, 1937]," located in the B'nai Israel File in the Synagogue Collection of the American Jewish Historical Society Library, Waltham, Mass.

73. Williams, *Arkansans of the Years*, 3:171; Interview with Rabbi Ira Sanders, October 21, 1976.

74. Ibid., pp. 170-71; *Arkansas Gazette* (Little Rock), September 10, 1899.

75. Higham, *Send These To Me*, p. 170.

76. See Evans, *The Provincials*, pts. 3, 4; Harry Golden, *Our Southern Landsman* (New York, 1974).

77. *Arkansas Gazette* (Little Rock), July 5, 1899.

78. Williams, *Arkansans of the Years*, 3:165; Jacobson, *Life Story of Jeff Davis*, p. 159. During the 1911 legislative session Jacobson introduced an appropriations bill for a Confederate reunion to be held in Little Rock and a second bill which appropriated funds to restore and maintain the muster rolls and records of Arkansas's units of the Confederate Army; *Journal of the Senate of Arkansas, 1911*, pp. 98, 192, 237, 241.

79. Williams, *Arkansans of the Years*, 3:171; Hempstead, *Historical Review of Arkansas*, p. 704.

80. Williams, *Arkansans of the Years, 3:170.*

81. *Arkansas Gazette* (Little Rock), May 26 and September 2, 1900; Dunaway, *Jeff Davis*, pp. 58-59; *Fayetteville Arkansas Sentinel*, March 25, 1902.

82. Some of Little Rock's leading Jewish businessmen in the early twentieth century were Charles T. Abeles, Charles S. Stifft, Mark M. Cohen, Max Heiman, Leo Pfeifer, Gus Blass, Arthur Pfeifer, and Dan Daniel. Williams, *Arkansans of the Years*, 3:171. Morris M. Cohn was president of the Little Rock Board of Trade in 1899. *Arkansas Gazette* (Little Rock), March 26, 1899. See also *Arkansas State Gazeteer and Business Directory 1906-1907* (Chicago, 1906), 5:229-43, 368-439, for a sense of the Jewish business community in Fort Smith and Little Rock.

83. Jewish businessmen led the anti-Davis protest meetings during the 1899 antitrust controversy. *Arkansas Gazette* (Little Rock), March 26 and April 13, 1899, April 15, 1899-April 1, 1904, describes the running battle between Davis and Arkansas businessmen, Jew and Gentile alike.

8.   Jews and Other Southerners

Stephen J. Whitfield

1. Willie Morris, *Yazoo: Integration in a Deep-Southern Town* (New York, 1971), p. 148; Welty quoted in C. Vann Woodward, *The Burden of Southern History* (New York, 1961), pp. 23-24.

2. William Faulkner, "The Bear," in *Three Famous Short Novels* (New York, 1961), p. 277.

3. Isaac Babel, *Collected Stories* (London, 1961), p. 163; Mark Zborowsky and Elizabeth Herzog, *Life Is with People: The Culture of the Shtetl* (New York, 1962), pp. 55, 301, 307; "Oscar Solomon Straus: A German Immigrant in Georgia," in Jacob Rader Marcus, ed., *Memoirs of American Jews, 1775-1865* (Philadelphia, 1955), 2:298.

4. Francis Bello, "The Physicists," in Editors of *Fortune, Great American Scientists* (Englewood Cliffs, N.J., 1961), pp. 7-8.

5. *New York Herald Tribune*, April 11, 1933, quoted in Dan T. Carter, *Scottsboro: A Tragedy of the American South* (New York, 1969), p. 244; Ludwig Lewisohn, *Up Stream* (New York, 1922), pp. 36-37; Joseph Salvador to Emanuel Mendes da Costa, January 22, 1785, quoted in Cecil Roth, "A Description of America, 1785," *American Jewish Archives* 17 (April 1965): 29, 30.

6. Wilbur J. Cash, *The Mind of the South* (New York, 1941), p. 50.

7. O'Connor quoted in Robert Coles, *Farewell to the South* (Boston, 1972), p. 136.

8. Harold Nicolson, *Diaries and Letters: The War Years, 1939-1945* (New York, 1967), 2:469.

9. William Alexander Percy, *Lanterns on the Levee: Recollections of a Planter's Son* (New York, 1941), pp. 17, 138-39.

10. William Faulkner, *The Sound and the Fury* (New York, 1956), p. 209; *Jewish Sentiment*, October 5, 1900, p. 3, quoted in Steven Hertzberg, "The Jewish Community of Atlanta from the End of the Civil War until the Eve of the Frank Case," *American Jewish Historical Quarterly* [*AJHQ*] 62 (March 1973): 285.

11. "Isidor Straus: A Young Confederate Businessman," in Marcus, ed., *Memoirs of American Jews*, 2:304.

12. Leonard Dinnerstein, "A Note on Southern Attitudes toward Jews," *Jewish Social Studies* 32 (1970): 49; John Higham, *Strangers in the Land: Patterns of American Nativism, 1860-1925* (New York, 1965), p. 92.

13. Watson quoted in C. Vann Woodward, *Tom Watson: Agrarian Rebel* (New York, 1938), pp. 438, 445.

14. James MacGregor Burns, *Roosevelt: The Soldier of Freedom* (New York, 1970), p. 431; Rankin quoted in John P. Roche, *The Quest for the Dream* (Chicago, 1963), p. 217.

15. William F. Holmes, "Whitecapping: Anti-Semitism in the Populist Era," *AJHQ* 63 (March 1974): 249; C. Vann Woodward, *Origins of the New South, 1877-1913* (Baton Rouge, La., 1951), p. 188; Louis Galambos, *The Public Image of Big Business in America, 1880–1940* (Baltimore, 1975), pp. 63-64.

16. John Higham, "Social Discrimination against Jews in America, 1830-1930," *AJHQ* 47 (September 1957): 30-31; Arnold Shankman, "Atlanta Jewry, 1900-1930," *American Jewish Archives* 25 (November 1973): 152.

17. Henry L. Mencken, *Prejudices: A Selection* (New York, 1958), p. 73.

18. Bernard Baruch, *My Own Story* (New York, 1957), pp. 48, 49; Stanley Marcus, *Minding the Store: A Memoir* (Boston, 1974), pp. 27, 32-33; Charles Herbert Stember, "The Recent History of Public Attitudes," in Stember et al., *Jews in the Mind of America* (New York, 1966), p. 224; Hartley quoted in Richard Hofstadter, *Anti-Intellectualism in American Life* (New York, 1963), p. 133.

19. Ruffin quoted in William R. Taylor, *Cavalier and Yankee: The Old South and the American National Character* (New York, 1961), p. 339.

20. Elizabeth Nowell, *Thomas Wolfe: A Biography* (Garden City, N.Y., 1960), pp. 86, 98; Cash, *Mind of the South*, pp. 333-34.

21. Russell Kirk, *Eliot and His Age* (New York, 1971), pp. 209-10; W. W. Thornton, *American Hebrew* 42 (April 4, 1890):191, quoted in Leonard Dinnerstein, "Introduction" to Dinnerstein and Mary Dale Paisson, ed., *Jews in the South* (Baton Rouge, La., 1973), pp. 17-18.

22. Hodding Carter, *Where Main Street Meets the River* (New York, 1953), pp. 185, 186; Cash, *Mind of the South*, p. 334; Woodward, *Tom Watson*, p. 433; Arthur M. Schlesinger, Jr., *A Thousand Days: John F. Kennedy in the White House* (Boston, 1965), p. 74.

23. Jonathan Daniels, *A Southerner Discovers the South* (New York, 1938), pp. 258-59; Wilson quoted in A. L. Todd, *Justice on Trial: The Case of Louis D. Brandeis* (New York, 1964), p. 138; Lawrence J. Friedman, *The White Savage: Racial Fantasies in the Postbellum South* (Englewood Cliffs, N.J., 1970), p. 164-65.

24. Eli N. Evans, *The Provincials: A Personal History of Jews in the South* (New York, 1973), p. 189; Dixon quoted in Raymond A. Cook, *Thomas Dixon* (New York, 1974), p. 63.

25. Hugh Sidey, "Impressions of Power and Poetry," *Time*, June 20, 1972, p. 31; Nathan Perlmutter, *A Bias of Reflections: Confessions of an Incipient Old Jew* (New Rochelle, N.Y., 1972), p. 66.

26. Hellman quoted in Eric Bentley, ed., *Thirty Years of Treason* (New York, 1971), p. 537; James K. Feibleman, *The Way of a Man: An Autobiography* (New York, 1969), p. 67; Arthur Krock, *Memoirs: Sixty Years on the Firing Line* (New York, 1968), pp. xii, 8.

27. Hortense Calisher, *Herself* (New York, 1972), p. 59; Ludwig Lewisohn, *Up Stream*, pp. 77, 101; Stanley F. Chyet, "Ludwig Lewisohn in Charleston, 1892-1902," *AJHQ* 54 (March 1965):312.

28. "Isaac Leeser: American Jewish Missionary," in Marcus, ed., *Memoirs of American Jews*, 2:68.

29. Evans, *The Provincials*, p. 276; Alfred O. Hero, Jr., "Southern Jews," in Dinnerstein and Palsson, eds., *Jews in the South*, p. 247.

30. Samuel Rosinger, "Deep in the Heart of Texas," in Stanley F. Chyet, ed., *Lives and Voices: A Collection of American Jewish Memoirs* (Philadelphia, 1972), p. 134; Ulrich B. Phillips, "The Central Theme of Southern History," *American Historical Review* 34 (October 1928): 30-43.

31. Feibleman, *Way of a Man*, p. 49. Bertram Wallace Korn, "Jews and Negro Slavery in the Old South, 1789-1865," in Dinnerstein and Palsson, eds., *Jews in the South*, pp. 123-25, 130.

32. David L. Cohn, *Where I Was Born and Raised* (Boston, 1948), pp. 20-21.

33. Tennessee Williams, *Penguin Plays* (London, 1962), pp. 301, 302, 303.

34. David Byck quoted in Harry Golden, *Travels through Jewish America* (Garden City, N.Y., 1973), p. 180.

35. Faulkner, "The Bear," p. 279.

36. James B. Pritchard, *Ancient Near Eastern Texts* (Princeton, N.J., 1955), pp. 376, 378.

9. Friend or Foe?

Arnold Shankman

1. John Cauthen, *Speaker Blatt: His Challenges Were Greater* (Columbia, S.C., 1965), pp. 27-28; Sylvia Orange, ed., *1974 South Carolina Legislative Manual* (Columbia, S.C., 1974), pp. 2-3; Solomon Blatt to Arnold Shankman, March 30, 1976.

2. Philip S. Foner, "Black-Jewish Relations in the Opening Years of the Twentieth Century," *Phylon* 36 (December 1975):359-76; Philip Foner, *American Socialism and Black Americans* (Westport, Conn., 1977); Lawrence Levine, *Black Culture and Black Consciousness* (New York, 1977); Eugene Levy, "Is the Jew a White Man? Press Reaction to the Leo Frank Case, 1913-1915," *Phylon* 35 (June 1974):212-22. Of lesser value is Oscar Williams, "Historical Impressions of Black-Jewish Relations prior to World War II," *Negro History Bulletin* 40 (July-August 1977):728-31, which cites few primary black journals in its notes. In unpublished form is David Hellwig's valuable "The Afro-American and the Immigrant, 1880-1930," (Ph.D. dissertation, Syracuse University, 1973), chap. 7, and Stephen Hertzberg, "The Jews of Atlanta, 1865-1915" (Ph.D. dissertation, the University of Chicago), chap. 8.

3. I have based my conclusions on work I have done on blacks and other immigrant groups. See, for example, "The Image of Mexico and the Mexican-American in the Black Press, 1890-1935," *The Journal of Ethnic Studies* 3 (summer 1975):43-56; " 'Asiatic Ogre' or 'Desir-

able Citizen'? The Image of Japanese Americans in the Afro-American Press, 1867–1933," *Pacific Historical Review* 46 (November 1977):567–87; "Black on Yellow: Afro-Americans View Chinese Americans, 1850–1935," *Phylon* 39 (March 1978):1–17.

4. T. Thomas Fortune, unsigned editorial note, *New York Age*, August 21, 1913. See also Thomas Clark, *Pills, Petticoats, and Plows: the Southern Country Store* (Norman, Okla., 1964), pp. 6–7; and Clark, "The Post-Civil War Economy in the South," in Leonard Dinnerstein and Mary Dale Palsson, eds., *Jews in the South* (Baton Rouge, La., 1973), pp. 159–69.

5. John Dollard, *Caste and Class in a Southern Town* (New Haven, 1937), p. 129. See also William Ivy Hair, *Bourbonism and Agrarian Protest: Louisiana Politics, 1887–1900* (Baton Rouge, La., 1969), pp. 158–60; Allison Davis, Burleigh Gardner, and Mary Gardner, *Deep South* (Chicago, 1941), p. 264.

6. Maurice Evans, *Black and White in the Southern States* (London, 1915), pp. 56–58, 105. See also Hortense Powdermaker, *After Freedom* (New York, 1939), p. 9; Steven Hertzberg, "The Jews of Atlanta," chap. 8.

7. Dollard, *Caste and Class*, pp. 4, 129–130. Dollard does not imply that by bargaining with blacks, Jews cheated or overcharged their Negro patrons. In Natchez, Mississippi, "When a few Jewish merchants in a Negro shopping area broke . . . caste rules [and called Negroes 'Mr.' and 'Mrs.,'] they were roundly condemned by other white merchants." See Davis, Gardner, and Gardner, *Deep South*, p. 459; see also Harry Golden, *Forgotten Pioneer* (Cleveland, 1963), pp. 33, 40; Hertzberg, "Jews of Atlanta," pp. 286–88.

8. Booker T. Washington, *The Man Farthest Down* (Garden City, N.Y., 1912), pp. 240–41; Eli Shepperd, *Plantation Songs* (New York, 1901), pp. 135–36; J. Mason Brewer, *American Negro Folklore* (New York, 1968), pp. 147–59; Charles Nichols, *Many Thousand Gone: The Ex-Slaves' Account of Their Bondage and Freedom* (Bloomington, Ind., 1969), pp. 96–97; Henry Feingold, *Zion in America* (New York, 1974), pp. 59–60. See also William Wells Brown, *My Southern Home* (New York, 1969), pp. 86–87; Kate Picard, *The Kidnapped and the Ransomed: The Narrative of Peter and Vina Still* (Philadelphia, 1970), passim, especially the introduction by Maxwell Whiteman; Levine, *Black Culture and Black Consciousness*, pp. 23, 43, 50.

9. Horace Mann Bond, "Negro Attitudes Towards Jews," in Meir Ben-Horin, comp., *Negro-Jewish Relations in the United States* (New York, 1966), p. 4; Kelly Miller, "The Cultural Kingship [*sic*] of Negro and Jew," *Richmond Planet*, April 20, 1935, hereafter cited as "Cultural Kinship." See also Benjamin Mays, *The Negro's God* (New York, 1968), pp. 25–28; James Weldon Johnson, *The Book of American Negro Spirituals* (New York, 1925), pp. 20–25.

10. Pinchback, quoted in *Alexandria* (Va.) *People's Advocate*, April 29, 1876; *Richmond Planet*, September 29, 1900. *Richmond Reformer*, n.d., quoted in *Savannah Tribune*, July 8, 1911. See also Raymond Gavins, *The Perils and Prospects of Southern Black Leadership: Gordon Blaine Hancock, 1884–1970* (Durham, N.C., 1977), p. 89.

11. Unidentified clergyman cited in speech of Booker T. Washington, in Louis Harlan, ed., *The Booker T. Washington Papers* (Urbana, Ill., 1972), 2:446. See also Hertzberg, "Jews of Atlanta," p. 305.

12. Washington, *The Man Farthest Down*, pp. 241, 257. See also, "The Hebrew Race in America," *The Voice of the Negro* (Atlanta) 3 (January 1906):20.

13. *Norfolk Journal and Guide*, January 14 and November 25, 1922, September 22, 1923.

14. Washington, *The Man Farthest Down,* p. 382. See also *Savannah Tribune,* May 4, 1912; *Atlanta Independent,* September 21, 1907; Booker T. Washington, *Putting the Most into Life* (New York, 1906), p. 33; *Indianapolis Leader,* n.d., quoted in *Alexandria* (Va.) *People's Advocate,* March 27, 1880; *New Orleans Louisianian,* August 6, 1881.

15. See, for example, C. E. Chapman's article on Memphis, "The Gristmill," *Kansas City* (Kans.) *Call,* December 27, 1935.

16. The advertisements mentioned above came from issues of the *Arkansas Mansion* (Little Rock) (1883-84); *Richmond Southern News* (1893); *Richmond Planet* (1913-15); *Georgetown* (S.C.) *Planet* (1873); *Raleigh Gazette* (1894, for Rosenbaum's of New Bern, N.C.); *Columbia* (S.C.) *Southern Indicator* (1921); *Atlanta Independent* (1906-1907); *Savannah Echo* (1883-84); *Savannah Tribune* (various years); *Norfolk Journal and Guide* (1916-23). Other cities in which Jews were prominent advertisers in black journals include Nashville, Tulsa, and Lexington, Kentucky.

17. *Columbia* (S.C.) *Southern Indicator,* August 6, 1921. There is no simple way to determine the religion of the owners of firms bearing such names as Peachtree Tailor Shop, Ace Jewelry, Sam's Drugs, or Queen City Clothing.

18. Harlan, *Booker T. Washington Papers,* 3:408-9; *Savannah Tribune,* September 26, 1914. See also Hellwig, "Afro-American and the Immigrant," p. 146.

19. *Columbia* (S.C.) *Southern Indicator,* October 15, 1921. See also *Norfolk Journal and Guide,* March 5, 1921; T. Thomas Fortune, "The Passing Show," *Norfolk Journal and Guide,* February 11, 1928.

20. Richard Bowling, "Jews and Discipline," *Norfolk Journal and Guide,* December 15, 1928. See also *Richmond Planet,* April 13, 1935; *Atlanta Independent,* October 22, 1931, and February 25, 1932.

21. *Atlanta Independent,* July 8, 1926; D. A. Hart, quoted in *Nashville Globe,* December 2, 1910. See also unidentified newspaper quoted in *Savannah Tribune,* December 13, 1923; *Chicago Whip,* n.d., quoted in *Savannah Tribune,* October 22, 1931; Kelly Miller, "The Negro and the Jew in Business," *Richmond Planet,* April 13, 1935 (hereafter cited as "Jew in Business"); *Houston Informer and Texas Freeman,* September 19, 1931.

22. *Savannah Tribune,* December 13, 1923. See also Hertzberg, "The Jews of Atlanta," p. 287.

23. *Savannah Tribune,* December 13, 1923; Miller, "Jew in Business."

24. See *Atlanta Independent,* October 7, 1926, January 20, 1927, and scattered issues for 1929.

25. Golden, *Forgotten Pioneer,* pp. 70-73, and Golden, *Jewish Roots in the Carolinas* (Charlotte, N.C., 1955), p. 47. See also Hertzberg, "The Jews of Atlanta," pp. 285-86.

26. Lorenzo Greene and Carter G. Woodson, *The Negro Wage Earner* (New York, 1969), p. 120; statement of Madden in *Report of the Fifteenth Annual Convention, National Negro Business League* (Nashville, 1915), pp. 164-65. Things had not always been so good for blacks and their Jewish employers. In Franklin, Tennesse, in 1868, the Ku Klux Klan lynched a liberal Jewish merchant and his Negro employee. See Morris U. Schappes, ed., *A Documentary History of the Jews in the United States, 1654-1875* (New York, 1952), pp. 515-17. On the lynching of Samuel Fleishman, who urged blacks to retaliate against the Ku Klux Klan, see Jessie Fortune, "Among the Children of the East Side Jews (1905)," ed. Arnold Shankman, *Jewish Currents* 29 (February 1975):4.

27. Miller, "Cultural Kinship" and "Jew in Business."

28. *Savannah Tribune*, August 7, 1924; "What Ben Davis Says," *Atlanta Independent*, March 5, 1931; Gordon Hancock, "Between the Lines," *Norfolk Journal and Guide*, October 11, 1930; *Norfolk Journal and Guide*, February 14, 1931.

29. W. E. B. Du Bois tells of a Russian Jew who cheated a rural Georgia black of his land and fled the scene, forcing the man to work on "his" own land for thirty cents a day. (Du Bois, *The Souls of Black Folk* [Chicago, 1931], pp. 133, 170). Jacob Schiff, Stephen Wise, and Morris Schappes called Du Bois's attention to the fact that some readers might see anti-Semitic implications in his unfavorable references to Russian Jews. After 1952, editions of *The Souls of Black Folk* omitted remarks that could mistakenly be considered anti-Jewish. Herbert Aptheker, "*The Souls of Black Folk:* A Comparison of the 1903 and 1952 Editions," *Negro History Bulletin* 34 (January 1971):15–17; Morris Schappes to Philip Foner, February 11, 1976 (copy in my possession); Schappes to Arnold Shankman, June 27, 1976. For other material on black images of Jews as money grubbers see Levine, *Black Culture and Black Consciousness,* p. 305; Hertzberg, "Jews of Atlanta," chap. 8.

30. Miller, "Jew in Business." See also *Norfolk Journal and Guide,* April 28, 1917; *Chicago Whip,* n.d., quoted in *Savannah Tribune,* May 25, 1922; Dr. H. R. Butler, "He Came to His Own, and His Own Received Him Not," *Atlanta Independent,* December 30, 1926, hereafter cited as "He Came"; S. B. Williams, "Cimbee's Rambles," *Houston Informer and Texas Freeman,* July 22, 1933.

31. *Atlanta Independent,* June 23, 1927; caption under pictures of Cohen's Saloon (whites only) and Abelsky's Saloon (colored only), in Ray Stannard Baker, *Following the Color Line* (New York, 1908), between pages 34 and 35. See also Hertzberg "Jews of Atlanta," p. 287.

32. *New Orleans Louisianian,* July 23, 1881; account of Brunswick incident in *Baltimore Afro-American,* October 18, 1902. *Tulsa Star,* December 12, 1914; *Savannah Tribune,* September 6, 1934; *Houston Informer and Texas Freeman,* August 18, 1934.

33. *Chicago Whip,* n.d., quoted in *Savannah Tribune,* May 25, 1922; Kelly Miller, "Jew in Business," and Miller, "Cultural Kinship." See also Dr. H. R. Butler, "The High Cost of Prejudice," *Atlanta Independent,* June 14, 1928; letter from Jackson McHenry of Atlanta, quoted in *Atlanta Independent,* October 31, 1914. It is the writer's impression that blacks were more willing to denounce Jewish businessmen than Gentiles for unfair treatment of Negro customers.

34. Editorial on Jews as the friend of blacks in *Savannah Tribune,* November 15, 1913. The topic of Jews helping blacks is well treated in Hasia Diner, "In the Almost Promised Land: Jewish Leaders and Blacks, 1915–1935" (Ph.D. dissertation, University of Illinois, Chicago Circle, 1975), chaps. 2, 3, hereafter cited as "Promised Land."

35. Praise of Solomon in *Savannah Tribune,* February 17, 1927. *Savannah Tribune* November 15, 1931, and October 27, 1927; Diner, "Promised Land," pp. 148–49, 164–65, 180, 196; *Richmond Planet,* May 13, 1899; *Norfolk Journal and Guide,* March 5, 1921, November 25, 1922; S. B. Williams, "Cimbee's Rambles," *Houston Informer and Texas Freeman,* April 8, 1933. For information on Josiah Morse, a Jewish professor at the University of South Carolina, see Marion Wright and Arnold Shankman, "Two Southerners Who Made a Difference," *Jewish Currents* 31 (February 1977):22–26, and Marion Wright, *Human Rights Odyssey* (Durham, N.C., 1978), pp. 4–6, 24–25. On Rabbi David Marx see Ann Ellis, "The Commission on Interracial Cooperation" (Ph.D. dissertation, Georgia State University, 1975), passim. Probably few Southern blacks in 1928 knew that the Association of Jewish Charities and Settlement Workers boycotted the annual meeting of the National Conference on Social

Work which was being held in Memphis. The reason for the boycott was that black delegates would be forced to endure segregated facilities. Nor did many blacks know that seven
years earlier, in 1921, the Workman's Circle refused to become chartered in several Southern
states because incorporation laws required that membership be limited to whites. The
Workman's Circle did not expect blacks to apply for membership, but it believed that
incorporation would imply sanctioning racism. Black journals seemed to ignore the contributions of Rabbi Ben Goldstein-Lowell. See Herman Pollack, "A Forgotten Fighter for Justice:
Ben Goldstein-Lowell," *Jewish Currents* 30 (June 1976):14–18.

36. Washington, *Man Farthest Down*, p. 255. In their efforts to be helpful, Jewish philan-
thropists even brought Aaron Aaronsohn, director of the Jewish Agricultural Experimental
Station in Palestine, to talk about farming to Tuskegee students. Diner, "Promised Land,"
pp. 148–49.

37. Letter from Leon Miller of Welch, West Virginia, to *Crisis* 43 (April 1936):122; letter
of J. E. Malone of Mobile, ibid. (March 1936):80; *Louisville News*, n.d., quoted in *Cleveland
Gazette*, May 1, 1926.

38. Editorial entitled "Our Lake Resorts," *New Orleans Louisianian*, July 23, 1881. The
Louisianian was the only paper located that regularly portrayed Jews in an unfavorable
light. The editor and correspondents to the paper seemed persuaded that Jews were among
the foremost opponents of the Negro. Rolla, the newspaper's Washington correspondent,
alleged, "It is a melancholy fact that the Jews in order to curry favor with the ruling classes,
are, except in a few sections, classed with the negro haters." Letter from Rolla, Washington,
D.C., September 20, 1879, quoted in the *Louisianian*, October 4, 1879. See also letter from
James Kennedy, sent November 10, 1879, while traveling through Delta and Water Proof,
La., ibid., November 15, 1879, and item printed ibid., June 25, 1881, p. 2.

39. Crosswaith, "Contrast Worth Noting," in both *Atlanta Independent*, September 25,
1930, and *Savannah Tribune*, October 2, 1930; *Norfolk Journal and Guide*, April 28, 1917.
See also Butler, "He Came"; Booker T. Washington, *The Future of the American Negro*
(New York, 1969), p. 183; Washington, *Putting the Most into Life*, pp. 30–31; address of
Washington at Hampton Institute, May 1905, quoted in *Southern Workman* (Hampton,
Va.) 34 (July 1905):405; Washington, *Man Farthest Down*, p. 263; *The Voice of the Negro*
3 (January 1906):20; *Savannah Tribune*, August 19, 1899, July 14, 1927.

40. *Savannah Tribune*, July 14, 1927. Blacks seemed unaware that many B'nai B'rith lodges
barred Russian Jews from membership before the 1930s. See unidentified black newspaper
quoted in *Alexandria* (Va.) *People's Advocate*, March 27, 1880; *Savannah Tribune*, November
15, 1913; *Houston Informer and Texas Freeman*, September 19, 1931, and May 27, 1933.

41. Article on a sermon by a rabbi on the way Judaism idealizes marriage, reported in *Houston Informer and Texas Freeman*, March 21, 1931; editorial comment on Jewish history in
Atlanta Independent, February 7, 1914.

42. T. Thomas Fortune, "The Passing Show," *Norfolk Journal and Guide*, February 11,
1928; *Savannah Tribune*, December 13, 1923. Plainly blacks underrated tensions between
parents and children on such questions as education, assimilation, and pride in one's heritage.
See also *Savannah Tribune*, October 12, 1889; *Norfolk Journal and Guide*, December 3, 1921;
Booker T. Washington, *The Man Farthest Down*, p. 263; Eugene Hayne, "The African in
America," *The Voice of the Negro* 3 (August 1906):565.

43. Baskerville, "Too Many Churches," *Atlanta Independent*, October 9, 1930; *Richmond*

Reformer, n.d., quoted in *Savannah Tribune,* July 8, 1911; Goodall's sermon quoted in *Savannah Tribune,* October 23, 1915.

44. The Reverend Ernest Hall, "Hall's Review," *Atlanta Independent,* June 17, 1926. *Savannah Tribune,* April 20, 1918, November 2, 1920, and October 22, 1931; *Richmond Planet,* November 10, 1934.

45. *Norfolk Journal and Guide,* January 14, 1922; *New Orleans Weekly Pelican,* November 2, 1889; Helen Chesnutt, *Charles Waddell Chesnutt* (Chapel Hill, N.C., 1952), pp. 22-23. See also Hair, *Bourbonism and Agrarian Protest,* pp. 158-60; William F. Holmes, "White-capping: Anti-Semitism in the Populist Era," *American Jewish Historical Quarterly* 64 (March 1974):245-61.

46. *California Eagle* (Los Angeles), May 8, 1925; *Chicago Defender,* July 7, 1928. For informa-tion on Negro reaction to the Frank lynching see Levy, "Is the Jew a White Man?" passim, and Levy, *James Weldon Johnson* (Chicago, 1973), pp. 158-59; Martinsburg (W. Va.) *Pioneer Press,* August 28, 1915. For more on Needleman see *New York Times,* March 30, 1925.

47. *Houston Informer and Texas Freeman,* October 4, 1930.

48. *Savannah Tribune,* April 11, 1929; *Richmond Planet,* May 14, 1910; J. A. Rogers, "News Commentators Ignorant of the Psychology of American Color Complex," *Savannah Tribune,* July 4, 1935. See also Hall, "Hall's Review," *Atlanta Independent,* June 17, 1926.

49. Crosswaith, "Contrast Worth Noting," *Savannah Tribune,* October 2, 1930. In 1912, when a dark-complexioned Russian Jew and a light-skinned white woman entered a fashion-able café in Arkansas, the man was mistaken for a Negro. Local whites were incensed, and had the Jew not been a rapid runner, he would probably have been lynched. *Pine Bluff* (Ark.) *Herald,* n.d., quoted in *Pittsburgh Courier,* February 24, 1912.

50. *Savannah Tribune,* November 15, 1913, April 11, 1929; "Colorful News Movies," *Savannah Tribune,* March 24, 1927; *Richmond Reformer,* January 27, 1900; *Norfolk Journal and Guide,* July 16, 1927. See also *Richmond Planet,* June 27, 1936.

51. Butler, "He Came"; *Norfolk Journal and Guide,* June 12, 1926.

52. *Savannah Tribune,* January 14, 1932; *Norfolk Journal and Guide,* May 22, 1926; *Atlanta Independent,* October 22, 1931.

53. *Houston Informer and Texas Freeman,* April 8, 1933; *Richmond Planet,* November 10, 1934. Similar comments can be found in *Richmond Planet,* March 24, 1934; *Norfolk Journal and Guide,* September 30, 1916; *Savannah Tribune,* May 30 and July 11, 18, 1903, August 26, 1905. See also Foner, "Black Jewish Relations," passim, and Foner, *American Socialism and Black Americans,* pp. 107-8; Arnold Shankman, "Brothers Across the Sea: Afro-Amer-icans on the Persecution of Russian Jews, 1881-1917," *Jewish Social Studies* 37 (1975):114-21.

54. Letter from Rolla, Washington, D.C., September 20, 1879, on Jews as "Negro haters," quoted in the *New Orleans Louisianian,* October 4, 1879; Richard Wright, *Black Boy* (New York, 1945), p. 215; "The Cameraman," *Richmond Planet,* January 31, 1925; Foner, "Black-Jewish Relations," pp. 365-66; Hertzberg, "Jews of Atlanta," p. 308; *Kansas City* (Kans.) *Call,* April 3, 1931.

55. Letter from Samuel Rosenberg, *Crisis* 43 (April 1936):122; Hortense Powdermaker, *Stranger and Friend* (New York, 1966), p. 195. Golden, *Jewish Roots in the Carolinas,* p. 47; Hertzberg, "Jews of Atlanta," pp. 297-98.

56. Charles Rubin, *The Log of Rubin the Sailor* (New York, 1973), p. 15. Vladeck also complained when he learned that Bernard Cone, a Jewish textile-mill owner in North

Carolina, had fired some black workers for joining a union. See Diner, "In the Almost Promised Land," pp. 409–10; Foner, *American Socialism and Black Americans,* p. 239. See also Hertzberg, "Jews of Atlanta," pp. 296–97.

57. Bond, "Negro Attitudes Towards Jews," pp. 3–4; *New York Times,* May 4, 1964. See also Hertzberg, "Jews of Atlanta," pp. 300–301; spiritual on the death of Jesus quoted in Brewer, *American Negro Folklore,* p. 161.

58. Another taunt went:

> Jew, Jew
> Two for five
> That's what keeps
> Jew alive. (Wright, *Black Boy,* p. 53)

Spiritual on Jews killing Jesus and placing him in a tomb quoted in the Reverend H. H. Proctor, "The Theology of the Songs of the Southern Slave," *Southern Workman* 36 (November 1907):587; spiritual on Jews and Romans hanging Jesus from Thomas Wentworth Higginson, "Negro Spirituals," *Atlantic Monthly* 19 (June 1867):685–94, quoted in Bruce Jackson, ed., *The Negro and His Folklore* (Austin, Texas, 1967), p. 90; Wright, *Black Boy,* pp. 53–54. For evidence of other spirituals and chants blaming the death of Jesus on Jews, see sources listed in note 57 above.

59. Butler, "He Came"; letter from Vass in *Richmond Planet,* April 29, 1899. The *Savannah Tribune* favored the "rehabilitation of Palestine by the Jews" in its September 5, 1929, issue.

60. Powdermaker, *Stranger and Friend,* p. 145.

61. "The Hebrew Race in America," *The Voice of the Negro* 3 (January 1906):20; Bowling, "Jews and Discipline," *Norfolk Journal and Guide,* December 15, 1928. See also *New York Age,* August 21, 1913.

62. Barry Supple, "A Business Elite: German Jewish Financiers in Nineteenth Century New York," *Business History Review* 31 (1957):151. Oscar and Mary Flug Handlin, *A Century of Jewish Immigration to the United States* (New York, 1949), p. 16.

63. Joseph Weill to Morris Waldman, December 16, 1907 [copy], Papers Relating to the Galveston Immigration Plan and the Industrial Removal Office, American Jewish Historical Society, Waltham, Mass.; David M. Bressler to Waldman, October 15, 1906, ibid. See also note 3 above.

64. B. C. Baskerville, "Too Many Churches," *Atlanta Independent,* October 9, 1930.

65. *Savannah Tribune,* May 13, 1893. See also *Norfolk Journal and Guide,* May 22, 1926.

66. T. Thomas Fortune, "The Passing Show," *Norfolk Journal and Guide,* February 11, 1928; *Atlanta Independent,* January 3, 1914. See also *Norfolk Journal and Guide,* May 22, 1926, July 16, 1927; S. B. Williams, "Cimbee's Rambles," *Houston Informer and Texas Freeman,* April 8, 1933.

10. Jewish Values in the Southern Milieu

Abraham D. Lavender

1. Robert Coles, for example, notes the Southern whites' resentment of "hypocritical and patronizing upper middle class Northerners": see Coles, "Jimmy Carter: Agrarian Rebel?"

New Republic, June 26, 1976, p. 18. Coles also notes that blacks are "increasingly disappointed by, if not enraged at, Northern pretensions and airs of superiority" (p. 17) and view the South as "home."

2. E. Brooks Holifield, "The Three Strands of Jimmy Carter's Religion," *New Republic,* June 5, 1976, p. 17.

3. This point has been made by several writers. See Leonard Dinnerstein, "A Note on Southern Attitudes toward Jews," *Jewish Social Studies* 32 (January 1970): 43–49; Alfred O. Hero, Jr., "Southern Jews, Race Relations, and Foreign Policy," *Jewish Social Studies* 27 (October 1965:213-36; and John Shelton Reed, "Needles in Haystacks: Studying 'Rare' Populations by Secondary Analysis of National Sample Surveys," *Public Opinion Quarterly* 39 (winter 1975-76):514-22.

4. Wilbur J. Cash, *The Mind of the South* (New York, 1941); Lewis M. Killian, *White Southerners* (New York, 1970); Willie Morris, *North Toward Home* (New York, 1967) and *Yazoo: Integration in a Deep-Southern Town* (New York, 1971); William Faulkner's books are numerous; for Thomas Wolfe, see especially *You Can't Go Home Again* (New York, 1942) and *The Hills Beyond* (New York, 1943).

5. William D. Workman, Jr., *The Case for the South* (New York, 1960), pp. 2–4.

6. Lillian Smith, *Killers of the Dream* (New York, 1949), pp. 79, 70.

7. James McBride Dabbs, *Who Speaks for the South?* (New York, 1964), p. 85.

8. Smith, *Killers of the Dream,* p. 83; Samuel S. Hill, Jr., et al., *Religion and the Solid South* (Nashville, 1972), p. 25.

9. Wallace M. Alston, Jr., and Wayne Flynt, "Religion in the Land of Cotton," in H. Brandt Ayers and Thomas H. Naylor, eds., *You Can't Eat Magnolias* (New York, 1972), pp. 101, 102, 111.

10. Alston and Flynt, "Religion in the Land of Cotton," p. 104.

11. Robert Sam Anson, "Looking for Jimmy: A Journey through the South, Rising," *New Times,* August 6, 1976, p. 34. Of the large number of popular-magazine articles on the South since Jimmy Carter's rise to national prominence, this is one of the best and appears in a special issue devoted to the South.

12. Workman, *The Case for the South,* p. 2.

13. Hill et al., *Religion and the Solid South,* p. 25; Anson, "Looking for Jimmy," p. 21; Thomas D. Clark, *The Emerging South* (New York, 1941), p. 138; Cash, *Mind of the South,* pp. 305, 342. A number of other writers—for example, Workman, Killian, and C. Vann Woodward—have also made this point.

14. Jacob R. Marcus, *The Colonial American Jew, 1492-1776* (Detroit, 1970), 1:361; Abraham D. Lavender, "The Sephardic Revival in the United States: A Case of Ethnic Revival in a Minority-Within-a-Minority," *Journal of Ethnic Studies* 3 (fall 1975): 21-31.

15. Abraham D. Lavender, "Disadvantages of Minority Group Membership: The Perspective of a 'Nondeprived' Minority Group," *Ethnicity* 2 (March 1975):99-119.

16. For a brief discussion of this, see Lavender, "The Sephardic Revival in the United States."

17. Nathan Glazer, "The New Left and the Jews," in Marshall Sklare, ed., *The Jewish Community in America* (New York, 1974), p. 307.

18. Marshall Sklare, *America's Jews* (New York, 1971), p. 87.

19. Charles S. Liebman, "Orthodoxy in American Jewish Life," in Sklare, ed., *The Jewish Community in America,* p. 140

20. Lawrence H. Fuchs, *The Political Behavior of American Jews* (Glencoe, Ill., 1956), p. 183.

21. Clyde B. McCoy and Jerome A. Wolfe, "A Comparison of Jewish and Non-Jewish Addicts in Institutional Treatment Programs," *Jewish Sociology and Social Research* 2 (spring/summer 1976)10-15; Joel Fort and Christopher Cory, *American Drugstore* (Boston, 1975), p. 24; Jon P. Alston, "Review of the Polls: Attitudes Toward Extramarital and Homosexual Relations," *Journal for the Scientific Study of Religion* 13 (December 1974):479-81.

22. Milton Himmelfarb, "Secular Society? A Jewish Perspective," in William G. McLoughlin and Robert N. Bellah, eds., *Religion in America* (Boston, 1966), p. 283.

23. Richard Reeves, "Is Jimmy Carter Good for the Jews?" *New York,* May 24, 1976, p. 12.

24. Charles Y. Glock and Rodney Stark, *Religion and Society in Tension* (Chicago, 1965).

25. Bill Walker, as told to Muriel Larson, "Conversion Results from Prayer," *Manning (S.C.) Times,* May 26, 1976, p. 8A.

26. Eli N. Evans, *The Provincials: A Personal History of Jews in the South* (New York, 1973), p. 124.

27. "A Jewish View on Segregation" (Greenwood, Miss.: Association of Citizens' Councils of Mississippi, n.d.), p. 9; Allen Krause, "Rabbis and Negro Rights in the South, 1954–1967," in Leonard Dinnerstein and Mary Dale Palsson, eds., *Jews in the South* (Baton Rouge, La., 1973), p. 363. See also Alfred O. Hero, Jr., "Southern Jews," in Dinnerstein and Palsson, eds., *Jews in the South,* pp. 217-50.

28. C. Vann Woodward, *The Burden of Southern History,* rev. ed. (Baton Rouge, La., 1968); Woodward, "W. J. Cash Reconsidered," *New York Review of Books,* December 4, 1969, p. 28; Jack Bass and Walter DeVries, *The Transformation of Southern Politics* (New York, 1976); Willie Morris, *Yazoo,* p. 148.

29. Evans, *The Provincials,* p. x.

30. Hero, "Southern Jews, Race Relations, and Foreign Policy," p. 230; Theodore Lowi, "Southern Jews: The Two Communities," in Dinnerstein and Palsson, eds., *Jews in the South,* p. 277.

31. "South Now Ideological Heart of GOP," *Washington Post,* August 18, 1976, p. A8.

11.   Ethnicity in the South

John Shelton Reed

1. George B. Tindall, "Beyond the Mainstream: The Ethnic Southerners," *Journal of Southern History* 40 (February 1974):8.

2. John Maclachlen, "Distinctive Cultures in the Southeast: Their Possibilities for Regional Research," *Social Forces* 18 (December 1939):210-15; J. Kenneth Morland, ed., *The Not So Solid South: Anthropological Studies in a Regional Subculture* (Athens, Ga., 1971).

3. Tindall, "Beyond the Mainstream" p. 8.

4. John Shelton Reed, " 'The Cardinal Test of a Southerner': Not Race but Geography," *Public Opinion Quarterly* 37 (summer 1973):232-40; Edward Shils, "Primordial, Personal, Sacred, and Civil Ties," *British Journal of Sociology* 8 (June 1957):130-31; Andrew M. Greeley, *Ethnicity in the United States: A Preliminary Reconnaissance* (New York, 1974), pp. 10-15.

5. *American Jewish Year Book 1970* (Philadelphia, 1970) 71:345-46. "The South" in this

paper refers to the eleven ex-Confederate states, Kentucky, and Oklahoma. See John Shelton Reed, *The Enduring South: Subcultural Persistence in Mass Society* (Lexington, Mass, 1972), pp. 13-17, for a discussion of regional definition.

6. Alfred O. Hero, Jr., *The Southerner and World Affairs* (Baton Rouge, La., 1965), p. 636. Bibliographies can be found ibid., pp. 636-39, and in Leonard Dinnerstein and Mary Dale Palsson, eds., *Jews in the South* (Baton Rouge, La., 1973), pp. 389-92.

7. Lewis M. Killian, *White Southerners* (New York, 1970), pp. 69-83; Dinnerstein and Palsson, eds., *Jews in the South,* p. 3.

8. The data were obtained from the Roper Center for Public Opinion Research, Williamstown, Massachusetts; the cooperation of the Center and its staff is gratefully acknowledged. A description of the sample and of the difficulties in constructing it can be found in John Shelton Reed, "Needles in Haystacks: Studying 'Rare' Populations by Secondary Analysis of National Sample Surveys," *Public Opinion Quarterly* 39 (winter 1975-76):514-22.

9. The NJPS is the first study, to my knowledge, which includes enough Southern Jews to allow for accurate description. See the articles by Fred Massarik and Bernard Lazerwitz in Institute of Contemporary Jewry, *Papers in Jewish Demography* (Jerusalem, 1973).

10. *Gallup Opinion Index* (44 [February 1969]:27 reports a demographic description based on pooled Gallup data from a period slightly earlier than the period of those employed here. Although the tables do not distinguish between Jews in Florida and other Southern Jews, the aggregate data are very similar to those here. However, their samples and mine are probably not independent, and although the size of their pooled sample is not reported, it is almost certainly smaller than 100.

11. Harold G. Grasmick, "Social Change and the Wallace Movement in the South," Ph.D. dissertation, University of North Carolina, 1973.

12. Norval D. Glenn, "Class and Party Support in the United States: Recent and Emerging Trends," *Public Opinion Quarterly* 37 (spring 1973):1-20; figures for non-Southern Jewish voters are based on 159 respondents to Gallup polls 779, 783, 789, 793, and 801. Both for Southern and non-Southern Jews, I have used weights for "at-homeness" supplied by the Gallup organization, although, in fact, these weights made very little difference in the resulting percentages.

13. Seymour Martin Lipset and Everett C. Ladd, Jr., "Jewish Academics in the United States: Their Achievements, Culture, and Politics," *American Jewish Year Book 1971* (Philadelphia, 1971) 72:119-20 (emphasis added); Herbert H. Hyman, *Secondary Analysis of Sample Surveys: Principles, Procedures, and Potentialities* (New York, 1972), p. 130.

14. Joseph H. Fichter and George L. Maddox, "Religion in the South, Old and New," in John C. McKinney and Edgar T. Thompson, eds., *The South in Continuity and Change* (Durham, N.C., 1965), p. 382; Killian, *White Southerners,* p. 81. The literature on Southern anti-Semitism is confusing and often contradictory, but it appears that such anti-Semitism may be qualitatively different from the non-Southern variety.

15. Theodore Lowi, "Southern Jews: The Two Communities," in Dinnerstein and Palsson, eds., *Jews in the South,* pp. 265-82.

16. Francis Butler Simkins, "The Rising Tide of Faith," in Louis D. Rubin, Jr., and James J. Kilpatrick, eds., *The Lasting South: Fourteen Southerners Look at Their Home* (Chicago, 1957), pp. 87-88; Hero, *Southern and World Affairs,* pp. 435-37; Fichter and Maddox, "Religion in the South," pp. 362-65.

17. Reed, *Enduring South,* p. 67, shows a fairly constant difference of 10 percent between church attendance of Southern and non-Southern white Protestants for the period 1957–64. The difference between Southern and non-Southern middle-class groups appears to be about the same.

12.   Southern Jews and Public Policy

Alfred O. Hero, Jr.

1. Reported in Charles O. Lerche, Jr., *The Uncertain South: Its Changing Patterns of Politics in Foreign Policy* (Chicago, 1964), and Alfred O. Hero, Jr., *The Southerner and World Affairs* (Baton Rouge, La., 1965). Data on Southern Jews in the early 1960s is summarized from chap. 13 of the latter book and from Alfred O. Hero, Jr., "Southern Jews, Race Relations, and Foreign Policy," *Jewish Social Studies* 27 (October 1965):213–36.

2. See Alfred O. Hero, Jr., "Changing Southern Attitudes toward United States Foreign Policy," *Southern Humanities Review* 8 (summer 1974):275–95.

13.   Utilizing the Southern-Jewish Experience in Literature

Ronald L. Bern

1. Gloria Goldreich, "Fact in Fiction," *Hadassah Magazine,* November 1975, p. 24.

2. Leo Tolstoi, *War and Peace* (New York, 1889), vols. 3–4, p. 365.

3. Seymour Epstein, "The Legacy," *New York Times Book Review,* February 29, 1976, p. 14.

4. Bob Talbert, "And Then He Wrote the Book," *Detroit Free Press,* November 19, 1975, p. 15-A.

5. David Sable, "New Novel, 'The Legacy,' Tells of Growing Up Jewish Down South," *The Jewish Post* (New York), December 5, 1975, pp. 3–4.

Contributors

Raymond Ostby Arsenault is instructor in history at the University of Minnesota, specializing in the area of Southern politics.

Ronald L. Bern is the author of *The Legacy*, a novel based in part upon his youth in a small South Carolina town. Mr. Bern, who holds A.B. and M.A. degrees from the University of South Carolina, currently heads his own consulting firm, with offices in New York and New Jersey. He is also the author of two nonfiction books.

Stanley F. Chyet is professor of American-Jewish history at the Hebrew Union College–Jewish Institute of Religion in Los Angeles. Among his numerous publications in the field of American-Jewish history are *Lopez of Newport* and *Lives and Voices*.

Eli N. Evans grew up in Durham, North Carolina, and—following an interest in his own family's history—wrote *The Provincials: A Personal History of Jews in the South*. A frequent commentator in national publications on Jewish affairs and on politics in the South, Mr. Evans recently became the first president of the new Charles H. Revson Foundation in New York.

Alfred O. Hero, Jr., is director of the World Peace Foundation in Boston and the author of many articles and monographs on intergroup relations, including *American Religious Groups View Foreign Policy* and *The Southerner and World Affairs*.

Abraham D. Lavender is assistant professor of sociology at the University of Miami, Coral Gables, Florida. He has written a number of articles on minority groups and edited *A Coat of Many Colors: Jewish Subcommunities in the United States*.

John Shelton Reed is associate professor of sociology at the University of North Carolina. In 1973–74 he was Fulbright-Hays Visiting Senior Lecturer in American Studies at the Hebrew University of Jerusalem and in 1977–78, while a Guggenheim Fellow, he held a visiting appointment at St. Antony's College, Oxford. He has written extensively on the American South; among his publications is *The Enduring South: Subcultural Persistence in American Society*.

Gladys Rosen serves as program specialist in the Jewish communal affairs department
of the American Jewish Committee. She is a frequent contributor to scholarly
journals. Her most recent publication is *Jews in American Life: A Guide to Local
Programming for the Bicentennial.*

Arnold Shankman is associate professor of history at Winthrop College, Rock Hill,
South Carolina, specializing in the Civil War period, ethnic history, and twentieth-century Southern history.

Byron L. Sherwin is associate professor of Jewish religious thought at Spertus
College of Judaica in Chicago.

Jack D. Spiro is rabbi of Congregation Beth Ahabah in Richmond, Virginia, and
adjunct professor of religious studies at the Virginia Commonwealth Univer-
sity. He was formerly national director of the Commission on Jewish Education.
He has contributed articles to a variety of Jewish magazines and is author of
A Time to Mourn and coauthor of *The Living Bible* and *Dialogue: In Search of
Jewish-Christian Understanding.*

Malcolm H. Stern served as rabbi of Congregation Ohef Sholom in Norfolk, Virginia, for seventeen years before becoming Director of Rabbinic Placement for
the national institutions of Reform Judaism. He is chairman of the Executive
Council of the American Jewish Historical Society, genealogist for the American
Jewish Archives, and president of the American Society of Genealogists. His
revised and enlarged compendium *First American Jewish Families: 600 Genealogies,
1654-1977,* is being published by the American Jewish Historical Society jointly
with the American Jewish Archives.

Richard S. Tedlow is assistant professor of American studies at Brandeis University.
He has contributed several scholarly articles in the areas of American business
history and the history of mass communications and has just completed a book
on the history of corporate public relations.

Melvin I. Urofsky is professor of history and is chairman of that department at
Virginia Commonwealth University in Richmond. He is coeditor of the *Brandeis
Letters* and author of several books on American Jewish history, including *American Zionism from Herzl to the Holocaust* and *We Are One!* He served as chairman
of the conference.

Stephen J. Whitfield is assistant professor of American studies at Brandeis University. He is the author of several articles that have appeared in scholarly journals
as well as of the book *Scott Nearing: Apostle of American Radicalism.*

Index